Thomas B. Curran, OSFS
Rockhurst University
1100 Rockhurst Road
Kansas City, MO 64110

The Jesuit *Ratio Studiorum*

The Jesuit *Ratio Studiorum*

400th ANNIVERSARY PERSPECTIVES

Edited by

VINCENT J. DUMINUCO, S.J.

Presented in a Seminar
at Fordham University
Graduate School of Education

FORDHAM UNIVERSITY PRESS
New York
2000

The Jesuit Ratio Studiorum of 1599: 400th Anniversary Seminar (October 14–15, 1999) and the publication of this volume were made possible through the support of the Graduate School of Education, Fordham University.

Library of Congress Cataloging-in-Publication Data

The Jesuit Ratio studiorum : 400th anniversary perspectives / edited by Vincent J. Duminuco.—1st ed.
    p. cm.
    Proceedings of a conference held in the fall of 1999 at Fordham University.
    Includes bibliographical references and index.
    ISBN 0-8232-2046-X (hardcover)—ISBN 0-8232-2047-8 (pbk.)
    1. Jesuits. Ratio studiorum—Congresses.   2. Jesuits—Education—Congresses.   I. Duminuco, Vincent J.
BX3704.Z5 J47   2000
371.071′2—dc21   00-039380

John O'Malley delivered a similar address under the same title, printed in *Jesuit Education 21: Conference on the Future of Jesuit Higher Education*, Martin R. Trepole, S.J., ed. Permission to print the overlapping text has been granted by St. Joseph's University Press, Philadelphia, Pennsylvania.

To the alumni/ae of Jesuit schools, colleges, and universities who have grown as people of competence, conscience, and compassion in the spirit of the *Ratio Studiorum*.

CONTENTS

INTRODUCTION

One of the hottest topics in the field of Catholic education in the late twentieth century concerned the *identity* of Catholic educational institutions. In connection with *Ex Corde Ecclesiae* and development of regional norms for implementation of this apostolic constitution, discussions and debates have occurred at the level of Catholic higher education.[1] At the level of Catholic elementary and secondary education, one need only cast an eye over the topics of presentations at the annual conventions of the National Catholic Education Association since 1980. The topic of identity occurs with striking frequency. It would seem that in our times of major value paradigm shifts in religious, civic, and professional circles on a worldwide scale, clarity concerning the effective identity of Catholic education and its mission becomes urgent for a number of reasons.

Significantly, increased numbers of lay staff and younger religious (who do not have deeply rooted understanding of the raison d'être and mission of schools, colleges, and universities that are Catholic) swell the ranks of faculty members and administrators. Emerging Boards of Trustees, well intentioned and committed, often are not clear concerning the identity and mission, which is the sacred trust of any Board at a Catholic institution. This confusion can result in less of a sense of distinctiveness in program and pedagogy, as well as inadequate criteria for evaluation. The call, therefore, has been as Vatican II set out over thirty years ago, that we return to the charism of our founders to rediscover the graced insights that spark and direct the service God's people need from us. In light of that rediscovery we are called to apply it to the real situations we face today.

---

[1] In 1990, the Vatican issued this papal document, which addressed the Catholic identity of Catholic colleges and universities throughout the world. While all agreed on the description of the values and challenges to be espoused by Catholic higher education, development of specific regional norms for the United States prompted years of debate and discussion among the Church hierarchy and presidents of Catholic universities. In November, 1999, the United States Catholic Conference of bishops finally adopted a set of regional norms.

This volume is part of an effort initiated by the Society of Jesus immediately following the close of the Second Vatican Council (1962–65). It seeks to recapture the initial insights and experiences that gave birth to Jesuit education—its identity and mission, together with its distinctive mode of proceeding, set forth in the *Ratio Studiorum* four centuries ago.

The year 1999 marked the 400th anniversary of the landmark *Ratio atque Institutio Studiorum Societatis Jesu*, "The Plan and Methodology of Jesuit Education," which became the guiding pedagogical document throughout the world of Jesuit education.

The effectiveness of this plan has been praised through the ages by scholars like Francis Bacon in the seventeenth century: "For the doctrine of school-learning, it were the shortest way to refer it to the Jesuits, who, in point usefulness, have herein excelled." And in the twentieth century, Gilbert Highet noted that the Jesuits worked out in the sixteenth century one of the most successful educational systems the Western world has ever seen. He specifies methods and practices developed by the Jesuits. More recently, Harry Broudy in his *Handbook of Research on Teaching* refers to the Jesuits as "masters of method": "The Jesuit schools are selected for discussion (as one of the ten historic exemplars of teaching method) because they illustrate how schooling can be organized and systematized to make materials, methods of instruction, and teachers uniformly effective over broad regions of space and time." Paul Shore observes: "Its tremendous influence on the development of education can be attributed to both the organization it provided to hundreds of schools that the Jesuits established worldwide, and to the vision of the teacher embedded in the *Ratio Studiorum*."

In the midst of a search for effective pedagogy in many countries around the world on the eve of the new millennium, it was fruitful to explore the foundational plan of studies of the Jesuits, which has effectively guided Jesuit schools, colleges, and universities in seventy-two countries over the last 400 years. Some scholars recently have spoken of Jesuit pedagogy as "a best-kept secret." They urge that we highlight the Jesuit development in pedagogy in order that we can share it with others.

And so, to commemorate the 400th anniversary of the publication of the first definitive *Ratio Studiorum* of Jesuit education, Fordham University presented a two-day scholarly seminar, which brought together an extraordinary group of scholars to address this topic. For many years they have focused much of their research and reflection in the field of Jesuit education.

They include world-renowned experts in Jesuit spirituality like Howard Gray, S.J. and George Aschenbrenner, S.J. Historians John O'Malley, S.J., John Padberg, S.J., and Gabriel Codina, S.J. have in recent years revolutionized historical research concerning the origins and early history of the Jesuits and education. Rosemary DeJulio presents a pioneering study of women's reactions to Ignatius and the *Ratio* in the personages of Mary Ward and Madeleine Sophie Barat. Critical reviews are presented in responses by Louis Pascoe, S.J. and John Elias, Ed.D., while Mrs. Jenny Go presents fresh lay person's perspectives in the era of growing lay-Jesuit cooperation in mission. And in the final presentation we look to recent developments affecting Jesuit education worldwide and their likely impact in a new, more comprehensive plan and method for Jesuit education that can be effective in a changed environment as we enter the new millennium. The Appendices provide the text of the major documentation involved in this aggiornamento: *The Characteristics of Jesuit Education* (1986) and *Ignatian Pedagogy: A Practical Approach* (1993).

It seems strange that a relatively unique worldwide system of schools, colleges, and universities founded by the Jesuits and serving close to two million students each year in seventy-two countries has not generated much recent study of its origins, purposes, plans, and methods. This volume hopes to contribute to the scholarship necessary to understand and grow in the spirit of the *Ratio Studiorum* today and tomorrow.

Of course this presentation would not be possible without the kindness and cooperation of a number of people. Among them the authors of the papers deserve special thanks, for without their quality research and reflection, this volume would not exist. The encouragement of Fr. Joseph O'Hare, S.J., president of Fordham University, of Dr. Robert Carrubba, academic vice president at Fordham, and Dean Regis Bernhardt of the Fordham Graduate School of Education enabled the seminar to move from proposal to reality. The generosity of our benefactors, including the Jesuits of Fordham, the alumni/ae of the Fordham School of Education, The Fidel Gotz Stiftung, and an anonymous family foundation made it possible to bring our scholars to this event and to provide hospitality to our capacity audience consisting of 150 invited representatives from thirty-four Jesuit educational institutions in the United States, Asia, Latin America, and Europe.

The secretarial help and generous welcoming committees at Fordham insured the warmth and personal welcome that is one of the characteristics of Jesuit education.

Vincent J. Duminuco, S.J.

1

The Experience of Ignatius Loyola: Background to Jesuit Education

Howard Gray, S.J.

IN 1933, Edward Fitzpatrick, Dean of the Graduate School of Marquette University and President of Mount Mary College, aptly summarized the formal education of Ignatius Loyola.

> The most interesting and most striking incidents of St. Ignatius' life are included in the eleven years of his student days, commencing when he was thirty-three years old (March, 1524) and extending into his forty-fourth year (April, 1535). He began with the study of grammar for two years at Barcelona. He continued (1526) with the study of philosophy at Alcala. . . .
>
> At Paris he repeated his studies in grammar and the humanities, and then philosophy for three and a half years, receiving the Master of Arts degree in Lent, 1533, at the age of forty-two. He then studied theology for about two years, discontinued it because of illness, and never completed it. His formal studies ended in Paris in 1535.[1]

Sixty-six years separate us from Dr. Fitzpatrick's perspective; however, I suspect that most professional educators would read the data similarly. It is this perspective that I want to engage as I establish some focus for the discussion of the experience of St. Ignatius as background to Jesuit education. In attempting to bring a particular focus to this discussion I do not want to minimize the importance of the eleven years that Ignatius spent as a student. These were the years of personal maturation and integration for him. They also were

---

[1] Edward A. Fitzpatrick, St. Ignatius and the Ratio Studiorum (New York: McGraw-Hill, 1933), 7–8.

years in which he forged enduring friendships with a group of remarkable fellow students who became his companions in founding
the Society of Jesus. We would not have had the Jesuit order as we
know it without the experience of Ignatius's student years.[2] But I
want to emphasize that *education* for Ignatius antedated those
eleven years and persisted until his death. It is the focus of life-long
education that I want to offer here as a constitutive perspective from
which to interpret the influence of Ignatius on Jesuit education.

This presentation has three major sections: (1) for Ignatius education was an *event* that came "from above," from within, and from
outside himself; (2) for Ignatius education was a *code* that socialized
his experiences so that others could share these; and (3) for Ignatius
education was an *apostolic enterprise* that would have an impact on
both the Church and civil society. I shall conclude with some explor-
atory reflections on what this might mean for Jesuit education today.

EDUCATION AS AN EVENT

In his dictated memoir, Ignatius summarizes an important aspect of
his time at Manresa in these words:

> During this period God was dealing with him in the same way a
> schoolteacher deals with a child while instructing him. This was be-
> cause either he was thick and dull of brain,
> or
> because of the firm will that God Himself had implanted in him to
> serve Him—but he clearly recognized and has always recognized that
> it was in this way that God dealt with him. Furthermore, if he were to
> doubt this, he would think he was offending the Divine Majesty.[3]

---

[2] Let me give just two examples. First, Ignatius saw the importance of order,
personal appropriation, and balanced judgment because he experienced both their
lack and their availability; cf. George E. Ganss, S.J., *Saint Ignatius' Idea of a Jesuit
University, A Study in the History of Catholic Education* (Milwaukee: Marquette
University Press, 1954), esp. chap. 9, "Principles in the Spirit of St. Ignatius' *Constitutions* on Education," 185–93. Second, Ignatius found in the life of the university
friends and the power of conversation; cf. Jose Ignacio Tellechea Idigoras, *Ignatius
of Loyola: The Pilgrim Saint*, translated, edited, and preface by Cornelius Michael
Buckley, S.J. (Chicago: Loyola University Press, 1994), chaps. 23–27, 309–36.

[3] Ignatius Loyola, *A Pilgrim's Journey, The Autobiography of Ignatius Loyola*, introduction, translation, and commentary by Joseph N. Tylenda, S.J. (Wilmington: Michael Glazier, 1985), no. 27, pp. 35–36.

Ignatius then cites five extraordinary instances of divine tutelage, climaxing in the pivotal illumination at the River Cardoner. Of this extraordinary divine intervention, Ignatius says: "He cannot expound in detail what he then understood, for they were many things, but he can say that he received such a lucidity in understanding that during the course of his entire life—now having passed his sixty-second year—if he were to gather all the help he received from God and everything he knew, and add them together, he does not think they would add up to all he had received on that occasion."[4]

Ignatius's account of his transformation strikes me as important not only because it represents a moral conversion but an intellectual reorientation, a way of viewing God as inspiration and the world as a source of knowledge. Moreover, the primitive exercise of discernment initiated at Loyola was becoming at Manresa a habit of heart. This graced intervention was a communication not merely about the things of God but of God Himself. Later, Ignatius struggled to articulate what this relationship meant, especially as he began to see that the process was one he could share with others. The God of revelation was a God who communicated in order to lead men and women to decisions about how they would live their lives, employ their talents, and direct their resources. Consequently, from this Manresa experience, Ignatius was to lay down an essential principle in the *Spiritual Exercises*:

> [D]uring these Spiritual Exercises when a person is seeking God's will, it is more appropriate and far better that the Creator and Lord Himself should communicate himself to the devout soul, embracing it in love and praise, and disposing it for the way which enable the soul to serve him better in the future. Accordingly, the one giving the Exercises ought not to lean or incline in either direction but rather, while standing by like a pointer of a scale in equilibrium, to allow the Creator to deal immediately with the creature and the creature with its Creator and Lord.[5]

In other words; out of his own experience of divine intervention, Ignatius came to understand the universality of God's desire to com-

---

[4] Ibid., no. 30, p. 39.
[5] Ignatius Loyola, *Spiritual Exercises of Saint Ignatius Loyola*, translation and commentary by George E. Ganss, S.J. (St. Louis: Institute of Jesuit Sources, 1992), no. 15, pp. 25–26.

municate personally with men and women, to engage their histories with a new interpretation, to reorient their imaginations with new possibilities, and to redirect their talents and opportunities toward new enterprises. He was to term this divine intervention *de arriba*, a gift not only of understanding God's descent into the human but of the human ability to rise to God from created reality.[6] It is this graced ability that became for Ignatius the habit of finding God in all things. As Hugo Rahner explains: "From [Manresa] on, his theological thought became a descending movement from God to creatures, in which created things and all earthly beauty, wisdom and righteousness were merely reflected splendour of what he had already grasped in the immediacy of his mystical contemplation of God Himself."[7]

But the privileged particularity of his illuminations did not inhibit Ignatius from constructing a system of prayer and reflection that would invite other men and women of good will to find how God could also enter their lives, *de arriba*, from above, and how this grace would enable them, too, to find God in all things. Thus, inherent first in the Manresa experiences and then in the processes he proposed to others through the *Exercises* was the reverence Ignatius had for teaching and learning as metaphors for God's way in guiding human decisions.[8]

There are important consequences for the way God instructs. If the divine can enter into human consciousness and reorient a life, then people can trust the effect this has within them. The gift from above becomes a gift within the human reality of the person. Indeed, the revelation of God to a man or woman demands personal appropriation. It is personal history that is reinterpreted, personal imagination that accepts new possibilities, and personal talents and opportunities that accept new enterprises. The Ignatian idea of an election, i.e., the choice that emerges out of the process of the *Exercises*, is not that of imposition but of mutual acceptance, human and

---

[6] Cf. George E. Ganss, S.J., ed., *Ignatius of Loyola, The Spiritual Exercises and Selected Works*, commentary by Ganss (New York: Paulist Press, 1991), no. 86, p. 474. The classic treatment is found in Hugo Rahner, S.J., *Ignatius the Theologian*, trans. Michael Barry (New York: Herder and Herder, 1968), 1–31.

[7] Ibid., 4.

[8] On the tradition, cf. Ben Witherington III, *Jesus the Sage. The Pilgrimage of Wisdom* (Minneapolis: Fortress Press, 1994).

divine. It is not just piety that prompts the Ignatian insistence that
a colloquy conclude the prayer of the *Exercises*. This intimate conversation between a man or a woman and God is sacred because here
is a privileged moment of mutual trust.[9]

Ignatius learned to trust his heart as a place of unique encounter
with God. In that experience he also learned to trust the hearts of
others as places for similar encounters. This movement represents a
complex set of confidences: in one's own interiority, in the goodness
of God, in the ability of others to find God too. From the opening of
the *Exercises*—which encourages both the one who gives the *Exer-*
cises and the one who makes them to trust one another throughout
the process[10]—to the intense conclusion of the *Exercises*—in which
the one who is making them holds the entire experience as an act of
divine love, human acceptance, and mutual surrender[11]—trust is the
glue that holds this spiritual education together. Trust is an essential
component in Ignatian spirituality. Trust, in turn, will permeate the
life and mission of the Society of Jesus. Trust will characterize the
way Jesuits deal with people, cultures, and other religious experiences. For if Ignatius saw God as one who taught, he also saw God
as one who taught out of trust for the unique reality of Ignatius's
own temperament, history, and talents. God for Ignatius was an
adapting God, a God who met created reality in trust. From God's
trust Ignatius learned to trust—himself first and others later.[12]

This Ignatian trust of other created reality—other people, cultures, religious, experiences—founds why he can speak of finding
God in all things and explains both the location and significance of
the Contemplation to Attain Divine Love at the close of the *Exer-*
cises. If one lives with God, then, one can find God's truth within
life, God's direction within created energy, God's love dwelling
deeply within creation. For Ignatius sin is the absence of God; it is
uncovered in falsehood and deceit, in reckless ambition and oppres-

---

[9] Alexandre Brou, *Ignatian Method of Prayer*, trans. W. J. Young, S.J. (Milwaukee:
Bruce, 1949), 119–21.

[10] *Spiritual Exercises*, no. 22.

[11] Ibid., no. 234.

[12] On the significance of adaptation and trust, see Walter Brueggemann, "Nouns:
Yahweh as Constant," in *Theology of the Old Testament* (Minneapolis: Fortress
Press, 1997), 229–66; Michael Ivens, "The First Week: Some Notes on the Text,"
The Way, supplement, 48 (Autumn 1983): 6–8.

sion, in enmity, bias, and indifference to human anguish.[13] The Manresa experience did not exhaust Ignatius's education in divine wisdom. His subsequent years of study and then his governance over the young Society of Jesus contributed their own enrichments. But Manresa symbolizes the foundation of Ignatian education. It was an event that was experiential; it was based on trust; and it invited a discovery of God in a variety of created realities. Consequently, when we emphasize, as we should, the importance of adaptation in the *Spiritual Exercises*, we are reflecting what Ignatius discovered at Manresa about God. God adapts to the human to teach truth, to encourage our trust in our experiences, and to enrich the ways in which all creation can become a revelation about God's presence and action. Manresa was an event in divine tutelage for Ignatius, revealing how he was to help others to respond to that tutelage in their lives.[14] How was this help to be accomplished?

CODIFICATION OF THE EXPERIENCE

Ignatius learned early the value of bringing inspiration into a system.[15] The *Spiritual Exercises* are an ordered set of instructions integrating the freedom necessary to any genuinely Christian religious experience with the guarantees that insure the experience is both authentically from God and respectful of human reason and dignity.[16] While these dual concerns are woven throughout the *Exercises*, Ignatius presents them most systematically in the twenty introductory reflections that he presents as aids to the one who gives

---

[13] The imagery of the Satan in the Two Standards Meditation is the imagery of one who is "the mortal enemy of our human nature," no. 136 in the *Exercises*.

[14] The key section in Ignatius's *Autobiography* is no. 29, p. 37 in the Tylenda edition: "It was likewise in Manresa—where he stayed for almost a year, after experiencing divine consolations and seeing the fruit that he was bringing forth in the souls he was helping—that he abandoned those extremes he had previously practiced and began to cut his nail and hair."

[15] *Constitutions of the Society of Jesus*, introduction, translation, and commentary by George E. Ganss, S.J. (St. Louis: Institute of Jesuit Sources, 1970), "Preamble to the Constitutions," [134]–[135], pp. 119–20.

[16] A classic statement on "their proper place in the history of Christian piety" is Hugo Rahner's in *The Spirituality of St. Ignatius Loyola: An Account of Its Historical Development*, trans. Francis John Smith, S.J. (Chicago: Loyola University Press, 1980), 88–96.

the *Exercises*. These instructions fall under three general headings: about prayer, about discernment, and about choices. For example, when Ignatius gives suggestions about how prayer should be presented within the experience of the *Exercises*, he clearly expects the one who leads this experience to give instructions.[17] However, he also cautions that these instructions are to be brief in order to allow the one who makes the prayer the freedom to discover for himself or herself whatever God chooses to reveal.[18] To use another example, Ignatius lays out careful guidelines to help the one giving the *Exercises* to assess the movements of spirit that inevitably arise within the experience of the *Exercises*.[19] But he is equally solicitous that this instruction gradually empower the one making the *Exercises* to develop his or her own ability to distinguish what is from God and what is not from God, what is enduringly good from what is only an apparent good.[20] As a final example, while Ignatius relentlessly places before the one making the *Exercises* the ideals of the gospel, Ignatius is equally careful to insure that any personal choice that the one making the *Exercises* embraces be done with freedom from bias, prejudices, or outside influences.[21]

The Spiritual Exercises emerged out of Ignatius's stay at Manresa and then were refined over a number of years.[22] Ignatius viewed them as a way to help others find peace and direction in their lives out of the inspiration of the gospels. They were never intended to be coercive or insinuating. Rather, they were designed for people of maturity, freedom, and openness of heart who would be willing to consider how they could live lives of more profound dedication and generous service to others. To that end, Ignatius insisted on a certain solitude of soul, a separation from distractions, a willingness to take time to pray and to reflect, and a docility of heart to someone who would guide this experience. At the same time he cautioned the instructor of the *Exercises* to adapt them to the temperament, age, and experience of each person. As a document of Christian formation, the *Ex-*

---

[17] *Exercises*, e.g., nos. 2, 6–10, 14, 17.

[18] Ibid., no. 2.

[19] Ibid., nos. 6–10; 14, 16–17.

[20] Ibid., nos. 2, 5, 15, 20.

[21] Ibid., no. 15, and especially the advice on the Election, nos. 169–87.

[22] Joseph de Guibert, S.J., *The Jesuits: Their Spiritual Doctrine and Practice*, A *Historical Study*, trans. William J. Young, S.J. (Chicago: Institute of Jesuit Sources, 1964), 113–22.

ercises teach. As the initial codification of Ignatian principles of instruction, the *Exercises* establish important guidelines for Jesuit teaching.

While I have painted with a broad brush, the design of Ignatian instruction is clear. An ordered, humane approach to God's revelation presumes the freedom to find God for oneself, but within a communal revelation. Moreover, the *Exercises* insist on a person's willingness to test personal experience in order to choose what will be an enduring commitment to what will most direct one to God.[23]

Although the *Exercises* have sometimes been criticized as being too individualistic, they are, in fact, relentlessly oriented toward the life one lives outside of solitude—in the arena of public life, to the future. For example, the Ignatian view of Christ is that of Christ on mission—preaching, teaching, healing.[24] The decision to follow Christ is to follow him as humble, poor, and rejected within a culture that values wealth, power, influence, and prestige.[25] The virtues Ignatius emphasizes are those of freedom, magnanimity, and self-sacrifice, which lead to doing great deeds in the world but for the sake of the gospel. Consequently, as an educational tool, the *Exercises* were and remain a remarkable instrument of engagement with the world and culture of one's times.

The second significant area of codification I emphasize is the *Constitutions of the Society of Jesus.*[26] Pope Paul III approved the Society of Jesus in 1540; and on April 8, 1541, Ignatius was elected its first Superior General. Ignatius was then fifty years of age and dedicated the remainder of his life to the direction of this new order. As Superior General, one of his chief responsibilities was to give oversight to the writing of the *Constitutions*, which would express the aims and means that identify the life and work of the Society. It is this document I want to consider now, especially as an expression of educational aims and processes within the Jesuit community. In this examination I center first on the principles that governed the formation of Jesuits and then on that which governed Jesuits who had completed their formation and were involved in direct ministry.

---

[23] *Exercises*, no. 169, the Introduction to the Election.

[24] Note the first prelude of the Call of Christ, no. 191, which establishes both a tone and a perspective for Week II of the *Exercises*.

[25] Ibid., II Standards, nos. 136–47.

[26] Cf. the Ganss edition for a succinct overview of the genesis and spirit of the *Constitutions*, 3–59.

There are three aspects of Jesuit formation that are crucial: the process of how to become a contemplative in action, the environment that promotes formation within the company, and the ways in which a man's ability to live Jesuit life and to do its ministry were assessed.

First, let me briefly explain this term "contemplative in action."[27] As we have seen, Ignatius valued the processes that led him to find God in the events of his life. He believed that the *Exercises*, if made well and in their integrity, could similarly help others to find God in their lives. He asked the same of the men who would be members of the Society of Jesus. In the *Constitutions* Ignatius spells out what the process might be that can dispose a man to become a contemplative in action.[28]

In Part III of the *Constitutions* Ignatius treats the spiritual formation of young Jesuits. In a remarkable section he counsels the importance of an asceticism that brings focus to a man's life, for example, silence, a certain self-composure, and effort to be at peace with oneself. Then he lays down the following wisdom directive:

> In everything they [the young Jesuits] should try and desire to give the advantage to the others, esteeming them all in their hearts as better than themselves [Phil. 2:3] and showing exteriorly, in an unassuming and simple religious manner, the respect and reverence befitting each one's state, in such a manner that by observing one another they grow in devotion and praise God our Lord, whom each one should endeavor to recognize in his neighbor as in His image.[29]

This directive centers on three constitutive operations: *constitutive* of ways in which the young Jesuit can open himself to God's presence and action within human relationships; *operations* as distinct ways to achieve a certain openness to this experience. The first is what I would call attention, the ability to be present to a relationship in its particularity. It stands for that presence in which one person allows another reality, here another Jesuit, to enter his awareness on his own terms.[30] It is acceptance of the reality, not an intrusion—

---

[27] Joseph F. Conwell, S.J., *Contemplation in Action: A Study in Ignatian Prayer* (Spokane: Gonzaga University Press, 1957).

[28] *Constitutions*, [250].

[29] Ibid.

[30] An important discussion of "attention" can be found in Pierre Hadot, *Philosophy As a Way of Life*, trans. Michael Chase, edited with an introduction by Arnold I. Davidson (Oxford: Blackwell, 1995), 126–44.

through fear or bias or lack of concentration—on that reality. The second operation is reverence, the ability to cherish the reality that reveals itself, here the other Jesuit, in all his integrity. It represents another level of acceptance, not only allowing the reality to be present to me but accepting that reality as different from, unique in his self-expression, worthy of his own integrity.[31] The third operation is actually the operation of grace. The word "devotion," which denotes this third step, is precious to Ignatius.

> Devocion: a word which Ignatius uses with great frequency in all his works, especially his letters, Spiritual Exercises, Spiritual Diary, and Constitutions. It expressed his attitude of profound respect before God to whom he was totally dedicated in love and service, and he used it with multitudinous connotations, often mystical. In the Constitutions, . . . the word expresses the personal or communitarian pursuit of spiritual progress. [It was for Ignatius] "the actualization of the virtue of religion by means of an affection for God which is prompt, compliant, warmly loving, and impelled by charity. Its goal is the worship of God which is accomplished in all things and actions of oneself and one's fellow men, since it gives worship to Him by finding and serving him in all things."[32]

In other words, through attention and reverence one can hope to be led to devotion, the ability to discover how God exists in another, here in another Jesuit.

What Ignatius proposes as the touchstone of Jesuit formation is an asceticism that focuses a young Jesuit on the ability to be present to another reality, to hold in acceptance and a kind of awe the reality as he finds it, and out of this orientation to be sensitive to how God speaks to him through that other reality. Moreover, this kind of formation was not something to be done only within the novitiate. Rather it was to be inculcated as an abiding apostolic process that helped the Jesuit to become a man who could find God in all things like studies, like other cultures, like people weighed down by sins, like art and music and science.[33] The ramifications of this formation directive are wide and rich, suggesting an important key not only to

---

[31] Charles O'Neill, S.J., "Acatamiento: Ignatian Reverence," Studies in the Spirituality of the Jesuits 8 (January 1976).

[32] Ganss edition of Constitutions, n. 5, pp. 155–56.

[33] A specific example of this is Timothy B. Toohig, S.J., "Physics Research: A Search for God," Studies in The Spirituality of the Jesuits 31 (March 1999).

the personal religious event of finding God in all things but to the apostolic mind set of expecting to find God in all people, places, and events. For what this education in attention, reverence, and devotion invites is an apostolic consciousness, a readiness to expect God to communicate his presence and intentionality within all created reality but especially within human relationships. For the Jesuit, then, the world became both a place of contemplation and a source for apostolic planning.[34]

In that same section of the *Constitutions*, Part III, Ignatius also describes the formation environment in which attention, reverence, and devotion can be best exemplified and taught. It is contained in his description of the Director of Novices:

> It will be beneficial to have a faithful and competent person whose function is to instruct and teach the novices in regard to their interior and exterior conduct, to encourage them toward this correct deportment, to remind them of it, and to give them kindly admonition; a person whom all those who are in probation may love and to whom they may have recourse in their temptations and open themselves with confidence, hoping to receive from him in our Lord counsel and aid in everything.[35]

I have referred to the importance of trust in Ignatian spirituality. This description of the Jesuit Director of Novices is but one more instance of this virtue. The Director of Novices models what he teaches in his relationship to his charges. Men learn attention, reverence, and devotion best when they see it exemplified in their own formation. This is as appropriate a place as any to call attention to how often Ignatius urges the power of good example to affect apostolic fruit.[36] People learn the gospel by seeing it lived out in their own regard. So, too, the Jesuit novices. By creating an environment of trust, the Jesuit Director of Novices makes the teaching about attention, reverence, and devotion credible and available.

The formation of men for the work of the apostolate, a work that

---

[34] John W. O'Malley, S.J., "To Travel to Any Part of the World: Jerónimo Nadal and the Jesuit Vocation," *Studies in the Spirituality of the Jesuits* 16 (March 1984); Brian B. Daley, S.J., " 'In Ten Thousand Places': Christian Universality and the Jesuit Mission," *Studies in the Spirituality of Jesuits* 17 (March, 1985).

[35] *Constitutions*, [263].

[36] Cf. the extensive citation of "Edification" in Index 1 of the Ganss edition of *Constitutions*, 380.

frequently demanded that Jesuits work alone and in places with min-
imum ecclesial safeguards and support systems, had to include a
component that would test the resiliency and fidelity of the novice.
Can this man live this apostolic life with benefit both to himself and
to the people he will serve? Can he practice attention, reverence, and
devotion outside the security of the novitiate? To answer these kinds
of questions Ignatius introduced a revolutionary form of novitiate
training called experiments. What are these and how do they operate?[37]

There are six novitiate experiments that "constitute the Ignatian
pattern of religious development into ministerial life."[38] Their aim
was apostolic integration. What does this mean? The overall aim of
the Society of Jesus was "to strive especially for the defense and
propagation of the faith and for the progress of soul in Christian life
and doctrine"[39] and to accomplish this through a variety of ministries, chiefly centered on the word of God.[40] Moreover, Ignatius envisioned a group able to work on the frontiers of the Church and even
in lands and in enterprises that were not part of Christendom, much
less Catholicism. In other words, the work of the Jesuits demanded
capability and flexibility. The novitiate (and tertianship) experiments, then, were ways to test the ability of young men to live this
kind of life with benefit both to themselves and to others.[41]

By "apostolic integration" we mean that there is "a peculiar structure internal to the experiments, that they possess their own organic
and evolving pattern, and that at their completion the novice or
tertian has moved from an event of the deepest interiority and solitude into the ministerial life of the Society."[42] In other words, there
is a harmony—psychological and religious—between the way a man

---

[37] The best treatment in English of the experiments is that of Michael J. Buckley,
S.J., "Freedom, Election, and Self-Transcendence: Some Reflections Upon the Ignatian Development of A Life of Ministry," in *Ignatian Spirituality in a Secular Age*,
ed. George P. Schner, S.J. (Waterloo, Ontario: Wilfrid Laurier University Press,
1984), 65–90.

[38] Ibid., 81.

[39] *Formula of the Institute*, in *Constitutions*, [3].

[40] Ibid.

[41] The apostolic centrality of the Jesuits demanded a long training begun in the
novitiate and climaxed by a final formation period now called tertianship. After
tertianship, the young Jesuit was eligible for final profession into the Society of
Jesus. Cf. *Constitutions*, Ganss's n. 4, p. 233 and n. 1, pp. 234–35.

[42] Buckley, "Freedom, Election, and Self-Transcendence," 81.

prays and orients his life and the kind of ministerial presence he brings to his work with other people.

The six experiments ranged from the thirty-days of spiritual exercises made under the guidance of an experienced Jesuit to work in a hospital, to a pilgrimage, to service within the Jesuit community, to teaching catechetics, to the ministries of preaching and hearing confessions. These latter two experiments were reserved for priest candidates or tertians. While a detailed analysis of the religious significance of these experiments is somewhat afar from the focus of this paper, their importance as an educational tool is not.

> [T]here is a more profound pedagogy at work here. . . . These experiments move from devotion, the ability to find God in all things, through experiences which call upon humility, abnegation, and poverty, and to engagement in the ministerial life of the Society. . . . They are patterned on the life and ministry of Jesus. There must first be a profound contact with Christ our Lord, one that has been developing within the exercitant since the first events of the Exercises. Within that contact there is the experience of choice, of being sent, of being schooled with the "way Christ calls and wishes for all persons under his standard. . . ." The call of Christ into discipleship possesses a pattern that his life embodies. Ignatius sees this pattern in the earliest contemplations of his life. . . . The movement of Jesus into his most profound ministry is through poverty and humiliations. The six experiments retrieve the structure of his life as the development of ministerial consciousness.[43]

These experiments, then, were part of the overall education of candidates into the Society of Jesus. They were part of a schooling for service. When these experiments were introduced, they contained "a great deal of daring and a considerable amount of novelty."[44] But Ignatius assumed that risk because he believed that only through concrete experiences of working for God and with God could a man learn how God works in life situations. As a result of this insistence of learning by doing, the Jesuit novice or tertian came to appreciate that his vocation was genuinely founded on what he himself possessed before God. On the other hand, the superiors of the Society of Jesus came to appreciate the kinds of men who had presented

---

[43] Ibid., 84–85.
[44] de Guibert, *The Jesuits*, 103.

themselves for the life and the ministry of the Society. This kind of formation established a climate in which Jesuits expected to learn from one another. Consequently, a pattern of mutuality in learning characterizes not only the life of candidates to the Society but the life of those who had taken final vows. To be a Jesuit is to learn from one another.

In discussing the educational pattern within the life and work of formed Jesuits, I emphasize the idea of union in the Society of Jesus.[45] For the early Jesuits union, not community, was the operative word. And while Ignatius centers his *Constitutions* on the apostolic end of the Society of Jesus, that is, what it was meant to accomplish for the Church and other people, what sustains this ministry is union, the union between God and the members of the Society and the union between the head of the Society and his fellow Jesuits:

> The chief bond to cement the union of the members among themselves and with their head is, on both sides, the love of God our Lord. For when the superior and subjects are closely united to His Divine and Supreme Goodness, they will easily be united among themselves, through that same love which will descend from the Divine Goodness and spread to all other men, and particularly into the body of the Society. Thus from both sides charity will come to further this union between superiors and subjects, and in general all goodness and virtues through which one proceeds in conformity with the spirit.[46]

As Ignatius indicates, this bonding of its very nature effects a mutuality of exchange both with the divine and with the human. The question emerges, then, how was the Society to keep this bonding alive; what means does it have to dispose itself both to the love of God and the love between the members? Clearly the fundamental means is the acknowledgment of the utter gratuity of such union, a grace given by God for a man to live this kind of life. Establishing that absolute priority, Ignatius then indicates a collection of human

---

[45] Central to the *Constitutions* are Part VII, on the apostolic work of the Society and Part VIII, on the union of the members. That an entire section of the *Constitutions* should be centered on union emphasizes the essential movement outside the community toward the labor of the Society. For an informative discussion of this, see Jean-Yves Calvez, S.J., "Union: Community for Mission," in *Constitutions of the Society of Jesus, Incorporation of a Spirit* (Rome: Secretariatus Spiritualitatis Ignatianae, 1993), 311–26.

[46] *Constitutions*, [671].

means to sustain an openness to this gift: selectivity of members; obedience; the exclusion of members who consistently undermine the unity of the Society; the moral, religious, and apostolic leadership of the Superior General of the Society; a healthy uniformity; communication through letters.[47] But the chief means is the General Congregation, a juridical assembly of worldwide Jesuit representatives, called either to elect a Superior General or "for matters of greater moment."[48] It is from this assembly that the Society of Jesus culls its directions for the future: its values, life style, and apostolic priorities. The rhythm of a General Congregation arises out of the willingness of the delegates to assess the data, to listen to one another, to articulate emerging common concerns and opportunities, and then to forge these into appropriate legislation or directives for future development by the Superior General. Consequently, the Congregation is primarily a learning session before it becomes a legislating session.

In its spirituality and its government the Society of Jesus depends on the ability of its membership to discern, that is, to make religiously motivated decisions about the most appropriate way to live gospel values and to put these into practical operation. Discernment is a learning process that involves the cooperation of human beings who try to relate their lives, talents, and resources to God's priorities.[49] Throughout the Ignatian *Constitutions* there is a respect for learning that emerges both out of the Ignatian reverence for a God who teaches through life experiences and out of a similar reverence for the ability of the human mind and heart to be taught. In tracking the experiences of Ignatius that influence Jesuit education, this radical reverence for learning as a divine-human partnership cannot be exaggerated. These religious principles founded his legislation on formal education, which constitutes the important fourth part of the Jesuit *Constitutions*.

EDUCATION AS AN APOSTOLIC ENTERPRISE

What I have attempted to isolate are those elements that influenced the educational outlook of Ignatius Loyola and, in turn, structured

---

[47] Ibid., [657]–[667], [673]–[676].

[48] Ibid., chaps. 2–7 treat the General Congregation.

[49] Ibid., esp. chap. 7.

the educational experience of the Society of Jesus. Those elements were:

- a *reverence* for the enduringly pedagogical character of God's revelation
- a *trust* that this process invited not only participation but imitation
- an assumption that this process was *mutually beneficial* both to the one who taught as well as to the one who learned
- in any learning experience the *confirmation* of God's presence was the way that it led a Jesuit to recognize his *ability to help people* as Christ had helped people and the way that it *united him* to the other members of the Society of Jesus.

Part IV of the *Constitutions* presents how Jesuits themselves were to learn within school systems and then how they were to conduct their own schools.[50] This is ground which has been magisterially analyzed by Fr. George Ganss,[51] and more recently expertly revisited by John O'Malley[52] and Michael Buckley.[53] I do not wish to re-present their work here. What I do want to underscore here is that there is a continuity between the divine pedagogy Ignatius experienced throughout his life and the emphases he offered in Part IV of the *Constitutions*. He adapted divine wisdom to the secular reality of education and the schools.

There are seventeen chapters in Part IV of the *Constitutions*. Chapters one through ten are concerned with the formal education of Jesuits; chapters eleven to seventeen are concerned with the ministry of education that Jesuits carried on for others.

For Jesuits the overriding aim of formal education was to help them to learn how to help other people. Ignatius is straightforward in describing how people were to be helped: "To achieve this pur-

---

[50] A most helpful treatment of the genesis of Jesuit education as intramural and then apostolic can be found in Pedro Leturia, S.J., "Why the Society of Jesus Became a Teaching Order," *Jesuit Educational Quarterly* 4, no. 1 (1941), 31–54.

[51] Ganss, *Saint Ignatius' Idea of a Jesuit University*.

[52] John W. O'Malley, S.J., "The Schools," in *The First Jesuits* (Cambridge: Harvard University Press, 1993), 200–242.

[53] Michael J. Buckley, S.J., *The Catholic University as Promise and Project: Reflections in a Jesuit Idiom*, Part 2, "The Universities of the Society" (Washington: Georgetown University Press, 1998), 53–147.

pose, in addition to the example of one's life, learning and a method of expounding it are also necessary."[54] This is a rich program. Education should produce character, "the example of one's life."[55] The way that Jesuits learned was part of their mission. Their esteem for truth, their commitment to study for its own sake, their ability to succeed academically without alienating themselves from the humility and availability of the Master they followed—these were part of the educational program for Jesuits.[56] This implies a great deal. The Jesuit scholastic was expected to integrate his formal education into the pattern of his apostolic life, to incorporate the empowerment of learning and professional competence into the availability of service to all people, the rich and the poor, the sophisticated and the simple, the young and the old. The good example that Ignatius presumes is not simply private virtue but rather a public persona that indicated a Jesuit was part of the human family he served. A Jesuit's education was supposed to enhance his apostolic labor, not his social status.

Presuming this sustained commitment to psychological and apostolic availability, Ignatius underscores two educational aims, learning and a method of expounding it. His own experience in education had taught Ignatius the value of sound learning—linguistic, literary, philosophical, theological. His experience of trying to explain the ways of God to men and women taught him the crucial importance of communication. He honored the need for adaptation, but demanded a structured program that insured educated ministers capable of touching the minds and hearts of people.[57] Formal education within the Society of Jesus was treated with deep reverence as an emblem of God's providence, part of God's plan to help people: "Therefore the human or acquired means ought to be sought with diligence, especially well-grounded and solid learning, and a method of proposing it to the people by means of sermons, lectures, and the

---

[54] *Constitutions*, [307].

[55] Ibid.

[56] See the extraordinary letter of Ignatius to the community at the Jesuit college in Coimbra. The young Jesuits there had embarked on a set of extreme penances and public testimonies that witnessed to great enthusiasm but not much prudence. Ignatius's letter is at once understanding of their good will but firm in reorienting their energies to the humbler abnegation of solid study for the more enduring good of the Kingdom. *Letters of St. Ignatius of Loyola*, selected and translated by William J. Young, S.J. (Chicago: Loyola University Press, 1959), 120–30.

[57] Cf. Ganss, *Saint Ignatius' Idea of a Jesuit University*, chaps. 4–6.

art of dealing and conversing with men and women."⁵⁸ University education undertaken for non-Jesuits "will aid toward the same end, as long as the method of procedure described in Part IV [440–509] is preserved."⁵⁹

Concerning these universities, there are three points I want to stress. First, the apostolate of education for "those outside the Society"⁶⁰ is a sharing in the gifts of Jesuit education. Second, Part IV clearly emphasizes that through the universities these gifts will "spread more universally through the branches taught, the number of persons attending, and the degrees that are conferred."⁶¹ Third, the hope is that such an apostolate would produce graduates "able to teach with authority elsewhere what they have learned well in these universities of the Society for the glory of God our Lord."⁶² In other words, the apostolate of Jesuit education is the expression of a mission that digs deeply into the traditions that identify Jesuit life and ministry. Like the giving of the *Spiritual Exercises* this reliance on a tradition does not mean replicating the experience of Jesuits for non-Jesuits. However, it does mean honoring the presence of God's spirit in human life and liberating the dynamism of God's healing and consecrating power in human enterprises. The authenticity of Jesuit education, then, does not rely primarily on the details of Ignatius's life but on the vision he offered of the dignity of teaching, of the authority inherent in sound learning, and of the power of communicating well what one has learned. Finally, this vision proves its validity when, as it did for Ignatius, it empowers us to use what we are and what we have to help others.

CONCLUSION

In describing the impact of Ignatius Loyola on his life, one writer, not a Jesuit, expresses it in these words:

> I have read every major biography and book about Ignatius, I have held his shoes in my hands, I have walked through his freshly restored

---

⁵⁸ *Constitutions*, [814].

⁵⁹ Ibid., [815].

⁶⁰ Ibid., [440].

⁶¹ Ibid. Cf. Buckley, "Ignatius' Understanding of the Jesuit University," in *The Catholic University*, 57–63.

⁶² Ibid.

rooms in the house next to what is now the Church of the Gesu, and I have next to me as I write this a nail that was in one of the walls. Supernatural prodigies have nothing to do with my rapt and consuming interest in him. I have simply been trying to figure out how to live my life magnificently, as Ignatius did, who sought in all his works and activities the greater glory of God.[63]

I like the description for two immediate reasons. The appreciation testifies to accomplishment and to challenge. Ignatius truly did great deeds, and education was at the heart of these. Ignatius invites us to similar deeds, and education ought to be at the heart of these. Let me unpack these reflections, using the unpacking as a way to orient what I have summarized to the present condition of Jesuit and Catholic education today.

An increasing number of educators laments the lessening of the religious and the spiritual and the Catholic in higher education today.[64] But alongside these uneasy reflections there is also a lively resurrection of interest and activity about mission and identity and values.[65] People care deeply about those traditions that have bound faith and culture together in an integrated view of education. Many want to reclaim an authenticity not only of goals but of means. I suspect that throughout these days we shall hear much more about both goals and means. But the ultimate question, I suggest, is how do we relate to traditions? If we believe that we possess them then we want to sustain their vigor. If we believe that we have lost them,

---

[63] Ron Hansen, "Saint Ignatius of Loyola, The Pilgrim," in A Tremor of Bliss: Contemporary Writers on the Saints, ed. Paul Elie; introduction by Robert Coles (New York: Riverhead Books, 1995), 112.

[64] For example: James Tunstead Burtchaell, C.S.C., The Dying of the Light: The Disengagement of Colleges and Universities from Their Christian Churches (Grand Rapids: Eerdmans, 1998). In his Preface, Burtchaell cites the "magisterial work already done by George Mardsen, Philip Gleason, and Douglas Sloan," ix–xiii. To this list I would add: Buckley, "A Conversation with a Friend," in The Catholic University, 40–51; David W. Gill, ed., Should God Get Tenure? (Grand Rapids: Eerdmans, 1997); Alvin Kernan ed., What's Happened to the Humanities? (Princeton: Princeton University Press, 1997); Warren F. Nord, Religion and American Education: Rethinking a National Dilemma (Chapel Hill: University of North Carolina Press, 1995).

[65] For example: The annual meeting of the Committee on Identity and Mission of the Association of Jesuit Colleges and Universities brings together a number of representatives, male and female, Jesuits and others, whose universities have delegated them to give specific oversight to the promotion of Jesuit and Catholic values in higher education.

then we want to recover their vigor. These are two different processes, but they are enlivened by a common inspiration: experience.

By experience I do not mean raw sense data nor a fleeting emotion
but a sustained process that engages the humanity of a person.[66] In
describing the processes of conversion, dedication, and accomplishment that characterize the life of Ignatius Loyola, I wanted to lay
out such an experience. I wanted to describe something that was
available to others in his day and remains available to us today. Do
we/can we have access to this kind of religious sensibility today?
Those of us involved in the work of mission and identity in our colleges and universities ask ourselves these questions daily. Those involved in development and fund-raising have to ask themselves these
questions frequently. The discussions surrounding *Ex Corde Ecclesiae* and its application to the United States have involved administrators and faculty in significant discussions about the identity and
mission of Jesuit, Catholic higher education.[67] In a pluralistic culture
how do we ask Ignatian questions and how do we present Ignatian
ideals and values?

In the May 22, 1999 issue of *America*, John Donohue reflected on
the significance of this 400th birthday of the *Ratio*. His conclusion
suggests a way, a means, whereby all of us in today's pluralistic culture can sustain or revive the Ignatian experience of education. "The
secret of the success of those Jesuit schools cannot be found in the
letter of the *Ratio*. It has been said that all the Renaissance school
plans looked pretty much alike on paper. What made the 17th century Jesuit schools effective could only have been the element that
is indispensable for every school that works well—good teaching."[68]

---

[66] Tad Dunne has provided a succinct overview of this in his contribution "Experience," in *The New Dictionary of Catholic Spirituality*, ed. Michael Downey (College-
ville: The Liturgical Press, 1993), 365–77. A more recent study, while focused on
spirituality, develops much of what I suggest in this presentation: Ronald Rolheiser,
The Holy Longing: The Search for a Christian Spirituality (New York: Doubleday,
1999).

[67] A recent issue of *Origins* provides both a copy of the National Catholic Conference of Bishops committee's most recent draft and a margin history of the discussion: "An Application to the United States of *Ex Corde Ecclesiae*," *Origins* 29
(September 30, 1999), 245, 247–54. James Burtchaell has provided a slanted, albeit
entertaining, résumé of the proceedings in *Crisis* for July/August, 1999; I received
my copy through the internet: http://www.catholic.net/rcc/periodicals/crisis/July–
Aug99/everything.html.

[68] John W. Donohue, "A School Plan's 400th Birthday," *America* 180 (May 22,
1999), 26.

I agree. In the climate of university and college culture today teaching frequently competes with research; and research wins, at least when it comes to tenure. But my experience has been that the publishing faculty and research scholars among us are also dedicated to teaching, to a mentoring of excellence that they hope will be passed to others. It is this care for the generation at the cusp of scholarship and/or adulthood that we face in all our discussions. We want what we do to help people. It is this experience that I sometimes desperately assert to Boston College when I speak with faculty, staff, and administrators about the Ignatian tradition. It is here where I place my primary trust in my negotiations with faculty and staff about the mission. It is here where I find the Ignatian strategy of attention, reverence, and devotion capable of bridging gaps and translating competing values into generous, shared concerns about creating a new kind of academic community in which we can speak to one another in order to learn from one another. It is here where we have to start in the relationships that bind a school together.

If we fear that this may not be enough, I am heartened by another observation in John Donohue's *America* piece: "*Magistri sint insignes*—'The teachers should be outstanding,' said a Spanish Jesuit writing some years before the *Ratio* appeared. Surely not all fully measured up. No doubt some were flat failures. It is a fair guess, though, that there were a fair number of competent teachers who did seriously care that their students should really learn and should also become good Christians."[69] Our aim today would be more ecumenical; but the concern is still there and the odds are that there are a large number who have remained in education because they believe in this care of the young, because they have an investment in the next generation of scholars and professionals. Would Ignatius believe that this basic experience of caring was foundation enough? Would he see in this kind of bond a union of minds and hearts? Would he believe that this common denominator can lead us to God? I believe that he would. I also believe that to ascribe to this vision and to foster the kind of conversation that invites a hunger and thirst for something more is to live in some ways as he did—magnificently.

---

[69] Ibid.

RESPONSE TO
HOWARD GRAY, S.J.

George Aschenbrenner, S.J.

Fr. Gray's stress on and development of an educational pedagogy, a tutelage, revealed in the whole of Ignatius's life experience is very enlightening and gets us off to a good start. This seminar will also focus on Ignatius's experience of the Parisian method, but it is important, here at the beginning, to recognize the educational method enshrined in Ignatius's lived daily experience. In the daily discerned life of Ignatius's pilgrim mysticism there was an educational event *de arriba*, from above, which affected his own deeply personal interior life, his relations with others, and, finally, everything within the ken of his life.

Manresa was central in this foundation of Ignatian education. And, yes, "trust is the glue that holds this spiritual education together." Manresa was a great school of trust. The divine schoolteacher tutored the "young" thirty-one-year-old child in a trust carved into his heart and soul.

I want to re-emphasize this central point of Fr. Gray in three ways: looking at the journey from Loyola to Manresa for Ignatius, looking at the absolutely radical trust to which he was invited and challenged at Manresa, and looking at some contemporary deceptions that can mislead when such radical trust is lacking.

THE TRIP FROM LOYOLA TO MANRESA

This journey, a matter of some 300 miles, involved a stretch of soul Ignatius could not have imagined. After the battle wound of Pamplona and the excruciating resetting of the bones of his leg, he met

Jesus at Loyola as never before. A methodical reading of the 181 chapters of Ludolph of Saxony's *Life of Christ* profoundly reoriented his soul and brought Christ alive in love as never before. At the same time, reading some of the lives of the saints in *The Golden Legend* fired his sense of heroism and magnanimity—qualities that had stirred his heart before but which were now sharply reoriented. He was emotionally on fire to do even greater things for God than Francis of Assisi and Dominic had done.[1] But there was a lot of self-throbbing in this determination to top the other saints. It rang with the same heroic competitiveness that had prevented his surrendering at Pamplona even though faced with insurmountable odds. The heroism of his heart had now been redirected, but it still revealed a lot of selfish prejudice.

Manresa would strip and purify him within an inch of his life. A series of desolations and struggles with scruples threw him in reliance on Jesus alone as he had never experienced before.[2] It was as if he were left with Jesus on the Cross, immersed in that rock-bottom foundational trust to which Jesus was reduced on the Cross. Ignatius left Manresa having been stripped of his willful, competitive desire to top the saints. Now he had only Jesus, and knew he was "glued" to him in a radical trust that could never fail. He would discern and follow whatever and wherever the Divine Majesty chose for his specially unique participation in God's Glorious Enterprise of transforming our universe.

Yes, Manresa was central and the issue was trust, but it built on Ignatius's Loyola experience.

A Monk at Lincoln Center: Alone with God Beyond the World

In March 1970, Fr. Joseph Whelan, S.J., then teaching at Woodstock in New York, and for almost twenty years after that involved in Jesuit administration culminating in five years as American Assistant to Father General, gave a conference to that Jesuit community in New York about the Jesuit as a monk in the world. He claimed "that a

---

[1] Ignatius Loyola, *A Pilgrim's Journey: The Autobiography of Ignatius Loyola*, introduction, translation, and commentary by Joseph N. Tylenda, S.J. (Wilmington: Michael Glazier, 1985), nos. 2–8, pp. 9–15.

[2] Ibid., nos. 22–23, pp. 31–32.

Jesuit belongs, and precisely as Jesuit, in Times Square and in Lincoln Center."[3] Here we are almost thirty years later in Lincoln Center reflecting on that Ignatian spirituality and its educational implications.

In that conference, Fr. Whelan made heavy use of an essay by Karl Rahner entitled "The Ignatian Mysticism of Joy in the World."[4] In that essay, Rahner speaks of an essential foundation for the Ignatian grace of finding God in all things. "Ignatian piety is a piety of the Cross . . . and, because it is Christian, is directed to the God *beyond* the whole world, . . . and it is precisely in the emphasis on this attitude that its peculiar character is to be found, as well as the foundation for the fact and the meaning of its joy in the world."[5] In his Calvary experience, Jesus reveals most dramatically and clearly that his identity and focus of heart are fascinated with and absorbed into a God of love whose essence is way beyond anything of this world. In this sense of being rooted and centered in God alone, far from the world, Rahner calls Ignatian piety "monastic." This is not meant in a juridical manner of life-style. Rather, "monastic" has a profound theological and religious sense.[6] It signifies a direction of life, a center of existence, an identity.

This monastic heart of Ignatian spirituality always involves an utterly foundational moment of choice and crisis: either God or the world. In this crisis, whether dramatically enfleshed in the threatening presence of an absurd catastrophe or gradually developed in the ripening of our spiritual awareness, we choose as clearly and decisively as we can God, yes, God over the world. This is a moment fraught with risk and tingling with the excitement of trust, a trusting faith in God alone. It is the trust of Jesus on Calvary, his feelings stinging with forsakenness, but in his core faith still in touch with and utterly abandoned to One he calls "my dearly beloved Father."[7] In fact, that profoundly core faith is all he has to cling to. As Psalms 62 and 63 put it: "Only in God will my soul be at rest." and "Your

---

[3] Unpublished comment from a New York conference.

[4] Karl Rahner, "The Ignatian Mysticism of Joy in the World," in *Theological Investigations*, vol. 3 (London: Darton, Longman and Todd, 1967), 277–93.

[5] Ibid., 281

[6] Ibid., 281

[7] George Aschenbrenner, S.J., "Monasticism of the Heart: The Core of All Christian Lifestyles," *Review for Religious*, 49 (July/August, 1990), 487–89

love is better than life itself." It is a trust stripped of emotion, stripped of self, stripped of all worldly satisfaction.

But it is a profoundly personal trust rooted in a loving God alone. This is Ignatius's most radical and challenging experience of God's trust. At Manresa, in the temptation to suicide, he clung to his trust in Jesus. Though Loyola had prepared him for this, he could never have guessed that God's trust would strip him so totally—and, finally, support him so faithfully. It was an experience beyond anything he had ever known. And it marked him for life with hope and trust into the future.

God over the world! How can this radical choice lead to joy in the world and to a spirituality meant to inspire a whole education that claims to find God in all things? This choice for God is not an unhealthy negation of the world. Rather, in its starkness, such an experience lifts our identity to the lengths of God greater than our world and makes us capable of God's own free passionate commitment to the world revealed in Christ. It is only by transcending the world into God's all-sufficient trusting love that we are ready to be sent, *always* ready to be sent, as Jesus was, from the heart of God back into a world marked by and sensitive to divine trust in all things. This stark, stripping, either/or choice makes possible a life of trusting service enlightened in a both/and vision—trusting and finding God both in the most likely and in the most unlikely situations of our world.[8]

The monk flees this world to be alone in and with God. Religiously and theologically this monastic experience is not world-denying. But it does shift the center of identity from a self too entangled with this world, to God way beyond this world. This shift of identity-center wrenches and purifies our soul. It is never automatic, nor easily slipped into. It is a journey we must all make, a tutelage we must all undergo, as Ignatius did in his movement from Loyola to Manresa.

There is a dynamic principle at work here in my reflections (based very much on those of Rahner in the article previously quoted). A mortification of self in all things makes possible finding God, instead of self, in all things. The experience of superabundant divine trust in finding all things in God comes first, and then facilitates the trusting freedom for finding God in all things. To overlook or shortchange this dynamic principle will usually have deleterious effects in the

---

[8] Ibid., 490–91

trusting educational pedagogy of a person's life. In the closing section of my response, I point briefly to some of these deleterious deceptions.

MISTAKEN IDENTITIES

When we try to tone down or avoid the radical challenge of *monastic* trust in God alone at the heart of Ignatian spirituality (and education)—and there is much in us all that wants to avoid such a challenge—then the presence of attention, reverence, and devotion in our hearts is dulled and complacently weighted toward self. This is not to deny a healthy belief in and acceptance of self as fundamental to any Ignatian pedagogy. The difference between a belief in self that is fundamental to healthy religious identity and one collapsed into a selfism absorbing all one's energies is often subtle and not easily detected. But such deception is rampant in much of contemporary western culture.

Let me sketch briefly, in conclusion, four examples.

1. In an overly therapeutic atmosphere, a healthy care for self can easily corrupt and fixate into a person's whole-life enterprise. This care for self can supersede and downplay much responsible stewardship for one another and for this universe of ours. Once this has happened, the "global dimension" of education and of human existence becomes simply trendy words.

2. Education for mature individual responsibility can misfire into the overly confident autonomy of today's brand of rugged individualism. And it is quite clear that this contemporary secular ideal of arrogant autonomy destroys hope for much union and sharing among us. I would suggest that the Christian version of autonomy is born in the experience of forgiveness in Christ crucified and risen and is, therefore, characterized by a gratitude eager to serve.[9]

3. Education for an appreciation of one's identity as gifted creature of God can also subtly misfire. Creatures gifted with a deep-hearted desire to be like God can easily be tricked into a desire, and

---

[9] George Aschenbrenner, S.J., "I Want To Be Like God: A Birthright for Autonomy," in *Handbook of Spirituality for Ministers*, vol. 2, ed. Robert J. Wicks (New York: Paulist, 2000).

even a decision, to *be* God. Though the similarity between these two desires is close, there is a world of difference with disastrous consequences when misunderstood.[10]

4. Education for Christian responsibility and service can be waylaid by a self-protective misuse of power for domination. In a culture of flagrant violence and super safety-consciousness, such personal power can seem sensible enough, almost even responsible, but often leaves a trail of abuse and domination that violates and makes hardly possible at all interpersonal trust, attention, reverence, and devotion.

All of this is not to criticize or denigrate Fr. Gray's vision. I applaud his closing masterful development of Ignatian spiritual education, and I agree wholeheartedly. In these few closing examples of potential mistaken identities (and there are quite a few more, I suspect), the issue is always the same: the person is not *monastic* enough, namely, centered in a dear God beyond our world, to be freely and fully present with an attention, a reverence, and a devotion that can discover a divine trust in some very unlikely and apparently untrustworthy situations.

I have explicated a basic foundation for the Ignatian servant-mysticism of finding God in all things, namely, being rooted, identified, and overwhelmed in God's love far beyond this world—an experience that gives enlightenment and fire, first, to avoid corrupt contemporary distortions of self-trust and, then, much more importantly, to live a trusting education we are all still learning together *de arriba*, from above. If we are careful and determined enough, this trusting education will always bear the stamp of that little converted Basque *hidalgo*—magnificently so.

---

[10] Ibid.

2

The "Modus Parisiensis"

Gabriel Codina, S.J.

First Stages

On April 8, 1548, after a difficult passage of three weeks, buffeted by rough seas and imperiled by Turkish pirates, Jerónimo Nadal and nine fellow Jesuits landed at Messina from Rome. It was a group carefully selected by Ignatius, destined to found what is considered to be the first Jesuit College for externs. To no other work of the Society had Ignatius given such consideration in assigning a team as numerous or as select. In doing so, Ignatius had to suffer the negative comments of Nicolás de Bobadilla, the most critical of Ignatius's companions, who was displeased with the loss of personnel in such an undertaking. Yet time would justify the intuition of Ignatius: Messina would become the prototype and model for all the other colleges of the Society, the first laboratory for Jesuit pedagogy.

The expectations of the city, which had sought insistently from Ignatius the creation of the College, could not have been higher. Within fifteen days the group had begun classes, thanks to the efficient organization of Jerónimo Nadal. The chronicler of the Society notes significantly that the College "gradually introduced the method of instruction of the University of Paris."[1] The reports, statutes, and documents of the College made repeated references to Paris: "following the method and order used in Paris," "according to the usage at Paris," "conforming everything to the method of Paris."[2] So many mentions of the *modus Parisiensis*, without any further ex-

---

[1] *Vita Ignatii Loiolae et rerum Societatis Iesu Historia*, vols. 1–6, *Monumenta Historica Societatis Iesu* [hereinafter *MHSI*] (Madrid, 1894–98), vol. 1, 282 n. 243.

[2] Cf. Gabriel Codina Mir, *Aux sources de la Pédagogie des Jésuites: Le "Modus Parisiensis"* (Rome: Jesuit Historical Institute, 1968), 262–68.

planation, remain enigmatic to us today. What exactly was the often-mentioned *modus?*

The expression might appear to us to be a bit arcane, but to the Jesuits making reference to the *modus Parisiensis*, the meaning was obvious enough. Neither was it necessary for them to describe what they meant. Ignatius, in one of his letters, refers to the *modus Parisiensis* as something commonly understood: "according to the so-called Paris method, [since it is] where the Society first studied, and so [it] knows the methods used there."[3] It had been at the University of Paris where the first companions of Ignatius shared the same classes and colleges as students; and it was there that they became familiar with the method of Paris and came to appreciate it—so much so that some years later they would choose it for their own colleges.

It all began on a cold day in February 1528, when a mature student of thirty-seven quietly entered Paris "alone and on foot" arriving from Spain. He had not heeded those trying to dissuade him from going to France by recounting tales of the great war occurring and how Spaniards were put on spits. Ignatius had lost too much time at Alcalá and Salamanca with his unorganized studies and problems with the Inquisition, and so finally he had decided to go to Paris to study. Arriving at the French capital, he found lodging in a house with some Spaniards, and "went to study humanities at Montaigu. . . . He studied with children following the order and method of Paris."[4]

Because of its renown, the University of Paris was a magnet for students from all over Europe. The migratory current from Spain and Portugal was one of the strongest. Some of the colleges, like Sainte Barbe, were considered veritable Iberian fiefdoms. This explains why the majority of the ten "first companions" were Spaniards and Portuguese. The bull of approval of the Society (1540) underlines the fact that the founders of the Society were "Masters of Arts, and graduates of the University of Paris." It was a new kind of citizenship for the ten companions. In a letter to Paschase Broët, Igna-

---

[3] *Monumenta Ignatiana* [hereinafter *MI*], Series 1, *Sancti Ignatii de Loyola Epistolae et Instructiones,*vols. 1–12, *MHSI* (Madrid, 1903–11), vol. 3, 604–5 (1551).

[4] *MI*, Series 4, *Fontes narrativi de Sancto Ignatio de Loyola et de Societatis Iesu initiis.* vols. 2–4, ed. C. de Dalmases (Rome: Institutum Historicum Societatis Iesu, 1951–65), n. 73.

tius stresses "the respect and love that we have for the University of Paris, which has been a mother to all of the first members of the Society," to the extent that the Jesuits considered themselves "sons" of this University.[5] The University of Paris and the French Parliament did not return these sentiments in kind. From the start they would oppose the Jesuits and slow the expansion of the Society of Jesus into France.

Nevertheless, the choice of the *modus Parisiensis* should not be attributed to the first Jesuits' affection for their alma mater, or as a type of devoted inertia. The *modus Parisiensis* was the object of a clear choice on the part of the Society. Initially, Ignatius had thought that young Jesuit scholastics might follow their course of studies at the great universities of the era. It seems as if he had thought to concentrate them in two educational centers, Paris and Rome. In fact, in 1540, we find a small contingent of young Jesuits beginning their studies in Paris, though soon the Spaniards in the group had to emigrate to Louvain as a result of the war between Francis I and Charles V. So the plan to have Paris as the center of Jesuit formation quickly fell apart.

Little by little, colleges exclusively for the education of Jesuits were established in the great university cities: Coimbra (1542), Padua (1542), Louvain (1542), Cologne (1542), and Valencia (1544). At first, these colleges did not offer classes, but were simply residences for the Jesuits who attended local universities.[6] However, complaints quickly began to pour into Rome from all over Europe, but especially Italy, concerning the lamentable state of studies in the universities where the young Jesuits were studying. At Padua, the most famous Italian University of the period, Juan de Polanco and André des Freux complained about the waste of time and lack of practical study exercises that would involve students more actively in their learning.[7] After having experienced Paris, Padua was a disillusionment.

---

[5] *MI*, vol. 9, 451 (1555), vol. 8, 541 (1555).

[6] "No studies nor lessons in the Society," according to the *Constitutions* of the Society of Jesus of 1541. Cf. Ladislaus Lukács, "De origine collegiorum externorum deque controversiis circa eorum paupertatem obortis," *Archivum Historicum Societatis Iesu*, vol. 29 (1960), 189–345, vol. 30 (1961), 61–89.

[7] *Monumenta Paedagogica Societatis Iesu: Nova editio ex integro refecta*, vol. 1 (1540–56), ed. Ladislaus Lukács (Rome: IHSI, 1965), 358–59.

To avoid these growing difficulties, little by little the colleges expanded beyond their residential function and began offering classes for the young Jesuits. Of course there would be requests from all of these schools for directions on how to organize these studies and the student life. In 1546, the first norms for Jesuit students appeared at Padua, probably the work of Diego Laínez, with specific reference to Paris.[8] But it is clear that the *modus Parisiensis* became definitively part of the Society of Jesus when Jerónimo Nadal establishes it as the rule for the College at Messina (1548). From there it became the norm for all Jesuit colleges, whether for formation of its own scholastics or for externs.

So, while for the early Jesuits the results would be obvious, what exactly did the *modus Parisiensis* consist of? How did it differ from other pedagogical methods, and why did the Jesuits prefer it to the other operative methods of the era? To respond to these questions it will be necessary for us to study the University of Paris at the end of the Middle Ages and the beginning of Renaissance humanism there. We will try to follow the broader strokes: (1) the general structures of the University and various colleges at Paris, (2) the methodological elements of the Parisian methodology, (3) the colleges of letters.

THE UNIVERSITY AND THE COLLEGES OF PARIS

The universities of medieval Europe shared a basic structure. Teachers and students constituted a community: *universitas magistrorum et scholarium*. But the organization of professors and students was not the same everywhere. Basically, there existed two university archetypes: Paris, the model for universities of teachers; and Bologna, the model for universities of students. In the Bologna model, predominant also in Spain, the students contracted the services of professors, the colleges of doctors and the colleges of students were separated, and the power remained in the hands of the students. In Paris, on the other hand, the professors offered their services to students for a determined fee, and, although the colleges were made up of both professors and students, the power remained in the hands of

---

[8] Ibid., 6–18. "Circa il modo di studiare li nostri di Padova" (Const. Schol. Patav.).

the professors. The Italian model responded to a society noted for its commerce and emphasized the professional aspects (law, medicine), while the Parisian model rested on a formation fundamentally centered on theology.[9]

The first Jesuits, some of whom had studied or taught at Bologna, Padua, or the Sapienza at Rome, did not like a plan of studies less systematic or dominated by the students, as in the Italian and Spanish systems, and so they opted overwhelmingly for the more organized and centralized system of Paris. In terms of the naming of authorities at Jesuit colleges and universities, Ignatius took a nonnegotiable position, establishing in the *Constitutions* that this remained in the competence of the Superior General. The same would be true for other officials and professors who, in the universities and colleges of the Society, were always named from above and never elected by the students.

In Paris, the control of the University extended to the colleges and the entire student environment. From the start, colleges of the "regulars" for the formation of members of various religious Orders proliferated: Dominicans, Minorites, Premonstratentians, Bernardites, Carmelites, Augustinians, Cluniacs.[10] Parallel to the colleges of the regulars were a profusion of secular colleges. At times they were simply hospices for poor students, or colleges with two sections: for the poor and for those with means or the beneficiaries of scholarships. Many of these colleges were accustomed to receive students from specific nations or cities, as for example the College of Sainte Barbe for the Portuguese.

By the time Ignatius and his companions arrived in Paris in 1528, dozens of colleges crowded the *rive gauche* of the Seine around Mount Sainte Geneviève. A wide variety of types existed there. Some of them were colleges "with complete exercises" following the full course of instruction; they were the schools that constituted the Faculty of Arts as such. Others provided only a certain part of the course. Theology was studied exclusively in the convents of the regulars, as for example the Dominicans at the College of St. Jacques (where Ignatius followed his studies), and at the secular colleges of the Sor-

---

[9] Codina, *Aux sources de la Pédagogie des* Jésuites, 59. Aldo Scaglione, *The Liberal Arts and the Jesuit College System* (Philadelphia: John Benjamins, 1986), 23.

[10] In what follows, we base our study on Codina, 50–190.

bonne and Navarre (also frequented by Ignatius and his companions).

All types of students passed through the narrow streets of the Latin Quarter. There were the *martinets* or extern (day) students. Ignatius was among them in the first year of his studies, living at the St. Jacques hospice and taking courses at the College of Montaigu. Then there were the *portionistes* (*convictores*, boarders) who paid a fee for lodging at a college. Ignatius joined these ranks later, lodging at the College of Sainte Barbe, as soon as he had collected enough resources in his summer trips to Flanders. The *boursiers* (*bursarii*) were students who benefited from a founded scholarship. Finally, there were the *caméristes*, or rich students, who leased a room or suite and hired their own servants and tutors. There were also the *galoches*, or "perpetual students," who dragged their feet through the halls and streets of Paris.

Beginning with the university reforms of 1452, the University of Paris had gradually imposed order and gained some control over all this motley and picaresque student life. When Ignatius came to Paris, the University had imposed complete control. The Rector of the University intervened in the name of the Principals and other authorities of the colleges, establishing rules and sending censors or visitors to check on discipline and studies. In short, he exercised a complete authority in everything touching the academic and disciplinary aspects of the colleges and their students.

The unity and efficiency of the educational system at Paris was due to a great extent to this organizational structure, and to the strong central authority exercised by the University over the colleges. Two other factors, however, also need to be mentioned: the progressive concentration of teaching in the colleges; and the boarding system, which allowed an enormous interaction between the students and their professors, and among the students themselves.

The statutes and rules of the colleges of Paris, following a quasi-conventual style, followed a common code. In a sense the whole city functioned as a great school, moving together from the sound of the Angelus in the morning, through to the evening, following the same rhythm of hours, calendar, rules, practices, customs, religious and student celebrations, and general style of life.

At the head of each college was an authority figure who wielded supreme power: *Primarius, Principalis, Magister*. In conventual (reli-

gious) terms, he might also be called *Provisor, Prior, Praepositus.* In
Renaissance Paris he also received the Hellenized title of *Gymnasiar-
cha.* The term Rector was not common. Nevertheless, it will be this
last term that will be taken by the Society for its own colleges and
universities, following in this point the Italian style.

The officials charged with studies and discipline were the *Magister
studentium.* (Nadal established in Messina a "maestro delli studii.")
This is the predecessor to the classic "prefect of studies" of the Jesuit
colleges. There were other offices that might even be held by the
students themselves, such as *praefecti (ordinum),* or class heads, the
correctores, notatores, or *decani,* who were also called not so happily
lupi (wolves).

Typical of the *modus Parisiensis* were the job descriptions for the
various offices. Rules and more rules detailed minutely the duties of
each of the responsible offices as well as the means to fulfill them.
The Jesuits remained faithful to this Parisian tradition taken from
medieval times. A sizable part of the first pedagogical documents of
the Order were made up of rules for various offices. The most famous
of these documents, without a doubt, is the *Rules for the Rector of
the Roman College* (1551). The main body of the *Ratio Studiorum*
(1599) is none other than a collection of thirty series of rules corresponding to distinct offices, counting no less than 467 articles.

Admission to the colleges required an entrance examination. It
was intended to verify precisely whether or not the applicant had a
sufficient grounding in grammar (*sufficienter fundatus in grammati-
calibus,* the statutes for the colleges stress repeatedly) to begin the
Course of Arts. This clause had cost Ignatius an extra year in Paris,
studying letters with children, because "he found himself very deficient in fundamentals."[11] The college students were then distributed
according to their level of knowledge and not in consideration of
their age. The Jesuit colleges adapted this as a norm, sanctioned by
the *Ratio,* always to administer an entrance examination for the student to determine which course to assign him.

The disciplinary rules were very strict, both within and outside the
colleges. They explicitly prohibited carrying arms or playing games of
chance, as well as enjoined a whole series of activities and spectacles
unwholesome for the students. Similar prohibitions, of course, are to

---

[11] *MI,* n. 73.

be found in the *Ratio* and in the rules for students at the various Jesuit colleges. Informing on one's companions, or to use a more euphemistic term, "fraternal correction," was the rule of the day. One example was the reporting of those who were not speaking Latin outside of class.

Physical punishment formed a part of the process of instruction at Paris. It has been noted that of the seven liberal arts portrayed in the portals of the cathedral of Chartres, only grammar clutches a rod. Letters come with blood; it did not matter the age of the students. We might recall how Diogo de Gouveia the Elder, Principal at Sainte Barbe, threatened to give the famous "room" punishment, that is, to whip publicly Ignatius Loyola, who was almost forty years old at the time. This was in response to the accusation that he had distracted his fellow students from their studies.[12] It is therefore not strange that the Jesuits incorporated physical punishment into their pedagogy as something quite normal, though they did add a few safeguards. First, it was to be used only as a last measure, after other means of persuasion had failed. Second, the corrector was not to be a Jesuit, but someone hired and paid by them. In this way, the Society passed the guilty party on to "the secular arm." This norm can be found in the *Constitutions* of the Society of Jesus.[13]

Fortunately, not only punishments but also rewards formed part of this stimulating pedagogy. Emulation played an important role in education, especially by means of the *concertationes* or academic presentations, the innumerable *disputationes*, and the other scholastic exercises in vogue in that period. This "healthy emulation" also entered into the *Constitutions*.[14]

It is difficult to calculate how much time the students actually spent in classes. Evidence indicates that lessons occupied two hours in the morning, and two hours in the afternoon. But before and after these, other extraordinary lessons might be offered, sometimes beginning as early as five in the morning. The almost limitless quantity of other scholastic exercises also extended the day considerably. Of course, the day inevitably began with Mass, and was sprinkled with many other pious exercises throughout the day. Referring spe-

---

[12] Ibid., n. 78.

[13] *Constitutiones Societatis Iesu et Normae Complementariae* (Rome: The General Curia of the Society of Jesus, 1995), nos. 397, 488, 500.

[14] Ibid., n. 383.

cifically to the *modus Parisiensis*, the first Jesuit colleges adopted the norm of three hours of class in the morning (without any intervening recreation), and another three hours in the afternoon.

Very little time was, in reality, dedicated to rest. Tuesdays, Thursdays, and Sundays brought the students a "moderate reduction," though classes were not entirely suspended. In the tradition of the Society of Jesus, Thursday prevailed (in many places even to our own days) as the day of rest during the week. Sundays were filled with the celebration of the liturgy, and dedicated to rest. The students would go with their teachers to take the sun in the fields around Paris, a scene that saw not a few skirmishes and gang fights between the collegians. Fortunately for the students, numerous religious celebrations lightened the academic calendar considerably.

The school year invariably began on the feast of St. Remi (October 1). The Jesuits maintained this typically Parisian tradition in the face of the Bolognese custom of beginning classes on the feast of St. Luke (October 18). Vacations began either on St. John's day or St. Peter's day. For Christmas, Easter, and Pentecost, there were also several days of break. It is possible that the celebration of the "second day" of these holidays in most European countries comes from this ancient medieval religious tradition, embedded in the scholastic tradition of Paris and the universities of the period.

THE ELEMENTS OF THE PARISIAN METHODOLOGY

We now enter into the substance of the *modus Parisiensis*. It is clear to us today that one of the most typical characteristics of Paris was the division of students into classes (*lectiones, ordines, regulae, loci;* and in Renaissance Paris: *classis*). Each class occupied its own place and was made up of its own teacher and regents or aides. Above all, in grammar the classes were large, sometimes counting a hundred students. From there, the students were subdivided into groups of ten within each class (*decuriae*), at whose head the responsible student was called a *decurio*. The institution of *decuriae* came from the College of Montaigu, one of the colleges most innovative from the methodological point of view, owing to the influence of the Brethren of the Common Life, as we will see later.

No one could be promoted to a higher class level without passing the fundamental ones. There was a sequence and progression in studies that obviously resulted from this. Ignatius learned this basic principle from his own experience in Spain: the lack of method followed during his studies there. In the *Spiritual Exercises* he would carefully note the need of laying a good foundation, with order and proper sequence, yet without anxiety about moving forward.

Concerning the actual methodology as such, which was followed in the courses, if we had to define it in one word, it would be the exercise. Exercises and constant practice, as a "spiritual gymnastics," put into play all of the faculties and resources of the human person. The variety of exercises used was amazing. The *lectio*, or lesson, was equivalent to the traditional lecture class. Reading, listening, and taking notes were typical in an age when printing was at its beginning and books were expensive, and paper scarce. But at the same time an amazing variety of other activities were developed which we know by their Latin names: *quaestiones* or planned questions for the instructor concerning proper understanding of the text; *disputationes* or debates arguing in favor or against a proposition or point of view, analyzing, distinguishing, making further distinctions of each subject. The *disputationes* came to be the ordinary exercise to which the students at Paris devoted themselves from the Middle Ages onward.

A specialized terminology of exercises developed around the *disputationes* which were used not only in the study of the arts and theology, but also in grammar and the humanities: *positiones, theses, themata, versiones, repetitiones, collationes, argumenta, compositiones, reparationes, conclusiones, conferentiae, concertationes, declamationes.* Public acts and theatrical representations—originally of a religious and moral type, and later of the classical sort—also formed part of the scholarly activity at Paris.

Paris did not have the monopoly on *disputationes* and the other exercises, for we find in the other European universities of the period much of the same system. But certainly the frequency, the celebration, and the importance that Paris assigned to this type of exercises gave it world renown. At the base of this methodology, naturally, was scholasticism. Erasmus, Vives, and the humanists of the period satirized the abuses of the scholastic method, and even Francis Xavier from India, like Jerónimo Nadal, criticized the speculative sterility of the doctors of the Sorbonne. Nevertheless, the Jesuits recognized that this active methodology characteristic of the *modus*

Parisiensis could be put to a good and intelligent use, and adopted it for their teaching.

Next to these exercises, we find other methods taken by the Jesuits from Paris: memorization (*pensum*); notebooks for noting citations of the best classic authors, thereby enriching their vocabulary (*copia verborum, loci communes, rapiarium, thesaurus*); the study of a theme in pairs so as to help learning (the *aemulus* is the companion of private study rather than its rival). Ignatius of Loyola, roommate of Francis Xavier and Pierre Favre at the College of Sainte Barbe, encountered in these men good study partners for helping his progress in the arts.

In Messina and in the first Jesuit colleges we find exactly these same practices and methods, and the same terms for them. The Parisian connection is clear. The pedagogy of Paris, primarily active and interactive, even with its indubitable exaggerations, proved to be an efficient method for advancing in one's studies. It is no surprise that the Jesuits chose it.

Nevertheless, it is necessary to underline the fact that it was not in Paris, but at the University of Alcalá, where Ignatius and the first Jesuits had their first contact with the *modus Parisiensis*. Founded by Cardinal Cisneros (1510) "in the image of the University of Paris," Alcalá became a major Renaissance center for Europe and was a Parisian island in the midst of predominantly Bolognese-model universities throughout the rest of Spain. Ignatius passed through there briefly (1526–27), and many of the other first Jesuits we later find at Paris first studied there: Alfonso de Salmerón, Diego Laínez (both students of the Trilingual College), and Nicolás de Bobadilla. Jerónimo Nadal and other early Jesuits such as Martín de Olave and Diego de Ledesma, who would have important roles in the development of the *Ratio Studiorum*, also studied at Alcalá.

All of these Jesuits first became familiar with the *modus Parisiensis* at Alcalá. From there, the majority of them transferred to the "mother" University of Paris. One cannot disregard the primordial role of Alcalá in the configuration of the *modus Parisiensis* for the Society of Jesus.[15] In a curious letter to his brother, who had consulted him concerning the best school for his son Millán, Ignatius

---

[15] Cf. Codina, *Aux sources de la Pédagogie des Jésuites*, 15–49.

responds plainly: The University of Paris, "which he will find more fruitful in four years than any other school (that I know of) in six."[16]

THE COLLEGES OF HUMANE LETTERS

The arrival of Ignatius and the first Jesuits in Paris coincided with a major turning point in history: the explosion of Renaissance humanism. Since the *Quattrocento*, the new currents born in Italy had begun to be propagated in all of Europe, thanks in large part to the development of printing, and entered into the University of Paris. The new humanist ideas and new theological orientations that knew no frontiers quietly invaded scholastic and medieval Paris. Suspicion against the novel and the whiff of heresy set the defenders of orthodoxy on their guard. Ignatius had already experienced difficulties with the Inquisition at Alcalá and Salamanca, where he was imprisoned on the suspicion of being an "alumbrado." In Paris, too, he had problems with various inquisitors from the Convent of St. Jacques, where he studied theology. He and his companions lived intensely these changing times. To adopt a humanist line was a risk. Greek was synonymous with Lutheranism, as Nicolás Bobadilla pointed out.[17]

From the atmosphere of Renaissance humanism, the Parisian colleges experienced an important transformation. Grammar, rhetoric, and the classical languages, together with the arts, continued to grow in importance and acquire their own substance. Thus was fixed the nucleus of what we today call "secondary education," as distinct from higher education. The colleges continued to depend on the Faculty of Arts, but to a lesser extent. From above all the other disciplines, theology, which was studied in its own Faculty, continued to reign. Renaissance humanism consolidated in the "colleges of humane letters," a preparatory stage for the higher faculties. It is this model that the Jesuits (and the Protestants) would take for their extern colleges, and which would become the model for the modern secondary schools.

The barbarian authors and grammars, among them the famous

---

[16] *MI*, vol. 1, 78. Cf. *MI*, 148–49.

[17] "Qui graecizabant lutheranizabant." Cited by François de Dainville, *La naissance de l'humanisme moderne* (Paris: Beauchesne, 1940), 25.

Doctrinale of Alexandre de Villedieu, so criticized by Erasmus, were beaten into retreat. Cicero, Julius Caesar, Virgil, Horace, Terence, Ovid, Tacitus, Salust, Homer, Sophocles, Demosthenes all replaced the obscure medieval manuals. We encounter the same authors in the program at Messina. The watchword was *optimi auctores*, studied directly in their original works. Texts, not rules. Experience, exercise, imitation, not theory. The *modus Parisiensis* is eminently inductive. The *praelectio*, inspired by Quintilian, became the method *par excellence* for breaking open a text and preparing a student to understand it in depth. The Jesuits adopted it as one of their key instruments for teaching. With the rebirth of *belles-lettres* in the reign of Francis I, the colleges vied with each other in the study of the three languages: Latin, Greek, and Hebrew. The first College of the Society in Messina was planned as a trilingual college, as would be the Roman College later.

Medieval logic and dialectic that seemed to have dominated all of the spheres of the University yielded the way to the rhetoric of Quintilian. *Quintilianus noster*, the master of the Renaissance pedagogues, was proposed as the supreme ideal of eloquence. Rhetoric became the art of arts, and the science of sciences, the culmination of all literary studies. For Erasmus, as for all the humanists, the study of grammar, Latin, Greek was all oriented toward the attainment of eloquence. It is not strange, then, that the Jesuits proposed eloquence as the ideal of their formation—*eloquentia perfecta* as it is called in the *Ratio Studiorum*. Jerónimo Nadal dreamt to the end of his days of a "Christian rhetoric," which would integrate the qualities of the classical pagan authors with the Christian virtues.

Eloquence was not a technique, but a style of life. The *vir bonus dicendi peritus*, as Cicero defined the orator, offered the perfect model for the humanism of the Renaissance. The ideal was not only to speak, write, and communicate one's ideas with propriety, ease, and elegance, but to reason, feel, and express oneself harmonizing virtue with letters.

Virtue and letters. This was the objective that coincided in all of the programs of the colleges of Paris: *Scientia et mores; doctrina, pietas, litterae; virtus et litterae*. This was the ideal that both Jesuits and Protestants sought to instill in their schools: the acquisition of true Christian wisdom. Christ, as the end of all erudition and all eloquence, was the ideal that Erasmus himself offered. For him, the reading of the ancient authors was only to be a preparation for the reading of Sacred Scripture.

But not all of the classical authors were recommended or edifying. The humanists of the Renaissance faced a difficult problem, joining Christian faith with the undeniable values of the classics. Some, such as Jean Standonck (not the most humanist), the severe Principal of Montaigu at the turn of the century, opted for the banishment of the more lascivious authors. Others sought to replace the pagan authors with Christian authors. This solution was completely rejected by Jerónimo Nadal and the more humanistic Jesuits, who considered it an impoverishment of humanism—though they did not discard the study of the Fathers of the Church, or the Christian orators.

How to "baptize" pagan humanism? The Jesuits followed in part the counsel of Erasmus and Luis Vives, partisans of the select editions with extracts of the classics. "Expurgated" editions were also edited, as for example those of André des Freux, who tried to convert the more libertine scenes of Terence into chaste conjugal relations. This attempt did not convince Ignatius, who preferred to simply omit those passages. In the *Constitutions*, he talks of taking advantage of the pagan authors "as the Israelites did with the spoils of Egypt"; and in the case of Christian authors, "even if a book is good in itself, it should not be read if the author is of ill repute, lest he become popular."[18] This statement of Ignatius evidently referred to none other than Erasmus and Vives, who were not looked upon well by him because of their sarcasm regarding institutions of the Church. Ignatius had not forgotten the mocking comments made by Vives in Bruges concerning ecclesiastical abstinence.

Despite the strictness of the *Constitutions*, in practice tolerance prevailed over the law. But the "selection of authors," so typical of the *modus Parisiensis*, was a constant source of discussion in the first Jesuit colleges.[19] Ignatius was not the consummate humanist, but he was a man of his times, open to the new world being born, and sufficiently intelligent to trust the Jesuit humanists who surrounded him. The attitude of Nadal on this point was definitive in the style of Renaissance humanism adopted by the Society of Jesus.

---

[18] *Constitutiones Societatis*, n. 359.
[19] Cf. Codina, *Aux sources de la Pédagogie des Jésuites*, 305–16.

THE INFLUENCE OF THE BRETHREN OF THE COMMON LIFE

To what extent can the *modus Parisiensis* be considered an autonomous and original pedagogical method? The Parisian method was certainly not the only one that existed in Europe. Bologna had its own method, which enjoyed ample influence throughout Italy, Spain, and the south of France. Sprinkled throughout all of Europe there were still a multitude of other Church schools, semi-secular public schools at both the primary and secondary levels, under the governance of the free communes. There were also diverse forms of boarding schools, and also private schooling of various types.[20] Between all of them and the *modus Parisiensis* existed an interplay of mutual influences difficult to untangle.

It would be absurd to pretend that the *modus Parisiensis* was absolutely independent and autonomous, or that the Jesuits received only its single and exclusive influence in Paris, without also experiencing the impact of the scholastic systems of the places where they found themselves established.[21]

Among these other influences, one cannot overlook the impact of the Brethren of the Common Life on the University of Paris, particularly through the College of Montaigu. Many of the elements of the *modus Parisiensis* have their origins in the pedagogical and spiritual currents of the Brethren. Without going into too much detail, we should at least consider some of the more important points of influence, direct or indirect, that the Brethren of the Common Life exerted not only in Paris but also on Jesuit pedagogy.[22]

Gerard Groote (1340–1384), an alumnus of the University of Paris and founder of the Brethren of the Common Life (also known as Jeronimites), initiated in the Low Countries a religious current that captured the populace and transformed their customs into what would become known as the *Devotio Moderna*. Groote, in the educational aspect of the Brethrens' work, occupied himself with the education of youth, and began at Deventer a student movement that

---

[20] Scaglione, *The Liberal* Arts, 11–12.

[21] Scaglione suggests that my teacher Dainville and I have omitted other possible influences, and that we overstate the originality and independence of the Jesuit system (Scaglione, 17, 54–58, 71–74). We do not deny other influences; they simply have not been the direct object of our studies.

[22] Codina, *Aux sources de la Pédagogie des Jésuites*, 151–90.

rapidly spread through the Low Countries, Germany, and the north of France. The Brethren brought with them a semi-monastic style of life, and their schools could be considered semi-secular, because of their ties with the local communities. The spread of this spirituality, inseparable from the Congregation of Windesheim, founded under the inspiration of Groote, overtook all of Europe. The impact of the Brethren on German humanism and the Reformation has been amply studied. Among their students are numbered Erasmus, Luther, Nicholas of Cusa, Gabriel Biel, and Paracelsus. The schools of the Brethren at Deventer and Zwolle were the most famous. Although harshly criticized by Erasmus as the schools of the barbarians, one cannot deny that they were little by little joining in the cause of humanism.

We might now call attention to some common points between the program of Messina and of the Brethren school of St. Jerome in Liège (1495). At some points there might even arise accusations of plagiarism. In reality, however, the influence was not direct but through the University of Paris. Concretely it is the College of Montaigu that is the vehicle for the penetration of the pedagogy of the Brethren into the University. The influence was exercised mainly by Jean Standonck, Principal and reformer of the statutes of the College of Montaigu (1499) and an alumnus of the Brethren at Gouda.

Montaigu introduced hitherto unknown elements to Paris, elements whose origins can be found in the Brethren. We might list among these the previously mentioned division of students into classes, the *decuriae*, examinations and promotions from one grade level to the next, the *rapiarium* or vocabulary notebook, the office of *notator* or student prefect. Another typical element of the Brethren we also find at Montaigu is the insistence on the religious formation of the youth, especially by means of the Bible. Paradoxical as it may seem, this was a novelty at the colleges of Paris. Groote was one of the major promoters of the *pietas litterata*. Theater, which certainly was not unknown in Paris, also took on major importance in the schools of the Brethren. Evidently the Brethren were not the inventors of all these innovations; the adoption of the system of *decuriae*, for example, attributed to the Brethren, was probably nothing more than the secularization of a monastic custom used to divide the work of the monastery.

It would appear that there are some contributions from the Brethren to the *modus Parisiensis*. But we would be mistaken to search for the origins of the *modus Parisiensis* in the schools of the Brethren. Their influence was not the only one, given that Gerard Groote and many other of their educators studied at Paris. But certainly Paris incorporated elements of their tradition, giving them its own seal of approval.

The College of Montaigu enjoyed an enormous ascendancy among the colleges of Paris, due mainly to the level of its studies and its rigorous discipline. Accordingly, it was said that the school was "sharp" (*acutus*) because of the geniuses it cultivated, sharp for the razorlike teeth of its hungry students. Eminent students such as François de Rabelais, Erasmus, Calvin, and, later, Ignatius Loyola passed through the halls of this austere College. Rabelais sarcastically referred to the "lousy College" where he studied. The period when Standonck was Principal was famous for its harshness. His successor, Noel Beda (1509), timidly introduced humanism. It was logical that many of the innovations begun at Montaigu would pass from there to the other colleges of Paris. It was during the period of transition from Montaigu's "barbarism" to humanism that Ignatius came to study there.

In addition to the pedagogical influences, it is important to underline the impact that the College of Montaigu had as a center for the spread of the *Devotio Moderna*, especially on Ignatius Loyola. The first contacts Ignatius had with this movement date considerably before his arrival in Paris. Already at Montserrat, Ignatius found himself in contact with the current from Windesheim, introduced there by the Abbot García de Cisneros. Studies have already been made on the relationship between the *Exercitatorio* of Cisneros and the *Exercises* of Ignatius. On the other hand, there exists undeniably a parallel between the Rule of Montaigu and the *Constitutions* of the Society of Jesus. In fact, for many years a legend circulated (sufficiently refuted now) that the Society of Jesus had its origins in a split from the Congregation of Montaigu.[23]

At any rate, it is certain that various pedagogical formulae of the Brethren of the Common Life entered into Jesuit pedagogy through the College of Montaigu, and that Montaigu constituted another opportunity for Ignatius to enter into contact with the *Devotio Moderna*.

---

[23] Dainville, *La naissance de l'humanisme moderne*, 14.

Secular and Reformed Colleges: A Strange Similarity

Renaissance humanism was now invincible. The model of the colleges of Paris and of the Brethren could not be avoided. The city councils and the more restless provinces clamored for the new type of education in accordance with the latest humanist innovations. Throughout Europe, colleges, schools, *gymnasia*, and academies began to multiply. Among them, of course, was the College of Messina, founded at the behest of Juan de Vega, the viceroy of Sicily, and the magistrates of the city.

One result of this humanist atmosphere was that various secular schools—many of them tied to the Protestant Reformation—were opening shortly before the school at Messina, almost contemporary with it. Their programs carried a strange similarity to that prepared by Jerónimo Nadal. We will mention only three similar schools: the College of Guyenne in Bordeaux, the College of Arts at Coimbra (both born under the influence of the Parisian College of Sainte Barbe), and the Gymnasium at Strasbourg. Their similarities speak of common origins. From whence comes this suspected resemblance?[24]

In addition to the College of Montaigu, the College of Sainte Barbe (its eternal rival) also enjoyed a notable reputation and exercised significant influence at Paris. At Sainte Barbe, governed by the Portuguese Gouveia dynasty, there was a sizable group of professors won over to the cause of the Reformation. Ignatius and five of the other first companions (Francis Xavier, Pierre Favre, Simão Rodrigues, Claude Jay, and Alfonso de Salmerón) were also students of Sainte Barbe.

In 1532, the city of Bordeaux decided to found a college "following the example, form, and manner of the colleges of the city of Paris." In 1534, they gave charge of the new College of Guyenne to the Portuguese André de Gouveia, nephew of Diogo de Gouveia the Elder. The new school was made into an exact replica of Sainte Barbe. The team of professors, many of them "Barbistes," was a select group. Quickly the College of Guyenne acquired an extraordinary fame as the "best school in France," in the judgment of one of its famous alumni, Michel de Montaigne. Guyenne was a successful

---

[24] For what follows, cf. Codina, *Aux sources de la Pédagogie des Jésuites*, 195–233.

example of the *modus Parisiensis*. Unfortunately the rules and program of studies for Guyenne during this period are no longer extant, but we do know the program of another college founded shortly after and in the footsteps of Guyenne: the College of Arts of Coimbra, also Parisian and "Barbiste" so it appears.

King John III of Portugal, a Renaissance man and patron of all the arts, carried forth an idea of founding next to the University of Coimbra a grand college for the study of arts and letters. It was only logical that he would call on the Portuguese of Sainte Barbe, the former beneficiaries of several royal scholarships. André de Gouveia could not resist the will of his sovereign, and in 1547 abandoned the direction of the College of Guyenne to return to Portugal. He was accompanied by an excellent team of professors, all out of the Parisian mold.

The College of Arts of Coimbra, which opened its doors in 1548—the same year as Messina—carried the unmistakable seal of Paris. The *modus Parisiensis* was not unknown in Coimbra, given that the king of Portugal had long ago reformed the university there according to the statutes of the University of Paris, from where he had also sought professors. When the Society of Jesus opened a college for young Jesuit scholastics in Coimbra in 1542, there was no difficulty with sending them to the university that Simão Rodrigues recognized as having literary and art classes that had nothing to envy of Paris.

In 1555, the king confided the College of Arts to the Society of Jesus. The Jesuits quickly found their beloved *modus Parisiensis* there, introduced not by them but by Gouveia and the Portuguese scholars from Sainte Barbe and Guyenne. Among the Jesuits who received their early acquaintance with the *modus Parisiensis* under the shadow of Coimbra, there were two who would later form part of the founding team at Messina: the Italian Benedetto Palmio and the Flemish Cornelius Wischaven. In this way, the College of Messina experienced indirectly the influence of Coimbra. Some of the Jesuits who would exercise the greatest influence on the course of studies in the humanities, arts, and theology for the Society of Jesus were alumni of Coimbra: the humanist Pedro Perpiñà, the theologian Manuel de Sa, the philosopher Pedro de Fonseca, the rhetorician Cipriano Soares, and the grammarian Manuel Alvares (the developers of the *Ratio Studiorum*); all passed through the school at Coimbra where they became familiar with the *modus Parisiensis*.

Another college with a Parisian stamp also opened its doors at almost the same time as Guyenne and Coimbra, though in a very different context: the famous Gymnasium of Strasbourg, founded by the reformer Johannes Sturm. Sturm had been educated in a school of the Brethren of the Common Life in Liège. Later he studied at Paris (1529–36) almost exactly at the same time as Ignatius and the first Jesuits. Won over to the cause of the Reform, he abandoned Paris, and, at the invitation of Martin Bucer, the German humanist and reformer, went to Strasbourg. There the educational authorities of the city entrusted him with the reorganization of the system of public instruction. In 1538, ten years before Messina, Sturm published his famous program, which would serve as a model for many other colleges of the Reform.

The structure of the Gymnasium of Strasbourg is based on the College of St. Jerome at Liège. Sturm himself said that it was the successor of the tradition of the Brethren of the Common Life. But it is also clear that Strasbourg fits as well into the lineage of Paris. There were similarities between Messina and Liège, but the similarity between Messina and Strasbourg was even more remarkable. For a long time it has been speculated that the Jesuits had plagiarized from the Protestants, or vice versa. Sturm himself marveled (1565) at the amazing similarity between the authors and exercises followed at the Jesuit colleges and the schools of Strasbourg, as if the Jesuits had been inspired by Strasbourg.

The Jesuits knew Sturm, and he knew the Jesuits, whom he praised for bringing classical studies into Germany. But it was not for this reason that he found them so frightening; rather, he criticized them for seeking the favor of emperors and kings. The Jesuits were not so friendly with him either. In a letter to Ignatius, Peter Canisius makes reference to the "eloquence" and at times the "pestilence" of Sturm's heresy, and that of the humanist reformers at Strasbourg.

Today the controversies that Jesuits and Protestants engaged in centuries ago about their mutual similarities seem to be sufficiently resolved. Nor is it necessary to appeal to plagiarism as an explanation for the resemblance between all of these colleges, at least in their initial stages. The explanation is in their common roots: The Brethren of the Common Life and the University of Paris. Certainly those two institutions shared much among themselves as well. To a greater or lesser extent it is possible to recognize a common genealogy in the Jesuit and Protestant schools, even if following distinct channels. The imprint of the Brethren appears stronger in the German countries, while the direct influence of Paris is felt more strongly in France and southern Europe.

In later stages, during the second half of the sixteenth century when Renaissance humanism was already well established throughout all of European education, it is both possible and probable that other common influences and examples of copies could be found. The family tree of pedagogy has many branches. Nor do pedagogical models exist in their pure state. Our thesis is simply to show how the *modus Parisiensis* marked Jesuit pedagogy from the beginning and influenced their option for Renaissance humanism.

"The Method That Is Familiar to Us"

Paris was the archetype that served as a model for the Jesuit schools, as well as for those of the Reformers and the communal schools of Europe, even though they did not share a single source of inspiration nor reach exactly the same final realizations. For the Jesuits, the *modus Parisiensis* was an excellent method, the best in their view, synonymous with an active pedagogy that engaged all of the capacities of the student, a plan of studies that was well-founded and organized. For these reasons they chose it. But there is something more than this. The *modus Parisiensis* was the means by which the first Jesuits had inserted themselves into the Renaissance humanism of their time. At a turning point in history, Ignatius of Loyola and the first Jesuits had the intuition to take part in the new culture of humanism, without leaving behind the wealth from the past. "Helping souls" was always the primary objective of Ignatius and the Society of Jesus. The desire to help students "in letters and good manners"[25] is what brought them to open their colleges to externs. They did so following the best model that they saw around them, that of Paris. And so were born Jesuit secondary schools.

In the final analysis, it is the old scholasticism that constitutes

---

[25] *Constitutiones Societatis*, n. 392.

many of the elements of the *modus Parisiensis* as a pedagogical method. But the contents are fully humanist. The Jesuits were not very original. They did not invent a new method, but took elements from a common pedagogical foundation that appeared to them most useful to create their own synthesis, stamped with their own seal. Other educators, especially the Reformers, did something similar, for other motives.

The *modus Parisiensis* was, for the Jesuits, a point of departure for the creation of their own pedagogy and educational system. The method systematized by Jerónimo Nadal in 1548 in the prototype school at Messina evolved and became diffused. From 1551 onward, the Roman College took, developed, and converted it into a model for the rest of the Jesuit colleges. The *modus Parisiensis* gradually ceded its place to the *modus Collegii Romani*. Later this would evolve into the *Ratio Studiorum*. Under new titles, and in successive editions, the Parisian roots of Jesuit pedagogy are unmistakable. At their origin are those ten Masters in Arts from Paris who had studied together "according to the method of Paris, where the Society first studied, and so [it] knows the methods used there."

RESPONSE TO
GABRIEL CODINA, S.J.

Louis B. Pascoe, S.J.

As one listened to Fr. Codina's paper in this afternoon's session, one could not help being impressed by the order, clarity, skill, and depth of analysis with which he summarizes the major sources, characteristics, and influence of the *modus Parisiensis*, especially as they relate to early Jesuit pedagogy. I might say in passing that the same characteristics can be used to describe his book.[1] Reading that book in the days before this conference was indeed an enlightening, enriching, and most pleasant experience for me. As in his book, Fr. Codina in today's paper has fleshed out the historical origins, context, and subsequent influence of a phrase that had been used so cryptically by early Jesuit educators. His paper has provided us not only with a comprehensive understanding of the *modus Parisiensis* but also with a solid foundation upon which to make further observations. In doing so, I will follow the major sequence of topics developed by Fr. Codina in his paper, namely, the University and the colleges of Paris, the elements of the Parisian methodology, and the colleges of humane letters.

With regard to the section on the University and the colleges of Paris, one wonders whether the high esteem of the early Jesuits for the University of Paris blinded them somewhat to the fact that the University had lost some of its pan-European stature and prestige as a result of the Avignon Papacy, the Great Schism, and the Conciliar controversies when it fell increasingly under the influence of the French crown and French nationalistic interests, becoming more the *filia regis* than the *filia ecclesiae*.[2] In this context, one also wonders

---

[1] Gabriel Codina Mir, S.J., *Aux sources de la Pédagogie des Jésuites: Le "Modus Parisiensis"* (Rome: Jesuit Historical Institute, 1968).

[2] As to the impact of all the above events upon the stature and reputation of the

how aware the early Jesuits at Paris were of the strong Gallican tradition of the theological faculty at the Sorbonne, the emerging conflicts between humanists and scholastics over the nature of philosophical and theological education, and the early inroads of Lutheran sympathizers in the University. Finally, while some of the early Jesuits complained about the academic program at the University of Padua, the fact is that the teaching of Aristotle in the Arts Faculty at Padua was more advanced than at Paris, especially with regard to the use of the Greek text in the classroom and the production in nearby Venice of more humanistically inspired Greek editions of Aristotle's works, as manifested in the *Editio Princeps* of the printer Aldo Manuzio.[3]

When one turns to the question of the administrative structures of the University of Paris, one is immediately struck by the fact that despite Ignatius's obvious awareness of the corporational organization and governance of the University of Paris, and, indeed, of medieval universities in general, he deliberately did not follow that model when establishing Jesuit colleges.[4] Ignatius preferred instead to rest the ultimate authority for the appointment of administrators and faculty in the hands of the Superior General rather than in the faculty itself, at least in the sense that it was the Superior General who appointed the rectors of the colleges who in turn possessed considerable authority as to the selection of other administrators and faculty.[5] The study of the administrative structure of several of the Parisian colleges, however, reveals that the corporational governing structures of the University were not as fully replicated in the colleges, especially as the colleges fell more and more under the control of the University after the reforms of Cardinal Estouteville in 1452.[6]

University of Paris, see E. Delaruelle et al., *L'Eglise au temps du Grand Schisme et de la crise conciliare*, Histoire de l'Eglise, 14 (Paris: Bloud and Gay, 1964), 472–73.

[3] See C. B. Schmitt, "Aristotelian Textual Studies at Padua: The Case of Francesco Cavalli," in *The Aristotelian Tradition and Renaissance Universities* (London: Variorum Reprints, 1984), vol. 13, esp. 287–94. See also Schmitt's *Aristotle and the Renaissance* (Cambridge: Harvard University Press, 1983).

[4] On the corporate structure and operation of the medieval university, see Walter Rüegg, "Themes," in *Universities in the Middle Ages*, ed. H. De Ridder-Symoens (Cambridge, Cambridge University Press, 1992), 35–41.

[5] Codina, *Aur sources de la Pédagogie des Jésuites*, 274–75.

[6] Hastings Rashdall, *The Universities of Europe in the Middle Ages*. 3 vols. New edition by F. M. Powicke and A. B. Emden, vol 1: *Salerno, Bologna, Paris* (Oxford: Oxford University Press, 1936), 497–539.

Was Ignatius's insistence upon the ultimate authority of the Superior General and the Rector as his appointee influenced by the changing administrative structures in the Parisian colleges? Was it in imitation of a model he may have witnessed at the Dominican Studium of St. Jacques? Was it the result of Ignatius's own organizational insights and skills? Or perhaps a combination of all three?

Turning now to the distinctive elements of the Parisian methodology, I believe that Fr. Codina rightly calls our attention to the fact that many of these elements were clearly drawn from the medieval scholastic tradition and passed down from the higher faculties to the colleges of humane letters, but we should not forget that many of these pedagogical methods also have earlier roots in the twelfth-century humanistic tradition. Evidence to this effect is clearly seen in John of Salisbury's description of the teaching methods used by Bernard of Chartres (ca. 1080–1130) in his grammar classes at the Cathedral School of Chartres. Here too we find clear evidence of academic exercises such as prelection, repetition, declamation, collations, memorization, and literary imitation.[7] Finally, the question can and should be asked whether in the *modus Parisiensis* we are dealing primarily with a pedagogical method alone or also in some degree with a philosophy of education?

One of the first questions that arises with regard to the colleges of humane letters at Paris relates to their historical evolution. On this point Fr. Codina's thesis is that these colleges emerged within the existing collegiate structures of the University as a result of the fact that logic and philosophy came more and more to dominate the curriculum of the Arts Faculty at Paris from the thirteenth century onward. As a result of this trend, the teaching of the liberal arts, more specifically grammar and rhetoric, came to be relegated more and more to the colleges, ultimately being reduced to a propaedeutic status in relationship to philosophy and theology.

The colleges of humane letters thus were essentially the traditional colleges of Paris as modified to meet the new curricular needs

---

[7] For the text of John of Salisbury, see his *Metalogicon*, ed. C. C. I. Webb (Oxford: Oxford University Press, 1929), Bk. 1, chap. 24. A translation of the *Metalogicon* can be found in *The Metalogicon of John of Salisbury: A Twelfth Century Defense of the Verbal and Logical Arts of the Trivium*, ed. Daniel D. McGarry (Berkeley: University of California Press, 1955).

of the late medieval and early modern periods. I believe that Fr. Codina's thesis in this respect still holds, but one wonders whether those who taught the humane studies were drawn from and remained part of the Arts Faculty or were somehow regarded as independent and separate from that faculty. In any case, they did not emerge as a fully distinct faculty of grammar, as Louis Paetow shows to have been the case in southern French universities, especially at the University of Toulouse.[8]

A second major question related to the colleges of humane letters is that of the origin and nature of humanistic influences at Paris from the fourteenth to the middle of the sixteenth century. Obviously, there must have remained some residue of twelfth-century humanism even though the schools of Paris were never as distinguished in the humanities as those of Chartres and Orleans. Yet there is no doubt that in the fourteenth and fifteenth centuries new forms of humanistic pedagogy and philosophies of education do emerge in Parisian colleges. Fr. Codina attributes these manifestations to the influence of the schools and pedagogy of the Brethren of the Common Life, especially as channeled into Paris through the College of Montaigu as a result of the reform of Jean Standonck.

While Fr. Codina's thesis has been criticized by Aldo Scaglione as neglecting the influence of Italian humanism and the school system of the Italian city-states, it must be said that Fr. Codina never intended his emphasis on the Brethren of the Common Life to be interpreted in an exclusive sense.[9] Both in today's paper and in his book he makes that position very clear. With regard to the Brethren of the Common Life, however, one can ask whether Fr. Codina would agree with the conclusions of R. R. Post who sees the Brethren not so much as originators of humanistic pedagogy but more as ac-

---

[8] Gordon Leff, "The Trivium and the Three Philosophies," in *Universities in the Middle Ages*, ed. H. De Ridder-Symoens, esp. 333–35; and Louis J. Paetow, *The Arts Course at Medieval Universities with Special Reference to Grammar and Rhetoric* (Champaign: University of Illinois Press, 1910), 54–66. A promising sign of the revival of interest in the arts faculties of medieval universities is to be seen in a new series of publications, *Studia Artistarum: Etudes sur la faculté des arts dans les universités médiévales*, eds., 0. Weijers and L. Holtz (Turnhout, Belgium: Brepols, 1944–); four volumes in this series have appeared thus far.

[9] Aldo Scaglione, *The Liberal Arts and the Jesuit College System* (Amsterdam: John Benjamins Press, 1986), 12, 17.

cepting and implementing the educational reforms proposed earlier by Dutch humanists such as Agricola (1443–1485) and Erasmus (1466–1536).[10]

Further insight into the origins of humanism in Paris can be gleaned from the work of Gilbert Ouy and his team of researchers at the Centre National de Recherche Scientifique in Paris. As a result of their research, the first appearances of humanism at Paris have been pushed back at least one hundred years to the latter half of the fourteenth century. In this context, the work of Ouy and his team have highlighted the humanistic dimensions of the writings of such prominent Parisian intellectuals as Jean de Montreuil (ca.1354–1418), Pierre d'Ailly (1350–1420), Jean Gerson (1363–1429), and Nicholas de Clamanges (ca.1363–1437), to name but a few. Many of these figures were associated with the College de Navarre, which Ouy has described as the "cradle of French humanism."[11] With regard to Pierre d'Ailly and Jean Gerson, I would add my own reflection that both of these former chancellors of the University of Paris were also strong supporters of the Brethren of the Common Life.[12]Consider-able clarification has also emerged from Ouy's work as to the degree of influence exerted on these Parisian personalities by humanist cir-cles at the papal court at Avignon, especially Petrarch (1304–1374) and those associated with him, not only in Avignon but also in Paris.

In a more recent article, Cesare Vasoli of the University of Flore-nce, following up on the work of Ouy and his team of scholars, clearly and emphatically rejects the extreme interpretations of the origins of humanism at the University of Paris either in terms of indigenous

---

[10] R. R. Post, *The Modern Devotion: Confrontation with Reformation and Human-ism*, Studies in Medieval and Reformation Thought, vol. 3 (Leiden: E. J. Brill, 1968), 551–631.

[11] Gilbert Ouy, "Paris: L'Un des principaux foyers de l'humanisme en Europe au début du xve siècle," *Bulletin de la Societé de l'Histoire de Paris et de l'Ile-de-France* (1967–1968), 71–98.

[12] Both D'Ailly and Gerson emerged as protectors of the Brethren of the Common Life at the Council of Constance in 1418, when the Dominican Matthew Grabow sought to restrict the Brethren's claim to the pursuit of Christian perfection because they did not profess the traditional vows of poverty, chastity, and obedience charac-teristic of the monastic and mendicant orders. For Gerson's views on this issue, see Louis B. Pascoe, S.J., *Jean Gerson: Principles of Church Reform*, Studies in Medieval and Reformation Thought, vol. 7 (Leiden: E.J. Brill, 1973), 165–67. Whether the influence of the Brethren on these two late medieval scholastic thinkers was purely in the realm of the spiritual or in the humanistic realm as well has not yet been sufficiently researched.

French influences or in terms of exclusively Italian influences. Vasoli also stresses the distinctive dimensions of early French humanism at Paris, especially the ability of Parisian thinkers to combine and synthesize their late medieval scholastic concerns with their newly discovered humanistic interests. Such academics, therefore, did not compartmentalize their scholastic and humanistic ideals and goals. Nor does Vasoli see this early humanism as aborted by the civil wars of France in the early fifteenth century but as continuing and intensifying in the sixteenth century through the royal support of Francis I (1515–1547) and the establishment of the College de France with its endowed professorships in classical languages and literatures.[13]

Finally, with regard to the goal of humanist and Jesuit education in terms of *doctrina* and *virtus*, that is, intellectual and moral formation, we must remember that these were also the goals of medieval cathedral schools and universities.[14] Too often we see the goals of the medieval university only in terms of intellectual and professional formation. Such a focus indeed reflects more our contemporary view of education than the medieval tradition. The task before us, then, is to distinguish more carefully between the similarities and the differences in the scholastic and humanist approaches toward a similar goal.

In conclusion, I would like to say that despite the complexity of the problems involved in our attempt to understand the late medieval and early modern University of Paris, Jesuits can still resonate with Ignatius's statement in a letter to Paschase Broët in 1555: *Il rispetto che teniamo et amore all' Università di Parigi, quale è stata madre delli primi della Compagnia.*[15]

---

[13] Cesare Vasoli, "Les débuts de l'humanisme à l'Université de Paris," in *Preuve et raisons à l'Université de Paris: Logique, ontologie, et théologie au xive siècle*, eds. Zénon Kaluza and Paul Vignaux (Paris: J. Vrin, 1984), 269–86.

[14] For a recent analysis of the importance of civic and moral formation in medieval cathedral schools, especially in the context of the charismatic teacher as model, see C. Stephen Jaeger, *The Envy of Angels:Cathedral Schools and Social Ideals in Medieval Europe, 950–1200* (Philadelphia: University of Pennsylvania Press, 1994).

[15] As cited in Codina, *Aux sources de la Pédagogie des Jésuites*, 258, n.4.

3

How the First Jesuits Became Involved in Education

John W. O'Malley, S.J.

In 1548, just a little over 450 years ago, ten members of the recently founded Society of Jesus opened the first Jesuit school in Messina in Sicily. That event would have immense repercussions on the character of the Society of Jesus, giving it a new and quite special relationship to culture; but it was also a crucial event in the history of schooling within the Catholic church and in western civilization.[1] Within a few years the Jesuits had opened some thirty more primary/secondary schools, but also the so-called Roman College, which would soon develop into the first real Jesuit university (Gregorian University). In 1585, they opened in East Asia a school in Macau that also soon developed into a university, and about the same time they founded in Japan a remarkable art school and workshop in which local painters were introduced to Western techniques. In Rome they hired Palestrina as the music teacher and chapel master for their students, and later in Paris they did the same for Chapentrier. They were the teachers of Descartes, Moliere, and, yes, Voltaire. In Latin America they had constructed magnificent schools of stone and brick, with huge libraries, before any serious school of any kind had been founded in the British colonies.

By 1773, the year the Society of Jesus was suppressed by papal edict, the Jesuits were in charge of some 800 educational institutions around the globe. The system was almost wiped out by the stroke of a pen, but after the Society was restored in the early nineteenth

---

[1] For general background, see Paul F. Grendler, *Schooling in Renaissance Italy: Literacy and Learning, 1300–1600* (Baltimore: Johns Hopkins University Press, 1989). For specific background, see John W. O'Malley, *The First Jesuits* (Cambridge: Harvard University Press, 1993), esp. 200–42.

century, the Jesuits with considerable success, especially in North America, revived their tradition.

Just as important as the work the Jesuits themselves accomplished in education has been their role, as the first teaching order within the Catholic church, in inspiring other religious orders to do the same. The seventeenth century saw an outburst of such foundations, as did the nineteenth. Most spectacular within the panorama, perhaps, is the model the Jesuits provided for women's Orders, beginning in seventeenth-century France. The Ursulines are only the best known among the many such institutions that had such an impressive impact upon Catholicism and upon women's roles in society—an impact about which we were almost without clue until the recent outpouring of writings on it from a feminist perspective. I refer you especially to Elizabeth Rapley's book on the subject.[2]

A word of explanation may be in order. What is meant by the expression "the first teaching order within the Catholic church"? What about the monasteries of the Benedictines in the Middle Ages, and what about the great Dominican and Franciscan teachers at the medieval universities? The Jesuits differed from these and similar prototypes in three significant ways. First, after a certain point; they formally and professedly designated the staffing and management of schools a true ministry of the order, indeed its primary ministry, whereas in the prototypes it never achieved such a status. Second, they actually set about to create such institutions and assumed responsibility for their continuance. Third, these institutions were not primarily intended for the training of the clergy but for boys and young men who envisaged a worldly career. No group in the church, or in society at large, had ever undertaken an enterprise on such a grand scale in which these three factors coalesced.

But here I want to deal more directly with how the Jesuit involvement in formal schooling originated, not about its impact. I do so because I believe there is something stabilizing, even invigorating, about being part of a long-standing tradition, if of course one understands both its achievements and its limitations and is therefore free to take from it what is life-giving and helpful and leave the rest.

Like all traditions, the Jesuit tradition has, to be sure, its dark

---

[2] Elizabeth Rapley, *The Dévotées: Women and Church in Seventeenth-Century France* (Montreal: McGill-Queen's University Press, 1990).

side. Its embodiment up to 1773 has been criticized for being elitist, paternalistic, backward-looking, religiously bigoted. In its restored form from the nineteenth century forward, it has been criticized for being reactionary and repressive, ghetto-enclosed.[3] Such criticisms are too persistent not to deserve attention. I merely call attention to them here so that you know I am keenly aware of them. But this afternoon I do not stand before you to criticize the Jesuit tradition or to praise it. I am here to sketch with very broad strokes how it began, what it was trying to accomplish, and how it developed especially in the foundational years. There will perforce be a certain amount of overlap with my two presentations because there is no way of talking about how the Jesuits got involved in education without dealing with the humanistic tradition, the subject of my other contribution.

I begin by describing for you two contexts for the founding of the school at Messina in 1548—the state of formal schooling in Europe at that moment, which I will develop more fully tomorrow, and the state of the nascent Society of Jesus. First of all, the state of formal schooling. Two institutions were confronting and trying to accommodate each other—the university, a medieval foundation, and the humanistic primary and secondary schools, which began to take shape in fifteenth-century Italy with great Renaissance educators like Vittorino da Feltre and Guarino da Verona.[4] These two institutions were based on fundamentally different, almost opposed, philosophies of education.

The universities, as you know well, sprang up in the late twelfth and thirteen centuries largely in response to the recovery in the West of Aristotle's works on logic and what we today would call the sciences—biology, zoology, astronomy, physics, and so forth. The universities almost overnight became highly sophisticated institutions with structures, procedures, personnel, and offices that have persisted with strikingly little change down to the present. They professionalized learning, something the ancient world had never really

---

[3] See John W. O'Malley, "The Historiography of the Society of Jesus: Where Does It Stand Today?" in *The Jesuits: Cultures, Sciences, and the Arts, 1540–1773*, eds. John W. O'Malley et al. (Toronto: University of Toronto Press, 1999), 3–37.

[4] Besides Grendler's *Schooling*, mentioned above, the best entrance into this world is still William Harrison Woodward, *Vittorino da Feltre and Other Humanist Educators* (1897; reprint, Teachers College, Columbia University, 1963).

known, and that professionalization was most evident in the creation
of what we today call graduate or professional schools like medicine
and law. Their goal, even in what we might call the "undergraduate
college" (the Arts Faculty), was the pursuit of truth. Their problem
was how to reconcile Christian truth, that is, the Bible, with pagan
scientific (or "philosophical") truth, that is, Aristotle. Great theologians like Aquinas believed they had achieved a genuine reconciliation, which meant recognizing the limitations and errors of
"philosophy" in relationship to Revelation.

The second institution was the humanistic schools first created in
Renaissance Italy in the fifteenth century, created to some extent as
a counter-statement to the university system. The humanistic
schools took not ancient scientific texts but ancient works of literature as the basis for their curriculum, the so-called *studia humanitatis*.[5] These works of poetry, drama, oratory, and history were
assumed not only to produce eloquence in those studying them but
were also assumed to inspire noble and uplifting ideals. They would,
if properly taught, render the student a better human being, imbued
especially with an ideal of service to the common good, in imitation
of the great heroes of antiquity—an ideal certainly befitting the
Christian. The purpose of this schooling was not so much the pursuit
of abstract or speculative truth, which is what the universities pursued, as the character formation of the student, an ideal the humanists encapsulated in the word *pietas*—not to be translated as piety,
though it included it, but as upright character.

This education, unlike that of the university that could be pro-
tracted until the student was in his thirties or forties, was concluded
in one's late teens. At that point the student could enter the active
life that was to be his future. By the early decades of the sixteenth
century these secondary schools had begun to spread outside Italy to
many other countries of Western Europe. When we think of the
sixteenth century, we automatically think of the religious controversies unleashed by Luther and of the great voyages of discovery and
conquest. What we also need to realize is that it was an age mad for
education, when support for it and belief in its therapeutic powers
for the good of society reached an almost unprecedented peak.

---

[5] See the insightful article by Craig R. Thompson, "Better Teachers than Scotus
or Aquinas," in *Medieval and Renaissance Studies*, ed. John L. Lievsay (Durham:
Duke University Press, 1968), 114–45.

That is the first context that I need to set. Now let us turn to the second, the founding of the Society of Jesus. As you know well, this began with the association together of six, then ten, students at the University of Paris in the early 1530s. Ignatius Loyola, a layman, was the leader of the group, their spiritual guide, who brought them all, one by one, to deeper religious conversion through the *Spiritual Exercises* he had already composed. These ten eventually decided they wanted to be missionaries to the Holy Land; but when that plan fell through, they went to Rome to place themselves at the disposition of the Pope, and then in 1539–40 decided on their own initiative to stay together to found a new religious Order.

The basic impulse behind the new Order was missionary. They formulated for themselves a special "fourth" vow that obliged them to travel anywhere in the world where there was hope of God's greater service and the good of souls—a vow often misunderstood as a kind of loyalty oath to the Pope, whereas it is really a vow to be a missionary. Even as the Order was receiving papal approval in 1540, St. Francis Xavier was on his way to India, thence to Japan, and almost to China before he died in 1552. The missionary impulse would continue to define the Order down to the present.

From the *Spiritual Exercises*, however, the Order had another important impulse, and that was to interiority, that is, to heartfelt acceptance of God's action in one's life through cultivation of prayer and reception of personalized forms of guidance in matters pertaining to one's progress in spiritual motivation and in purity of conscience. Derived from the *Exercises*, this impulse was a kind of recapitulation of the early religious experience of Ignatius. This call to interiority was one of many alternatives in the sixteenth century to the almost arithmetic and highly ritualized forms of religious practice that were in great vogue. It is important to note that the Jesuits did not begin because of some mandate from above or even because they wanted to deal with institutional issues besetting sixteenth-century Christianity, but because each of them sought peace of soul and a more deeply interiorized sense of purpose that they hoped to share with others.

The impulse to interiority manifested itself even in the way the Jesuits went about the teaching of catechism to adults and children, one of the first ministries they undertook. Catechism meant teaching the rudiments of Christian belief and practice with a view to living a devout life. The contents of the teaching was the Apostles Creed, the Ten Commandments, and basic prayers, but also included the so-called spiritual and corporal works of mercy—feeding the hungry, clothing the naked, welcoming the stranger. These were ultimately derived from the 25th chapter of Matthew's gospel, where Jesus said that to do these things for the needy was to do them to *Him*. The motivation was powerful. In the sixteenth century the practice of these works, this art of Christian living, was called *Christianitas*—and in my opinion was what the Jesuits were fundamentally all about once they began to work together, that is, persuading and teaching others how to be Christians in the fullest sense, with a special awareness of social responsibility.[6]

Three aspects of the spiritual development that Ignatius Loyola himself underwent are pertinent here. The first I would call the primacy of personal spiritual experience. While Ignatius underwent his great conversion at the castle of Loyola in 1521 when recovering from his battle wounds and especially when immediately thereafter spending months in prayer and contemplation at the little town of Manresa outside Barcelona, he became convinced that he was being taught by God alone—taught through his experience of joy and sadness, of hope and despair, of desire and revulsion, of enlightenment and confusion. Through all this God was trying to communicate with him, in a personal and direct way, so as to guide him in his life and choices. It was on this conviction that the *Spiritual Exercises* were based, for this action of God was somehow operative or wanted to be operative in every human life.

An important conclusion follows from this premise that had—or at least ought to have had—some importance for the Jesuit tradition of education. That is, it is of the utmost importance for every human being to attain personal, inward freedom, so as to be able to follow the movements toward light and life that God puts within us, or, if you prefer a less religious formulation, to allow us to live our lives in ways that satisfy the deepest yearnings of our hearts.

The second aspect, also related to Ignatius's personal evolution into spiritual maturity, we can call his "reconciliation with the

---

[6] For a description of *Christianitas* and its importance in the Middle Ages, see the brilliant article by John Van Engen, "The Christian Middle Ages as an Historiographical Problem," *The American Historical Review*, 91(1996): 519–52.

world." At the beginning of his conversion at Loyola in 1521 and the early months at Manresa, he gave himself over to severe fasting and other penances, let his hair and his fingernails grow, dressed himself in rags. But as his spiritual enlightenments continued, he began to modify this behavior and then give it up altogether, as he grew to love and see as a gift of god the things he earlier feared. He changed from being a disheveled and repulsive-looking hermit to a man determined to pursue his education in the most prestigious academic institution of his day, the University of Paris. He was on the way toward developing what might be called a world-friendly spirituality.

While at the University, he, at least in some limited way, studied the theology of Aquinas, in which he would have found justification for this change, for of all Christian theologians Thomas was the most positive in his appreciation of this world—intent, as I indicated, on reconciling nature and grace, reconciling Aristotle and the Bible, reconciling human culture and religion, so that they are appreciated not in competition with each other but in cooperation, both coming from God and leading to God. Ignatius must have found in Aquinas confirmation for the last and culminating meditation in the *Exercises*, the meditation on the love of God, for it contains insights along this line. The conclusion Ignatius drew from these insights was that God could be found in all things in this world, for they were created good, found in all circumstances (except of course in one's personal sin). The Jesuit *Constitutions* would later specify Aquinas as the special theologian to be cultivated in the order.[7]

As Saint Ignatius evolved in his own life from being a hermit to being reconciled with the world, he simultaneously developed the third aspect of his spirituality that is pertinent for our topic. He ever more explicitly and fully saw the Christian life as a call to be of help to others. This desire appeared in the earliest days of his conversion at Loyola, but became ever stronger and more pervasive. No expression appears more often in his correspondence—on practically every page—than "the help of souls." That is what he wanted the Society of Jesus to be all about.

As the years wore on, he also evolved into a believer in social insti-

---

[7] See John W. O'Malley, "Early Jesuit Spirituality: Spain and Italy," in *Christian Spirituality: Post-Reformation and Modern*, eds. Louis Dupré and Don E. Saliers, vol. 18 of *World Spirituality: An Encyclopedic History of the Religious Quest* (New York: Crossroad, 1989), 3–27.

tutions as especially powerful means for "the help of souls." This is exemplified most dramatically in his work in founding the Society of Jesus and in saying goodbye to what he called his "pilgrim years" to become the chief administrator in that institution from 1541 until his death in 1556. This change in Ignatius has been little emphasized by historians, but it is obvious and of paramount importance. From 1521, the year of his conversion, until practically 1540, he was either on the road or leading the rootless life of a student. That ended with the founding of the Society, and it can be taken as a symptom in him of a deeper psychological shift. This evolution prepared the way for the Jesuits undertaking formal schooling as their primary ministry.

The road to that decision, however, was not easy or straight. The original ten founding members of the Society were, "cumulatively," an extraordinarily learned group, all graduates of the University of Paris, which was still the most prestigious academic institution in Europe. As they envisaged the Society in the foundational documents of the earliest years, they not only did not foresee Jesuits as schoolteachers, but they expressly excluded it as a possibility for themselves. In fact, they decided that they would not even teach the younger members of the Order but send them to already established universities.

Nonetheless, they gradually began to offer some instruction to younger Jesuits, and from this humble beginning the idea began to arise in the Society and to some extent outside the Society that members might do some formal teaching—on a restricted basis and in extraordinary circumstances. This gentle but momentous shift of perspective took place within a three- or four-year period, leading up to 1547.

By that year, the Society of Jesus had several hundred members, many of them with humanistic secondary education and many of them located in Italy. Those who had been trained outside Italy, especially in Paris, realized that they had learned some pedagogical principles practically unknown in Italy and that allowed students to make fast progress. This was the so-called "Parisian method," about which Fr. Codina, the international expert on the subject, has so well informed us. Most of the elements have persisted in schools up to this day to the point we cannot imagine education without students being divided into classes, with progress from one class to a higher one in a graduated system. We also at least pay lip service to the idea that the best way to acquire skill in writing and speaking is not simply to read good authors but to be an active learner by being forced to compose speeches and deliver them in the classroom and elsewhere. Particularly important for the Jesuit system was the specification that it was not enough to read great drama; students should act in them, and such "acting" often had to include singing and dancing. This Parisian style of pedagogy would give the Jesuits an edge in Italy that made their schools more attractive than the alternatives.

Thus the stage was set for the Jesuits to enter the world of formal education. In place was an educational theory compatible with their self-definition, that is, the *pietas* of the humanists correlated with the inculcation of *Christianitas* that was their mission. Moreover, schools were a ready-made institution in which to perform one of the works of mercy—instructing the ignorant. When St. Ignatius spoke of the schools, he in fact described them as a work of charity, a contribution to what he called the "common good" of society at large. The schools were a way of "helping." He and other Jesuits also saw that the schools gave them a special entree into the life of the city and into the lives of parents of their students. Finally, the Jesuits had techniques and pedagogical principles that would make them especially successful teachers. In other words, it was something that by talent, background, and training they were highly qualified to do.

Yes, the stage was set, but there was no guarantee the play would be performed. The Jesuits could very easily have stuck to their original resolve and not become involved in offering instruction on any regular basis. There is no indication from these early years that Ignatius was guiding the Society in this direction or that he entertained any thoughts that formal schooling might be a venture the Society might explore. Why should he? No religious Order had ever undertaken such an enterprise. The Jesuits, I think we have to admit, got into education almost by the back door.

In 1547, some citizens of the city of Messina, prompted by a Jesuit named Doménech, who had been working in Sicily for some time, asked Ignatius to send some Jesuits to open what we would call a secondary school in the humanist mode to educate their sons. Somehow, in the minds of Doménech and other influential Jesuits, this idea had been germinating. Negotiations opened, with the citizens of Messina offering to supply food, clothing, and lodging not only for the five Jesuit teachers but also for as many as five young Jesuits who might also study there. Ignatius accepted the invitation, surely in part because he saw it as an opportunity to get funding for the education of Jesuits themselves; but he must also have sensed something more profound, though we have no information as to what was passing through his mind at the time. In any case, he gathered for the venture ten of the most talented Jesuits in Rome. The school opened the next year, and, despite many tribulations, it was in the main a resounding success. A few months later, the senators of the city of Palermo petitioned for a similar institution in their city, and Ignatius acquiesced—with similarly happy results.

With that, enthusiasm for this new ministry—new to the Jesuits and new to the Catholic Church—seized Jesuit leadership, and school after school was opened, including the Roman College in 1552, which as I said would develop into the first real Jesuit university. It seems that once they made the decision to create schools of their own, they easily accepted the idea that some of these might be universities where the so-called "higher disciplines" like theology and philosophy would be taught.

By 1560, a letter from Jesuit headquarters in Rome acknowledged that the schools had become the primary ministry of the Society, the primary base for most of the other ministries.[8] The Order had in effect redefined itself. From a group imaging itself as a corps of itinerant preachers and missioners it, without ever renouncing that ideal, now reframed it with a commitment to permanent educational institutions. By 1773, the Jesuit network of some 800 educational institutions had become the most immense operating under a single aegis on an international basis that the world had ever seen.

What did the Jesuits hope to accomplish by these schools? Why did they do it? It is often said that in them the Jesuits wanted to oppose Protestantism and promote the reform of the Catholic Church. Certainly these reasons came to play a role, and in certain parts of Europe the defense of Catholics against Protestantism and then a counterattack played a large role in Jesuit self-understanding and mission, especially by the end of the sixteenth century and into the seventeenth. But these reasons were not at the core of their moti-

---

[8] See O'Malley, First Jesuits, 200.

vation, especially when they worked in territories where Protestantism was not seen as a threat, which are the territories in fact where
most Jesuits lived and worked.

Their real goals for their secondary schools were those I have already suggested, borrowed more or less from the humanists themselves. Pedro Ribadeneira, one of the important early Jesuits,
explained the purpose of Jesuit schools in a letter to King Philip II
of Spain by saying *institutio puerorum, reformatio mundi*—I will tone
him down a little bit by translating it as "the proper education of
youth will mean improvement for the whole world."[9] Ribadeneira
was simply echoing the principal article in the humanists' creed—for
their faith in their style of education was ardent and their expectations high. Exaggerated though those claims might sound today,
even ridiculous, like any great faith they had a certain self-fulfilling
dynamism. Don't you agree: an educator who has no faith in the
high potential of the enterprise, no matter how defined, is hardly an
educator at all?

Other early Jesuits were more modest and down to earth than
Ribadeneira in what they expected, while still believing firmly in the
value of the schools for society at large. In this regard they rode
the enthusiasm of their times. Juan Alfonso de Polanco, executive
secretary of the Society from 1547 until 1572, at one point drew up
for his fellow Jesuits a quasi-official list of fifteen reasons for the
schools, in which, it is interesting to note, opposing Protestantism
and reforming the Catholic Church are not even hinted at. Among
Polanco's reasons are that poor boys, who could not possibly pay for
teachers, much less for private tutors, will make progress in learning
and that their parents will be able to satisfy their obligation to educate their children. The final reason he gives is the most encompass-
ing and reveals the social dimension of the whole undertaking:
"Those who are now only students will grow up to be pastors, civic
officials, administrators of justice, and will fill other important posts
to everybody's profit and advantage."[10]

The schools, in other words, were, as I said earlier, undertaken as
a contribution to the common good of society at large. This was true
as well for the Jesuit universities, where the cultivation of the sci-

---

[9] Ibid., 209.
[10] Ibid., 212–13.

ences would be especially noteworthy, for, we need to remind ourselves, "philosophy," that central plank in the "undergraduate" curriculum, meant for the most part "natural philosophy," that is, the sciences. Moreover, the basic design for the universities, in accordance with the tradition of the University of Paris, put theology as the preeminent "graduate school," the culmination of the system. In the religiously turbulent sixteenth century, the Jesuits realized the importance of well-trained theologians.

The Jesuits were a Roman Catholic religious order, and they of course retained their religious aims. But, especially with the schools, they began to have an altogether special relationship to culture and to have a more alert eye for what they called "the common good." In other words, the "help of souls" was not just help in getting people to heaven, but it included in a noteworthy way concern for the well-being of the earthly city. It was thus less exclusively "churchy" than we have sometimes been led to believe, partly because, I am convinced, of their spiritual vision of the world as "charged with the grandeur of God."

One of the special features of the Jesuit schools was that they were open to students from every social class. This was made possible by Ignatius's insistence that, in some fashion or other, the schools be endowed, so that tuition would not be necessary. In their ministries he wanted the Jesuits to minister to anybody in need, regardless of social status or socioeconomic class. Regarding the schools, he specifically enjoined that they be open "to rich and poor alike, without distinction."[11]

Jesuit schools even in the beginning are usually described as catering to the rich, and there is no doubt that over the course of the years and then of the centuries most of the schools tended to move in that direction. But this was far, far from the original intention, never actualized in the degree usually attributed to it, and insofar as it occurred was the result not so much of deliberate choices as of the special nature of the humanistic curriculum. That curriculum postulated the Latin and Greek classics as its principal subject matter, with appreciation for literature and eloquence as its primary focus. Such an education simply did not appeal to many parents and potential students, who preferred a more "practical" education in

---

[11] Ibid., 211.

the trades or in commercial skills. The same could be said *a fortiori* for the kind of training the universities offered. In any case, while the Jesuits of course had no idea of what we today call "upward social mobility," the schools in fact acted in some instances as an opportunity for precisely that. The Jesuits were aware of this reality and in a few instances had to defend themselves against critics who thought the prospect corrosive of the stability of society.

Were the Jesuit schools, then, identical in every way with other schools? Did the Jesuits simply do what others were doing, but with the considerable advantage that students did not have to pay tuition? No, I think that is a simplistic reading of what happened. It is true that in their secondary schools, as well as in the few universities they ran, they in the main conformed to the consensus of their age about what constituted a good education. This is a fact often overlooked when people today ask what a "Jesuit education" is. But there were some features that were special, if not quite unique, to them that began to give a special character to what they did, so that we no longer speak of them as following the Parisian style in the education but as developing their own Jesuit style.

I will describe only one of those features. Unlike some of their contemporaries, they did not oppose humanistic education to scholastic (university or professional) education, as if these were two incompatible systems or cultures. They saw them, rather, as complementary. They esteemed the intellectual rigor of the scholastic system and the power of the detached analysis it provided, and they believed in its goal of training highly skilled graduates in the sciences and in the professions of law, medicine, and theology. They saw this graduate training as especially appropriate in theology for their own members and even for a few select students for the diocesan clergy. In this instance they saw it as a help to a more "professionally" reliable ministry, for they shared the goal of both Protestant and Catholic leaders to produce a literate, more learned clergy.

They at the same time esteemed in the humanist system (primary and secondary education) the potential of poetry, oratory, and drama to elicit and foster noble sentiments and ideals, especially in younger boys; they believed in its potential to foster *pietas*—that is, good character. Moreover, this system taught eloquence, for rhetoric was at the center of the curriculum; that is, it taught oratory, the power to move others to action—action in a *good* cause.

Furthermore, from both these systems of education they appropriated the conviction that human culture and religion were not competing but complementary values, each enriching and challenging the other. Both systems taught in fact that philosophical, ethical, and to some extent even religious truths were available outside Christianity, and that these truths had to be respected. They were both thus reconciliatory in their ultimate dynamism. In the philosopher Aristotle the scholastic Aquinas found truths about the universe and human morality. In Virgil and Cicero the humanists found truths about human nature and its destiny. I do not know of any Jesuit going so far as the humanist Erasmus did in his famous prayer, "O, St. Socrates, pray for us," but some of them came close.

I am not the only scholar to suggest that the benign attitude Jesuit missioners like Matteo Ricci took toward Confucianism in China and Roberto De Nobili toward Hinduism in India related in some way especially to the humanist education that the Jesuits cultivated for their own members to a degree no other Order ever did—they had to, for practically every Jesuit was called upon at some point to teach "the humanities," that is, the Latin and Greek literary classics.

My impression is that the Jesuits, for all that, saw the boundaries between these two educational philosophies, unlike the blur that occurs in North America today where the undergraduate college both is the direct heir of the humanistic system and at the same time, by being part of the university, partakes of the technical or even vocational training reserved to "professionals." What is education for? It is for many things, according to one's philosophy, but it is difficult to be successful in it if it is seen to be for many things competing at the same time for the same person.

The Jesuits, I believe, wanted to preserve the best of two great educational ideals, the intellectual rigor and professionalism of the scholastic system and the more personalist, societal, and even practical goals of the humanists. I am not trying to say they were successful—or unsuccessful—in doing so. Indeed, I wonder if a final resolution of such disparate goals is possible within any educational vision and, unless we clearly opt for one of the two alternatives, if we are not perpetually condemned to some compromise rather than synthesis. Already in the sixteenth century, a certain ambivalence about the purpose even of university education was introduced by the Jesuits and others, and that ambivalence persists even today, though the terms in which it manifests itself are of course quite different.

By 1599, in any case, the Jesuits had had enough experience in education to try to codify their methods and ideals, and they did so by producing the famous *Ratio Studiorum,* or plan of studies, whose anniversary is the occasion for this conference. They had tried to produce it earlier but were not able to bring it about. The *Ratio* would serve them as a guide throughout the world, really down to the nineteenth century. Basically a codification of curricular, administrative, and pedagogical principles, it had all the advantages and the many disadvantages of any such codification. It provided a firm structure and assured a certain level of quality control. It ran the danger of dampening initiative and inhibiting needed changes as the decades and then the centuries rolled on. At a certain point it desperately needed revision, but revision was resisted. Perhaps most important, it failed to highlight the larger vision and deeper assumptions that had originally animated the Jesuit educational undertaken—partly because it took them for granted, partly because they were half-forgotten. Much scholarly commentary on Jesuit education has taken the *Ratio* as almost the only document studied, with the result that what I consider most important in Jesuit education has been slighted or even altogether missed.

There are two further aspects of the Jesuit enterprise that the *Ratio* and most scholarship has missed and that I think are crucially important. I have become increasing aware of these in recent years, and especially during the international conference that I helped organize two years ago at Boston College, entitled "The Jesuits: Cultures, Sciences, and the Arts, 1540–1773." Most of the papers from the conference—some thirty-five of them—have just been published in a volume from the University of Toronto Press.[12]

The first aspect of which the conference made me increasingly aware is the attention the Jesuits gave to the arts. Official Jesuit legislation and directives in this regard are generally quite deceptive, for they are few, and those few tend to be cautious and restrictive. The importance of Jesuit theater has long been recognized, but it has

---

[12] O'Malley, *The Jesuits* (see note 3 above). See also Gauvin Alexander Bailey, *Art on the Jesuit Missions in Asia and Latin American, 1542–1773* (Toronto: University of Toronto Press, 1999).

been little recognized in the American scholarship and generally treated as a subject in itself, not integrated into the educational enterprise as such.

In any case, the more I study the history of Jesuit education, the more integral to the program of the schools the arts seem to be, many of them consequences of the early Jesuit commitment to theater—which of course was itself part of the Parisian style, which the Jesuits interpreted to mean that the plays of Terence should not simply be read but be performed. The plays, besides inevitably entailing music and dance, sometimes required elaborate sets and other paraphernalia of dramatic productions. The arts took the form of what we would today call extra-curriculars, but they were done in many of the schools in a way that fitted them into a clear program—and often carried out with great expense. The great collegiate churches attached to Jesuit schools often employed architects, painters, and sculptors of the highest local standing for their construction and decoration—but not only of local standing, for the Jesuits employed in the early seventeenth century the most celebrated artist of the day, Rubens, and after Rubens's death, the subsequently most celebrated Gian Lorenzo Bernini. Thus, education took place outside the often narrow confines of the classroom.

Louise Rice wrote in the Toronto volume on the celebrations that took place at the Roman College in the seventeenth century on the occasion of academic disputations or degree defenses of the lay students.[13] These were great public affairs, with distinguished guests, who were entertained with instrumental and vocal music at various moments in the program, with the hall sometimes elaborately decorated according to the design of a local artist. An unexamined field in the history of architecture, it seems to me, is the development of formal school buildings as almost a new genre. The Jesuits sparked this development. At least in Italy before the Jesuits opened their schools, no such buildings existed for primary or secondary education, for "schools" were such informal institutions, usually meeting in the house of the schoolmaster. One of the great changes that the Jesuits helped promote was the development of teams of teachers—a real faculty—for such schools, which might range from five or six

---

[13] Louise Rice, "Jesuit Thesis Prints and the Festive Academic Defence at the Collegio Romano," in The Jesuits, ed. O'Malley et al., 148–69.

teachers up to thirty or forty. A faculty of such size required many classrooms, and hence required a building specially constructed for that scope.

A second aspect called to my attention by the Boston conference is the working of the very network itself, that is, the working of the communication of Jesuit schools with one another; or, even more impressive, communication with Jesuits working "in the field" in newly discovered lands. Steve Harris has published, again in the Toronto volume, an article on this subject, which he calls the Jesuit "geography of knowledge." Harris is a historian of science, and his specialty is Jesuit science in the seventeenth and eighteenth centuries, a subject now experiencing an upgraded evaluation among many such historians. Jesuits were committed to the university program in place at Paris and elsewhere, whose lower college was that of the arts, that is, of philosophy, that is, as I said, of natural philosophy or science. It is this curricular fact that accounts for the many Jesuit astronomical observatories and laboratories in their larger schools and for a certain Jesuit preeminence in this domain.

But one advantage the Jesuits had over others was the reports from the overseas fields of their brethren, who also had had good training "in philosophy" as astronomers, geographers, and naturalists. These reports often took the form of the "edifying letters" the Jesuits sent to broad audiences to win support for their work abroad. In Harris's opinion, it was not only the quantity and frequency of this correspondence that gave some Jesuit centers a privileged access to new information about the natural world. It was also the quality of the observation and the dependability of remote agents in executing requests from the Jesuit scientists back home for measurements, descriptions, and the sending back to Europe of natural objects, which could be examined and then put on display. The Jesuits shared this information with colleagues who did not share their own confessional allegiance. As Harris says, at least within the history of science, Jesuit letters can be found in the correspondence of every major figure from Tycho Brahe in the sixteenth century to Kepler, Galileo, Descartes, Newton, and Leibniz in the seventeenth, and to similarly distinguished figures in the eighteenth.

When the Jesuits opened their first school in Messina, Europe was not only in the throes of the great religious turmoil in the wake of the Reformation but also at one of the great turning points in the history of formal schooling. The fifteenth-century humanists in Italy had set in motion a movement that bit by bit was creating a brand-new institution—the primary/secondary school pretty much as we know it today. This new institution was of course derived from principles enunciated in ancient Greece and Rome, but it was being put into a systematic form that Cicero and Quintilian did not know. The Jesuits arrived on the scene at just the right moment to capitalize on what was happening, and they play an important role in the development of the new system. They were far from being alone in such development, but because of the way they were organized, because of the special backgrounds they came from and then devised for themselves, their role was special. I have tried to indicate a few ways in which this was true.

These schools must of course be placed in the context of what we can call the confessionalization of Europe, for they became confessional schools, intent on establishing for their students clear Roman Catholic identity. But they had other aspects to them that were broader in their scope, as I hope I have suggested, that helped lift them out of the special context of the sixteenth and seventeenth centuries.

The Jesuits also appropriated the older institution of learning—the university. This too gave them a special role in European culture, of which science was a particularly important and perhaps somewhat surprising manifestation. By the seventeenth century, the universities began to undergo important changes, as science moved away from the text of Aristotle to more experimental modes, in which individual Jesuits took part even as the Jesuit educational institutions tended to remain fixed in the more text-bound mode.

I exaggerate when I say that the Jesuits got into formal schooling almost by a series of historical accidents, but there is at least a grain of truth in it. I find that they were not always clear in explaining to themselves or others why they remained in it or what they hoped to accomplish—sometimes repeating what sound suspiciously like bromides. But let me put words in their mouths.

First, they were convinced that formal schooling was a good thing for society at large. They were content through their schools to contribute to the common good. Second, they believed that ethical and religious formation should not be confined to the pulpit, for it was a concern much too broad for such a boundary. Third, they were not fundamentalists, for, though not uncritical, they saw culture and education not as enemies but as friends. They derived this last conviction from the basically reconciliatory dynamics of the Thomistic system of scholasticism and from the reconciliatory dynamics of the humanists' attitude toward good literature. They derived it as well from the founder of their Order who, a few years after his conversion, decided that he needed a university education in order, as he said, "better to help souls."

RESPONSE TO JOHN W. O'MALLEY, S.J.

John Elias

I have tried many times to write a response to John O'Malley's excellent paper. I have read his paper many times and have even read and reread his monumental book *The First Jesuits*. Yet, I have not come up with a satisfactory response that is worthy of John O'Malley's paper. He has written the last word on the subject. I should express my gratitude to him and simply allow him to talk longer. But since I do not want to disappoint Fr. Duminuco, who has graciously asked me to respond, I will offer you what I have: a number of abandoned beginnings to responses. A good talk, according to Jesuit and accepted principles of eloquence, should have a beginning, middle, and an end. This talk will have six beginnings, no middle, and no end.

RESPONSE ONE

I am the wrong person to give this response. Why did I agree to it in the first place? I am not a Jesuit; I did not study under the Jesuits; I am not a scholar of Jesuit history; nor am I even a historian. Yes, I have taught in a Jesuit University for many years and have learned a number of things about some Jesuits and their educational institutions. I can say that my daughter Rebecca attended Fordham University for her undergraduate degree and is proud of having had a Jesuit education: talks and sermons by Jesuits, especially Frs. O'Hare and McShane, classes with Frs. Massa and Pascoe, and especially weekly liturgies and annual retreats with "Padre," Fr. Mullin. One cannot go very far with such a beginning, so I decided to abandon this approach.

RESPONSE TWO

Eureka! In the process of preparing this talk I discovered that I actually have undergone a Jesuit education. My formal Jesuit education consisted of an entire weeklong conference in 1967, entitled "Search and Service," at the Jesuits' Woodstock College. Those were heady days right after the Second Vatican Council. My Jesuit education, while not extensive, was intensive and of the highest quality. My eminent teachers were Avery Dulles, John Courtney Murray (recently returned home from Rome after his success as a Vatican Council peritus), George Wilson, Felix Cardegna, Giles Milhaven, and William Lynch. While I have vivid recollections of all of these Jesuits, it was Fr. Lynch who kept coming to my mind as I read O'Malley's paper and book. He embodies for me many of the high ideals of the first Jesuits. He was a man of interior spiritual depth that came through in his writings and person. He was a dedicated humanist who knew the Greek plays as well as any person I have known. He was a creative and imaginative theologian. He was a man of arts and imagination, a man of faith and hope. I am grateful to the first Jesuits who began a process that nurtured such a man and many others like him. Unfortunately, I found nowhere to go from here.

RESPONSE THREE

The more I have thought about the first Jesuits in the last few months, the more I realized that I have actually received an extensive informal Jesuit education. A pilgrimage to the shrine of the Jesuit martyrs in Auriesville was a deeply spiritual experience for me as a young man. I never made the Spiritual Exercises, but I did read and meditate on the book often. Furthermore, many of my intellectual interests have had powerful Jesuit inspiration: Scripture from John McKenzie and Joseph Fitzmyer, ecumenism from Augustin Bea and Gus Weigel, liturgy from Gerard Ellard and Joseph Jungmann, love of the Fathers from Henri duLubac, theology from Bernard Lonergan, Karl Rahner, Avery Dulles, and Juan Segundo. In philosophy, in my days as a Thomist, among my favorites were Joseph Donceel, Norris Clarke, and Gerald McCool. In my primary field of teaching and research, religious education and catechetics, I am greatly indebted to Joseph Jungmann, Johannes Hofinger, and Vincent Novak, my dean in the Graduate School of Religion and Religious Education. It was the reading of Hofinger's *The Art of Teaching Christianity* that fired me to be a teacher of religion. The list could go on and on. Yet, this does not appear to be a fruitful line to follow. What does all this have to do with John O'Malley's paper on how the first Jesuits got into education?

RESPONSE FOUR

I have recently published an article, "Whatever Happened to Catholic Philosophy of Education?" In my research for this article, I learned that while the chief writings in this area are by non-Jesuits, Jacques Maritain and Etienne Gilson, Jesuit educators were most prominent in this country in developing and promoting this Catholic philosophy of education. This philosophy has not continued in any significant fashion after Vatican II. Changes in philosophy departments and especially in the field of philosophy of education have contributed to this situation. It appears to me that the first Jesuits hammered out an educational theory that has much relevance for education today. They attempted to reach the heart, the mind, and the will. They were mystical and speculative, theoretical and practical, committed to both religious and secular values. They strove to educate for the eloquence of the orator and the depth of the philosopher. They were committed to the culture of humanism as well as to the culture of science, as they understood it. Alas, this sounds more like a response to Fr. O'Malley's second presentation to be given tomorrow.

RESPONSE FIVE

The Jesuit educational tradition has been a mixed one. Praise has come from many quarters. Francis Bacon in his *Advancement of Learning* noted, "For the doctrine of school-learning, it were the shortest way to refer to the Jesuits, who in point of usefulness, have herein excelled." The philosopher Harry Broudy praises their schools for developing the habits of speaking, writing, thinking, and judging.

The historian James Bowen comments that the Society of Jesus was so successful in its conduct of grammar schools that its members came to enjoy the title of "schoolmasters of Europe" and to have for a time a virtual monopoly of schooling in Catholic lands, including those of the New World. Even the acerbic Voltaire, who is otherwise so critical of Jesuit education, could bring himself to admit: "During the seven years that I lived in the house of the Jesuits, what did I see among them? The most laborious, frugal and regular life, all their hours divided between the care they spent on us and the exercises of their profession. I attest the same as thousands of others brought up by them, like myself; no one will be found to contradict me."

There is, however, another side of Jesuit education. It was disappointing for me to learn that the first Jesuits did not make much use of the writings of Augustine and did not recommend his *Confessions*. Bowen charges that they accepted the thought of their day as permanently viable and then regularized this into a rigid system. Broudy notes that when success in the world came to be expressed in terms of technology and industrial power, Jesuit education based on the Greek model became anachronistic. But attendees at this conference, and especially Fr. O'Malley, are well aware of the light and the dark of Jesuit education, as well as the strengths and the weaknesses of the 1599 *Ratio* whose publication we are today commemorating.

RESPONSE SIX

One final beginning. Each night for the past month or so I have thought about my response, on going to sleep and in waking moments during the night. One night I got an inspiration. For my response I would muse about what the first Jesuits would think if they came to Fordham Prep and Fordham University to see how their educational enterprise turned out. Would they be happy that the Jesuits are now teaching in coeducational institutions or that they have given up ownership of many of their educational institutions? Would these arrangements be in keeping with their way of proceeding and their spirit of accommodation? Would they find enough *Christianitas*, helping souls and reforming the world? Would they encounter sufficient Jesuits for the task? Would they discover a truly humanist curriculum in Fordham Prep and Fordham College?

Would they consider the faculty and students sufficiently steeped in *pietas literata* that came from extensive study of the ancient languages and the classical authors? Would they be disappointed that so little of Thomas Aquinas or other scholastics appears in the curriculum? What would they make of the offerings and the reduced requirements in the philosophy and theology curriculum? Would they be pleased with the addition of professional schools? The next morning, when I told my wife Eleanor about this nocturnal inspiration, she remarked that this tack might be seen as being too critical or too negative. Reluctantly I dropped this approach.

I had two other thoughts about this response. I would appeal to the assurance of Jesus: *Dabitur vobis quid dicetis* (It will be given to you what you will say). I was not totally sure I could count on this divine help. I also wondered, What if the citizens of Messina had requested the Jesuits to come to their city to establish not a school but an institution for converted prostitutes? The Jesuits were involved in this ministry in Rome. What would have been their contribution to civilization if this had been the case? Where would we all be today? Perhaps the School of Social Service would be sponsoring this event.

Last night after the New York Mets lost a heartbreaking game to the Atlanta Braves and before the New York Yankees took the field to play the Boston Red Sox, I put these unsuccessful attempts at a response on paper. This afternoon I humbly and with some sense of embarrassment submit them to you and John O'Malley.

4

Development of the Ratio Studiorum

John W. Padberg, S.J.

WHEN THE SOCIETY OF JESUS was founded in 1540, it had no schools and, as far as the records go, no intention of founding them. Eight years later, at Messina in Sicily, the Jesuits opened their first school, primarily designated for lay students. By the time of Ignatius Loyola's death in 1556, there were forty Jesuit schools throughout the world. By 1599, the year of the approval of the definitive version of the *Ratio Studiorum*, there were more than 200 such colleges in Europe alone.

However great the demand for such schools, and it was indeed great, it would have been impossible to staff them without a parallel or even greater growth in the number of Jesuits themselves. Remember that the Society started in 1540 with ten members. In 1556, at the death of Ignatius, there were approximately 1,000 Jesuits in the world, most of them at that time still in various stages of formation. Ten years later there were 2,770. Ten years after that, in 1576, there were more than 4,000, and by 1599, the year of the definitive edition of the *Ratio*, there were 8,272 Jesuits living and working throughout the world. In other words, in forty-five years there had been a ninefold increase in the number of members of the Society of Jesus. Of course, they staffed not only colleges but also churches, foreign missions, and houses of formation; and engaged in administering the sacraments, teaching catechism, preaching missions all throughout Europe, writing and publishing, visiting prisons, reforming convents, and founding confraternities.

Almost from the beginning, the Society of Jesus had to provide the training for its own members. Contrary to the circumstances of the first ten such Jesuits who were all university graduates, a very great number of those entering the Society in subsequent years had not had such an educational background. Thus, for the training of the members of the Society, the first Jesuit schools were colleges or residential houses situated at other universities. By 1544, Jesuits were at seven such universities: Paris, Coimbra, Padua, Louvain, Cologne, Valencia, and Alcala. The very earliest document of the Society on education is the 1541 *Fundacion de collegio,* a draft of an order of studies for Jesuit scholastics. Then in 1545 came the *Constitutiones Collegii Patavini* for the scholastics at Padua, with explicit mention of practices adopted from the University of Paris, which Ignatius highly esteemed. During the period 1547–50 came the so-called *Industriae et Constitutiones Collegiorum* by Juan de Polanco, the Secretary of the Society, all still for scholastics; and, finally, between 1553 and 1556, the provision for studies in the Jesuit *Constitutions* themselves. Eventually, the Society opened schools for teaching extern students, partly in response to a demand on the part of lay people and partly as a way of finding the financial resources to pay for the training of its own members. These changes in the type and number of colleges and the number of Jesuits should be kept in mind as a background to the central topic of this presentation: the stages in the development of the *Ratio Studorium.*

In a sense, the Society produced four *Ratios* between 1565 and 1572. First came an informal, so-called *Ratio Borgiana* in the time of Francis Borgia; then the formal *Ratio* of 1586; a revised version of that *Ratio* in 1591; and the definitive *Ratio* of 1599. I shall say something about each of them. But first a few words about their antecedents.

The *Ratio Studiorum* has a two-fold ancestry. On the one side, a series of rules multiplied in the Society of Jesus for every imaginable function, from provincial to master of novices, to beadle of a class, to the person responsible for the dining room or the clothes room. The other side of that ancestry is the plans of studies that the early individual colleges wrote, such as the statutes for Gandia and Messina, or such plans that were written for a particular province. They were desperately needed as schools multiplied and young, inexperienced Jesuit teachers were sent to staff them. An early example of such a plan was Jerónimo Nadal's *Disposition and Order of Studies*, which he wrote in 1552–53.[1]

At this point, a few brief words are in order on the *modus Parisiensis*, or the practices of the University of Paris. The *modus Parisiensis* stood in contrast to the *modus Italicus*. In the sixteenth century at Paris, the faculty took precedence over the students in determining the practices of the university; in Italy, the student body more directly ran the university. In Paris, classes were given in colleges or residential houses attached to the university; in Italy, the classes were given in the university itself. In Paris, there was much more order, regularity, and discipline; in Italy, the students had much more freedom in determining such matters. In Paris, the progress of students came through a set program that the teacher and the students followed; the professors lectured frequently; the students engaged in academic exercises following the lectures; the students were divided into specific classes according to the state of their academic ability and preparation; each class had its own specific teacher attached to it and specific material which it had to get through; students moved up from one class to another after examinations. All of this involved the personal knowledge and concern of the teacher and helped the young student progress more surely and more quickly through the course of studies. These characteristics were, as far as possible from the beginning, part of the structure of studies and programs in the Jesuit schools. We accept these practices as fairly normal today, but they were an innovation in the sixteenth century, an innovation spread widely throughout Europe as the Jesuit schools spread widely throughout the continent and later into the mission lands and colonies of European powers.

What were the developments that brought these methods into use in Jesuit education? During 1557–58, at the Roman College, the "mother and model school," so to speak, of the Society, the teachers, at the request of Diego Laynez, the second Superior General of the Society, had written a brief account of their classes and how they

[1] *Monumenta Historica Societatis Jesu*, vol. 92, *Monumenta Paedagogica* [hereinafter *MP*], ed. Ladislaus Lukacs. S.J. (Rorne, 1965), vol.1, doc. 13, pp. 185–210. This present study owes much to the data presented is the several volumes of *MP* as well as to *Ratio Studiorurn: Plan raisonné et institution des études dans la Compagnie de Jésus*. Edition bilingue latinfrançais. Demoustier, Adrien and Dominique Julia, Léone Albrieux, Dolorès Prolon-Julia, M-M Compère (Paris, 1997).

taught them, and a set of rules for the prefect of studies, the teachers, and the students. In 1562–63, Nadal produced an *Ordo Studiorum Germanicus*, an adaptation of the Roman College rules, a series of instructions written on the occasion of his visit to the colleges of upper Germany. They became rules for all of Germany up until 1570, and were used by one of the other earlier Jesuits, Oliver Manaraeus, in his official visit to France, also in 1563.[2] Just a few months after Nadal had written that series of rules for Germany, Diego Ledesma, prefect of studies at the Roman College since the previous year, was asking that Nadal be assigned to Rome to preside over writing a manual "that would set down the whole order of studies . . . class by class, subject by subject and task by task in a distinct and detailed way of proceeding."[3] Laynez agreed to the request, and Nadal briefly took charge of the Roman College in February 1564. Meanwhile, the members of the faculty of the college had revised the rules that they had done in 1558 and then produced another set of them in 1564. And Ledesma, too, had written a vivid account of how discouraging life could be for the Roman College teachers in the absence of any general norms for studies:

> Not only will studies fail but, at times, certain of the teachers and others who have taken on that responsibility will be shocked or troubled or will make bad decisions or will lose heart or will no longer do anything or at least nothing important because they see that the requests or the proposals that they deem useful and that they have often reiterated are subject to change and that nothing at all happens. Finally and at last, having set everything down in their letters, they just wait to see what is going to happen.[4]

Isn't this all too familiar even today?

The order of studies and regulations that Ledesma had written for the Roman College after the faculty consultation of 1563–64 he gave to Francis Borgia, the new Superior General, along with his summary of the remarks that came out of that series of consultations.[5] In addition, ever indefatigable, he also wrote comments on how to improve studies, on conduct at the Roman College, on vacations, on rules

---

[2] See *MP* (Rome, 1974), vol.2, pp. 85–133.

[3] Ibid., doc. 70, p. 484.

[4] Ibid., doc. 69, p. 467.

[5] Ibid.

for non-Jesuit students, on teaching philosophy, on how to improve studies in the lower classes, etc., etc.[6]

After all of this, there came from his hand the first document to have the word *Ratio* in its title, 161 pages of details on the classes in the humanities, *De Ratione et ordine Studiorum Collegii Romani.*[7] This has been called the *Ratio Studorium Borgiana* because, after some redoing, Borgia sent it out in 1569 with the recommendation to adapt the text "to places and particular circumstances." That last phrase, "places and particular circumstances," was to be of utmost importance in the actual implementation of the *Ratio.* That text went out on September 29, 1569 to the provinces of Spain, France, Aquitaine, Austria, Germany, Rhineland, Flanders, Lombardy, Sicily, and Naples. As for adaptation, Borgia wrote to Everard Mercurian, the visitor for France and the man who was to succeed him as fourth Superior General of the Society, telling him "to put into effect the order of studies which was sent to the two Provinces of France and Aquitaine, in adapting it especially to the circumstances of the place when necessary, in leaving to the teachers the faculty to critique a particular rule if they have something to say about it and in putting it into effect without waiting to consult us."[8]

In 1571, similar instructions on philosophical studies were sent out to some of the provinces.[9] As for theological studies, a commission of Jesuits close to Borgia, including especially Nadal, reviewed a draft document, but it was never promulgated. This was due to two circumstances. First, Borgia was absent from Rome, sent by the Pope on missions to Spain, Portugal, and France, only to return to Rome to die in September 1572. Second, and probably more important, a serious and prolonged controversy had earlier arisen in the Society of Jesus about the freedom of choice on what opinions, both in philosophy and theology, to teach, and that controversy still continued. Doesn't this, too, sound familiar?

For instance, already in 1563, just seven years after the death of Ignatius, Nadal had set down only very general recommendations about great prudence in the way Jesuits spoke about theology, especially because of the struggles against not only the Lutherans but

---

[6] Ibid., doc. 70–75, pp. 481–519.
[7] Ibid., doc. 76, pp. 515–627.
[8] Ibid., 183.
[9] Ibid., 184 and doc.32, pp. 253–65.

other heretics too. His recommendations included following St. Thomas and teachers approved by the church and by Catholic universities (note how universities enter into the *magisterium* here), watchfulness against odd or rash opinions and against being too attached to one's own view, but rather proceeding with humility, modesty, and simplicity, without a list of propositions to defend or proscribe.[10] But a year later, Ledesma was advocating a list of such propositions to defend and positions to take on such matters as the sacraments, free will, grace, original sin, justification, predestination, and perhaps also on the Trinity and the Incarnation. And for years on end he defended the desirability and necessity of such a list.[11] Borgia took Ledesma's view, and in November 1565 he put out an ordinance that for the first time made precise "the opinions which should be held and taught by our members."[12] Even so, the Province Congregation at Rome in 1563 had harsh words to say about the danger to unity of doctrine in the Society: "The main cause of the ignorance and disease is that in the philosophy courses sure and certain interpreters are not explained, but rather that young and untried teachers make up everything on their own." For the other major discipline, theology, Miro, the assistant for Portugal, could write, "Newness in theology is the worst of things."[13]

This was all part of a very long debate throughout the Society, which lasted at least up until the definitive *Ratio* of 1599. In setting up a program of teaching with certain texts to study, how was one going to strike a balance between the *Libertas opinandi* and the *Orthodoxia doctrinae* in which the former left it to each teacher to choose what propositions were dangerous and the latter sought to maintain the unity of the Society and the orthodoxy of a faith under attack by the reformers. Add to that the difficulty of trying to maintain such doctrinal uniformity in a society in a rapid expansion of membership without curbing the serious intellectual research work of its members. Some of the most famous Jesuits of the latter part of the century were involved in several sides of the controversy, even such as Toledo (later Cardinal Toledo), Gagliardi, Hoffaeus, de Va-

---

[10] Ibid., doc. 17, pp. 127–33.

[11] Ibid., doc. 73, pp. 500ff.

[12] Ibid., vol.3, doc. 244, pp. 382–85. The propositions set down here are similar in many respects to those of Ledesma.

[13] MP (Rome, 1981), vol.4, 8.

lencia, and Suarez. The problem was never going to be fully solved, and it is too complicated to enter into here and now in a presentation as brief as this.[14] All through the terms of office of Everard Mercurian, the fourth Superior General of the Society, these circumstances prevented the serious, widespread consultation that he and the congregation that elected him wanted to have before a definitive order of studies could be prepared.

When Claudio Aquaviva became Superior General of the Society in 1581, deliberate work on the preparation of an order of studies common to the whole Society began in earnest. The Province Congregations before the 4th General Congregation that elected Aquaviva asked insistently for such an order of studies and also for norms on choosing what philosophical and theological opinions were to be held in the Society of Jesus.[15] A twelve-member commission set up at the General Congregation to "write an order of studies" could hardly do so in the brief time limits of such a meeting. But Aquaviva himself was convinced that the task should be taken in hand. When he began to do so, it was in the context of a wholesale rule-making effort in the Society of Jesus throughout the years of his Generalate. For example, already in 1581 the Canons of the General Congregations had been published. In 1582, the "Rules of the Society of Jesus" appeared in print, regulations for all of the various offices in the Society. In 1583, a new edition of the *Constitutions* was published. By 1599, when the final edition of the *Ratio Studiorum* appeared, so did the official *Directory of the Spiritual Exercises*, among other such documents.

After Aquaviva set up a first working group to try to pursue the subject of a *Ratio*, he found out that it was not going to be an easy or a quick task. On the question of theological and philosophical opinions, the Roman College professors, for example, thought it best to keep to a few very general rules. For example, one was to deviate

---

[14] See the two works mentioned here for further details. On the teaching of theology, A. Mincia, S.J., "La controvensia con i protestanti e i programmi degli studi teologici nella Compagnia di Gèsu, 1547–1599," in *Archivim Historicum Societatis Jesu*, (Rome, 1985), vol.54, 3–4 and 209–66. On the teaching of philosophy, Luce Giard, "La 'libertas opinionun' dans les colleges jésuites," in *Sciences et religions de Copernic à Galilei: Actes du colloque international* (Rome, 1986) to appear in la Bibliothéque de l'ecole française de Rome.

[15] *MP*, vol. 7, doc. 33, pp. 288–92 for such requests in *Acta congregationurn provincialium de studiis*.

from St. Thomas only rarely and for good reasons; if someone wished to teach a differing thesis, he would have to have sufficient justifying authorities or, if not that, he would have to refer the question to his superior. As for the Borgia theses, the Roman College professors thought they ought to be suppressed or greatly reduced in number.[16] Interestingly, Alfonso Salmeron, the last living member of the first Jesuits, thought that the Society of Jesus should not choose a single authority, even St. Thomas, whom it had to follow to the letter; that only in the books of Sacred Scripture was there nothing to be rejected; and that if a Jesuit theologian in the future came up with a new theory, "which Blessed Ignatius of happy memory expected," he should not be opposed. And besides, according to Salmeron, in his letter of September 1, 1582 to Aquaviva, a catalog of forbidden propositions was hardly opportune, as experience demonstrated.[17]

At the beginning of 1583, Aquaviva set up a commission of six Jesuits and charged it "to draft a single set of rules and an order of studies intended to establish uniformity, solidity, and the usefulness of the material taught when dealing with speculative questions, and to prescribe in the practical order the way of treating the subjects and the matter to be taught with all of the fruit and profit which our Institute proposes to itself."[18] The six men, who set to work after receiving a special blessing from Pope Gregory XIII, came from the provinces of Spain, Portugal, France, upper Germany, and Austria and had held such offices as professor of theology in Spain, prefect of studies at the Roman College, professor of Sacred Scripture at Evora in Portugal, professor of philosophy and theology in Paris, professor of Sacred Scripture and of theology and of cases of conscience in Austria, and professor of theology in Rome. After nine months of work, from December 1583 to August 1584, they had produced two documents. The first of them, *Delectus Opinionum*, put together 597 propositions from the *Summa Theologica* of St. Thomas and classified them as some left to the freedom of the teachers who would not he forced to follow them and others as precisely prescribed to be taught. The text was sent to the teachers at the Roman College, who reduced the 597 propositions to 130 and accompanied the whole

---

[16] Ibid., vol. 6, doc. 1, pp. 3–11.
[17] Ibid., doc. 6, pp. 21–24
[18] Demoustier, *Ratio Studiorum*, Edition bilingue, 37.

document with their own *Commentariolus*, which was published at the head of the very first Society-wide edition of the *Ratio Studiorum* in 1586.[19] The second of the treatises produced in 1583–84, *Praxis et ordo Studiorum*, was also reviewed by the faculty members at the Roman College. It set down the order in which material was to be taught, beginning with theology (Sacred Scripture, scholastic theology, controversies, and cases of conscience) and then went on to deal with philosophy and the humanities.[20]

This 1586 edition of the *Ratio* was published at Rome under the care of the Roman College and there are only a very few examples of it still extant, possibly only as many as fourteen. Perhaps there are so few copies because this edition, destined for commissions of revisers in the various provinces, was meant for a limited public. In addition, Father General, in sending to the provinces the definitive version of the *Ratio* in 1599, recommended that they burn all of its preceding versions. To understand the structure of this first official *Ratio*, one has to know the intention of its authors and the function of this 1586 version. The six authors knew perfectly well that they were producing a provisory text intended to be submitted for consultation by and observations from the various Jesuit provinces. In presenting the material, therefore, they deliberately chose to deal more with what was to be taught, how it was to be taught, and the means to be employed, rather than putting their attention on the teachers who would be the ones responsible for doing the teaching itself. The 1599 *Ratio*, on the other hand, did exactly the opposite.

According to a letter that the Superior General sent, each province was to set up a commission or committee of men in the province, most eminent in knowledge and in judgment, and they were to be charged with examining with care and diligence the text of this *Ratio* and with sending written observations about it, especially on what ought to be added to it or said more strongly or ordered more appropriately both in the speculative as well as in the practical part of the document. These observations were to go to Rome as quickly as possible, and the Superior General said that he hoped the delegates who would participate at the next General Congregation could leave Rome at the end of that congregation with a complete and definitive order of studies.[21]

---

[19] MP, vol.5, 6–33, "De opinionum delectu."

[20] Ibid., 34–158.

[21] Ibid., 160–62, "De deputandis Patribus . . ."

The material on the study of humanities provides a good example of what the members of the Roman commission accomplished and how they did it. A first series of chapters deals with the questions common to all of the classes of humanities. Then the document descends to the material proper to each of the classes of the humanities. The general chapters deal with the separation of the upper faculties (theology and philosophy) from the study of humanities, the qualities necessary in those who teach the humanities, the type of grammar to be used, the concurrent teaching of Greek and Latin, the type of exercises to be done in teaching of Greek and Latin, the ways to excite competition or emulation, the movement from a lower to a more advanced class in the course of studies, the books to be used, vacations, and, finally, discipline and piety in the schools. It is only after these general materials have been dealt with that the *Ratio* goes on, class by class and within each class order by order, to deal with the exercises to undertake in the text, the rules of grammar to study, the way in which to distribute the material hour by hour in the morning and the afternoon, and the *modus agendi* that ought to be employed in accord with individual circumstances.

It is perfectly obvious that such a compendium of practice in the Society could hardly pretend to be original. Quite the contrary, a large tradition of texts preceded this particular document, and from that tradition the members of the committee had very conscientiously drawn. They also knew that they had to put into some form the results of the past fifty years of ongoing experience. They themselves explained how they had gone about their work (in the absence of tape recorders and photocopiers):

> In order to produce a definite plan and consistent ways in which each discipline and all of the matter would be treated, we read aloud to each other the deliberations of our Fathers who had set down what they had done in these matters and what had been established in the best known colleges of the Society, whether they were at Rome or at other places and in other circumstances. Then we went on to review the letters and the projects, the rules of the universities, and other documents of various types which either in the more distant past or quite recently had been addressed to the Superior General by most of the provinces, whether Italian or Spanish, whether from France or Germany or Poland. We re-read the fourth part of the Constitutions and we examined it in a desire to obey its provisions exactly. We fol-

lowed the same procedure with regard to the canons of the General Congregations, the rules and statutes of various schools, and in addition, the usages and customs of the Roman College, so that a single book would include the whole ensemble. From all of these texts we retained for the most part the older ones, adding to them the more recent ones, suppressing a certain number of others. If here and there some doubt arose, each of us put before the eyes of the other members of the commission both the particular and the common ways things were done in his own province, the usage and examples of the schools there, their customs and their results and pointed out their advantages and their disadvantages.[22]

In this 1586 version, then, we are in the presence of a work that dealt in various languages not only with all of the foundational texts of the Society, and in particular the *Constitutions*, but also with all of the educational experience accumulated over the years in the Society both from its origin in Rome, at the Roman College and the German College, as well as in the whole ensemble of the Jesuit provinces. On the one hand, current experience, or rather current experiences rooted in the various provinces, and, on the other hand, experiences of the past confronted each other. When the reading of such texts brought up a particular doubt or hesitation, the committee members described to each other the current and particular usages of their own province. As they said very well, "With such numerous and varied means used for our inquiry and for our discernment, it was easy to do detailed research on the remedies to be applied to the various difficulties that came up and to establish among ourselves the foundations of a mutual community of views."[23]

After Aquaviva sent out the 1586 version, committees in each of the provinces regularly met through the summer and the autumn of that year. At the end of their work they sent to Rome their comments, classified according to the order of the material in the *Ratio* itself. Fifteen provinces responded. Only the province of Castile was not able to, because the Spanish Inquisition had ordered that all of the copies of the *Ratio* be sent to it. As a result, a considerable amount of material, something like thirty fascicles, came to Rome. Those texts were worked over attentively during almost the entire

---

[22] Ibid., 4–5.
[23] Ibid.

next year by the six committee members who had participated in the original work of 1583–84 and who had remained in Rome. From this consultation came a new and entirely redone text, in which the material presented was completely turned around and which the Superior General, in October 1587, proposed sending again to the provinces.

As a matter of fact, the two parts which had initially made up the *Ratio* in 1586, the *Delectus Opinionum* and the *Praxis et Ordo Studiorum*, took separate paths here. The Superior General sent out a letter to the Province Congregations asking whether a General Congregation ought to be convened with the sole purpose of ratifying the *Ratio Studiorum*. The Province Congregations almost unanimously judged that the question was not of sufficient importance to justify such a General Congregation. Some of them even maintained that the text of 1586 be actually put into use *ad experimentum*.[24]

In the meantime, the *Delectus Opinionum* was redone by one of the original 1583–84 committee members and corrected by three of the Jesuits at the Roman College and then sent in 1590 to Pope Sixtus V, perhaps to keep it out of the hands of the Spanish Inquisition. When Sixtus died, his successor, Gregory XIV, sent this text to the Holy Office of the Inquisition in Rome. The Holy Office, in turn, forbade the printing of the document because of the polemics that would follow in many universities from the classification of the propositions of St. Thomas into the categories to be held as definitive, or probable, or of free choices. Such a classification would involve serious censure of the teachings of Thomas, who, according to the opinion of the censor at the Holy Office, "has been judged conformable to the faith, received in full force and vigor and approved in all schools and universities."[25] In July 1582, the Superior General had sent manuscript copies of the *De Delectu* to the Provincials to serve as rules for the professors of theology. But the commission "for the revision of the *Ratio*," which Robert Bellarmine, Rector of the Roman college, had been presiding over since the 5th General Congregation of 1593, returned to the option of ten very general directives on the choice of opinions, half dealing with theology and half

---

[24] Ibid., vol. 7, doc. 36, pp. 311–26 for the *Acta* of these Province Congregations.

[25] This opinion of the members of the Holy Office is in *MP*, vol. 5, p. 24, and the text of the June 12, 1592 decree of the Roman Inquisition on the speculative part of the *Ratio* is in ibid., vol. 77, doc. 11, pp. 86–87.

with philosophy. For three reasons the commission refused to publish a detailed catalog of propositions to be held or to be prohibited. First, one might in the future have to revoke a statement that mentioned that a certain proposition was to be held definitively; second, an open conflict with other religious Orders might eventuate in a case in which the Society would defend certain propositions that were condemned by authors in those other Orders; third, there was the example of certain universities which had seen propositions that they affirmed later condemned or refitted.[26]

As for philosophy, Aristotle was the author whom the professors were to follow in all questions of any importance except those that were contrary to the orthodoxy of the faith. Averroism was severely condemned, and whenever a commentary of Averroes was used, it was to be done without any praising of it. In theology St. Thomas would be the author to follow, and in the future no one was to be named to chairs of theology in Jesuit schools except professors well affected to St. Thomas. At the same time, those who exhibited less zeal or affection for him were gradually to be replaced. In questions not treated by St. Thomas, the sense of the church and of received tradition was to be followed. In addition, unless they consulted their superiors, professors were to refrain from introducing new questions even in matters that presented no danger to the faith or to propriety. The General Congregation accepted these prudential positions that basically repeated the provisional rules Aquaviva had sent to the provinces in 1582. It added to those decrees a brief preface giving advice that certainly would have pleased Salmeron: "Let our fathers not think that they have to be so attached to St. Thomas to the point that they cannot differ from him in any manner, because even those who most openly declare themselves Thomists sometimes differ from him, and it would not be appropriate to tie Ours to St. Thomas more strictly than the Thomists do themselves."[27]

So, after so long a period of consultation and of editing and re-editing of propositions that had often enough been requested by the provinces themselves and after more than ten years of work on the

---

[26] See *MP*, vol.7, doc.39, pp. 347–55 for the text of the pertinent *Acta* of the General Congregation. Bellarmine also personally sent a letter to the Superior General in which he summed up the reasons for not listing what propositions were to be held definitively.

[27] Ibid., 350.

matter, the General Congregation simply decided on a framework of general directives in theology and philosophy. They were certainly firm, but nonetheless they left to provincial superiors and to official visitors the responsibility of deciding on disputed questions and for the consequences that could follow upon such decisions. The varying reactions in the provinces when they had first received the document *Delectus Opinionum* gave evidence of how much opinions differed on theological and philosophical positions. But these general statements were undoubtedly the most practical way at the time to take care not to confine intellectual work inside a rigid skeleton and also to maintain at least a minimal consensus inside the Society. Unfortunately, later generations of Jesuit philosophers and natural scientists were to suffer under the preeminence given to Aristotle in philosophical questions, which, you will remember, then included the natural, physical, and mathematical sciences. The most egregious example was the Galileo case, of course. But that is too long and painful to go into here.

As for the second part of the *Ratio Studiorum* of 1586, the *Praxis et Ordo Studiorum*, through the years 1589 and 1590 it underwent a complete redoing that turned around its whole structure. The original 1586 text, as one will recall, arranged its material around the levels of instruction, starting with Sacred Scripture in theology and proceeding down to the classes in philosophy, and then for the humanities moving upward from the lowest class therein to the highest. The *Ratio* of 1591,[28] of which perhaps only eight copies now exist in the whole world,[29] took into account the comments of the Province Congregations on the content of the 1586 book. But then it took those contents apart and rearranged them systematically into a new structure, not by subjects to be taught but by the various offices of persons engaged in the teaching.

This 1591 *Ratio* had two parts. The first or practical part dealt with each of the offices in the Society concerned with education. It

---

[28] The full text is in *MP*, vol. 5, in two parts, the "Ordo et praxis studiorum," 229–313 and the "Pars speculativa," 314–29.

[29] One copy each in the Jesuit general archives in Rome, at The Gregorian University, the National Library of Italy, the Vatican Library, a Jesuit theologate at Louvain, the Jagellonian Library in Cracow, and perhaps a copy in the London library and the Cambridge University Library.

opened with the rules and responsibilities in education on the part of the Provincial. It then continued on with those of the Rector of the college; the rules of the two prefects of studies, that is, of the upper and lower classes; and then the rules of the professors, the professor of Sacred Scripture being first in order, followed by the professors of theology and professors of philosophy. In contrast to the descending order, the rules for those responsible for the study of grammar and the humanities reversed that treatment. They started with the lowest or third class of grammar and went up to the uppermost class, that of rhetoric. And then, finally, this whole part of the book finished with the rules proper to the Jesuit scholastics. The second or speculative part of the 1591 *Ratio* dealt again with propositions from St. Thomas, and with the way to treat the canon of Scripture, the Church councils and Popes, and authoritative theologians. Then, in an example of local adaptation right at the beginning of this *Ratio*, a group of appendices followed with rules proper to Italy, France, Portugal, Germany, and non-European lands; rules for certain classes; and examples of prelections.[30]

The *Ratio Studiorum* of 1599 came about as a result of a decision of the 5th General Congregation of 1593–94 that such an edition of the *Ratio* should finally be prepared.[31] The Congregation decided not to include what had been called the speculative part of the *Ratio*, the list of propositions that up to now had been part of the project. But that still left an immense amount of work to do on the practical part of the project. Three members of the Society were called to Rome to address this project. Their work, from 1595 to 1598, generated a whole series of drafts that, fortunately, are extant in the archives of the Society of Jesus in Rome and will give the researcher a clear idea of the process by which this order of studies came into being.

The three editors took seriously the suggestions, comments, and desires that had come from the various provinces. What turned into an almost unanimous request was that the text be abbreviated and that the number of rules be made much shorter. The editors agreed, as can be seen in comparing the *Ratios* of 1591 and 1599. In the earlier one there were 837 such rules; in the 1599 version only 467.

---

[30] Ibid., 330–54.
[31] The full text is in *MP*, vol. 5, 355–454.

To take as an example just one office, the rules for the Provincial had been ninety-six; now they were only forty.[32] The provinces also almost universally asked that there be much less rigorous uniformity in applying the *Ratio*. Already after the 5th General Congregation, Aquaviva gave frequent permissions to provinces asking for exemptions or changes in certain of the 1591 regulations. The 1599 *Ratio*, in the midst of all its details, has much more often phrases such as "if the occasion demands" or "to vary in accord with the customs of the region" or "where there is need for it" or "the decision of the teacher."

As mentioned before, this 1599 edition of the *Ratio* did not have a speculative part, or *Delectus Opinionum*. What the General Congregation had ordered in this matter was sent in manuscript form to the provinces, but nothing of this kind appears in the *Ratio* itself except for some principles that the rules for the professors of Sacred Scripture and scholastic theology should maintain. Once the document was published, the Superior General gave individual or particular permissions directed to individual provinces to derogate from applying the *Ratio* in particular circumstances. They were thus individually given in order to emphasize the temporary character of such permissions and therefore the possibility of changing them when the need to do so was obvious.

The first edition of this new and definitive *Ratio* appeared at Naples in 1599. Others appeared rapidly in the following years:[33] for example, at Munich in 1600, a second edition at Naples in 1603, and at Rome in 1608, 1610, and 1616. The 7th General Congregation in 1616 made some slight revisions to the text in regard to the studies of the scholastics, left the rest of the text as it was, and again gave an authoritative approval to it. This text stayed the same for 175 years, up until the suppression of the Society in 1773.

Because of this lengthy textually unchanged status of the *Ratio*, many have regularly accused the Society of Jesus of a quite imprudent educational immobility for all of that period. It may be true that later Jesuit generations forgot, to a degree, the principle that

---

[32] Ibid., 33.

[33] For the various editions, see Carlos Sommervagel, S.J., *Biblothèque de la Compagnie de Jésus* (Bruxelles and Paris, 1890), vol 1, Col. 488–89 (under "Aquaviva" as author because he was Superior General of the Society at the publication of the *Ratio*).

Ignatius had set down in the *Constitutions* and that the 5th General Congregation had defined for the future, namely, that a *Ratio Studiorum* was to be adapted to the needs of the Society of a particular time. But in practice, especially in the eighteenth century, as a matter of fact many profound changes took place. To take only two examples: First, in the province of Austria, in 1773, the year of the forced suppression of the Society, despite the small or absent space given to the following subjects in the *Ratio* itself, in twelve of the colleges in that province the French language was taught, in seven of them German, in three Italian, in two Czech, in six Hungarian. In two of the colleges German literature was taught. Five of them taught history, one taught geography, three taught architecture, three taught advanced mathematics, two taught mechanical drawing, five taught engineering, one taught hydrography, one taught agronomy, and two taught economics. As for a second example, in the French provinces history and geography were taught in the seventeenth and eighteenth centuries in college after college.[34]

What did the 1599 *Ratio* consist of? As with the 1591 text, it was structured around the official responsibilities of those concerned with Jesuit education. It started with the rules of the Provincial and went on to those of the Rector and the prefect of studies. Then it dealt with the regulations common to all of the professors of the advanced faculties, followed by those specific to the professors of Sacred Scripture, Hebrew and scholastic theology, and cases of conscience (what we might now call moral theology). Then came the regulations for the professors of philosophy, with a few of them specific to the professor of moral philosophy or ethics, followed by those of the professor of mathematics.

The regulations for the lower classes, or what we might call the secondary school classes, took up by far the greater portion of the *Ratio*. They legislated for everything from the number of classes or years in the school to material on repetitions, new students, exams, grading practices, promotions, books, and time for private study. Remember that while we take such practices for granted today, in great part we owe them and their later widespread use to the *Ratio*. In

---

[34] For the Austrian colleges, see L. Szilas, S.J., "Die österreichische Jesuitenprovinz, 1773," cited in *MP*, vol. 5, 34; for France, see François de Dainville, S.J., "L'enseignement de l'histoire et de la géographie et le 'ratio studiorum,' " in *L'éducation des jésuites* (Paris, 1978), 427–54.

addition, there was material on disputations, the academies and public prizes, the corrector, the classrooms, the school church or chapel, the way in which exams were to be written, and the conferring of prizes or recognitions for academic accomplishment. Each class then had its own rules, including those, for example, of the professor of rhetoric, the professor of humanities, the professor of grammar. At that point, the rules of the scholastics of the Society appeared, followed by the regulations for those who would do a biennium, or two of years, of advanced study after the ordinary course. The class beadle, the externs, that is to say non-boarding students, the various academies, groups of the more studious among the pupils who met regularly for special academic activities, in turn had their own detailed regulations.

Overall, this 1599 *Ratio* was the product of experience, active participation in that experience, and consultation about it. Those characteristics helped produce a document that put a method and a structure at the service of an apostolic enterprise, formation in learning and virtue.

When Giacomo Domenichi, the Secretary of the Society, sent the new *Ratio* of 1599 to the Provincials on behalf of Fr. General Aquaviva, he concluded his letter by remarking that "our teachers should diligently see that the regulations of the latest plan be put into effect with easy acceptance" and that the Superior General "asks insistently that superiors lend every effort to assure that it be observed willingly and exactly."[35]

Let me conclude this presentation on the development of the *Ratio* with three quotations. The first statement in the *Ratio* of 1599 is as follows: "It is the principal ministry of the Society of Jesus to educate youth in every branch of knowledge that is in keeping with its Institute. The aim of our educational program is to lead people to the knowledge of our Creator and Redeemer."[36] This is a noble end, and the Society of Jesus, seeking to find God in all things, knows that it can be attained through the whole panoply of human knowledge. It is an end that the Society, one hopes, will constantly keep in view.

That ultimate end has to be reduced to immediate practice, how-

---

[35] MP, vol. 5, 356.
[36] Ibid., 357.

ever, and when that happens, the real world makes its appearance and its demands. Six years after the promulgation of the 1599 *Ratio*, Pedro de Ribadeneyra, one of the very early Jesuits, in defending the apostolate of education as proper to the Society, had to admit nonetheless that a lot of people contended:

> [I]t is a repulsive, annoying, and burdensome thing to guide and teach and try to control a crowd of young people, who are naturally so frivolous, so restless, so talkative, and so unwilling to work, that even their parents cannot keep them at home. So what happens that our young Jesuits, who are involved in teaching them, lead a very strained life, wear down their energies, and damage their health.[37]

Finally, however, through all of the editions of the *Ratio* and through all of the years of practice that have followed, what Diego Ledesma said in a statement in the 1586 version still holds true, I hope, as to the purpose of Jesuit education—why the Society was to conduct schools:

> [F]irst, because they supply people with many advantages for practical living; secondly, because they contribute to the right government of public affairs and to the proper making of laws; third, because they give ornament, splendor and perfection to our rational nature, and fourth, in what is most important, because they are the bulwark of religion and guide us most surely and easily to the achievement of our last end.[38]

If this is what Jesuit schools, at their best, did in the past, in fulfillment of the *Ratio Studiorum*, they merit our admiration. If these four purposes—practical, social, humanistic, and religious—are what Jesuit schools, at their best, want to attain in the present and in the future, they merit our support.

EDITOR'S NOTE: At the conclusion of his presentation, Fr. Padberg shared with the participants at the seminar an outline of the *Ratio* (see page 100). He took it from Fr. Allan P. Farrell's introduction[39] to his English translation of this document; Farrell explicates the structure of the *Ratio* descriptively and then schematically:

---

[37] Pedro de Ribadeneyra, S.J., "Tratado en el qual se da razon del instituto de la religion de la Compañia de Jesus" (Madrid, 1605), 510.

[38] Diego de Ledesma, S.J., *MP*, vol. 2, 528–29.

[39] *The Jesuit Ratio Studiorum of 1599*, trans. Allan P. Farrell (Washington: Conference of Major Superiors of Jesuits, 1970).

There are four principal areas contained in the *Ratio Studiorum*, namely, administration, curriculum, method, and discipline. It begins with administration by defining the function, interrelation, and duties of such officials as the provincial, rector and prefects of studies. It outlines a curriculum by placing in their proper sequence and gradation courses of study in theology, philosophy and the humanities. It sets forth in detail a method of conducting lessons and exercises in the classroom. It provides for discipline by fixing for the students norms of conduct, regularity and good order.

The following detailed analysis of the *Ratio*, according to sets of rules, will illustrate these four main divisions.

AN ANALYSIS OF THE *RATIO STUDIORUM* OF 1599

I {
  A. Rules of the Provincial (1–40)
  B. Rules of the Rector (1–24)

C. Rules of the Prefect of Higher Studies (1–30)

D. Common Rules for all the Professors of Higher Faculties (1–20)

E. Special Rules for Professors of the Higher Faculties
    Ea) Prof. of Scripture (1–20)
    Eb) Prof. of Hebrew (1–5)
    Ec) Prof. of Theology(1–14)
    Ed) Prof. of Moral Theology (1–10)

F. Rules for Professors of Philosophy
    Fa) General Rules (1–8)
    Fb) Courses, Texts, etc. (9–20)
    Fc) Prof. of Theology (1–4)
    Fd) Prof. of Moral Theology (1–3)

II {

M. Rules for Students of the Jesuit Order (1–11)

N. Rules for those Reviewing Theology (1–14)

O. Rules for the Class Beadle (1–7)

Q. Rules for the Academies
    Qa) General Rules (1–12)
    Qb) Rules of the Prefect (1–5)
    Qc) Academy of Theology and Philosophy (I–II)
    Qd) Prefect of the Academy (1–4)

G. Rules of the Prefect of Lower Studies (1–50)

H. Rules for the Writing of Examinations (1–11)

J. Rules Governing Awards (1–13)

K. Common Rules for Teachers of the Lower Classes (1–50)

III {

L. Special Rules for the Teachers of the Lower Classes
    La) Rhetoric (1–20)
    Lb) Humanities (1–10)
    Lc) Grammar I (1–10)
    Ld) Grammar II (1–10)
    Le) Grammar III (1–9)

P. Rules for Extern Students (1–15)

Q. Rules for the Academies
    Qe) Academy of Rhetoric and Humanities (1–7)
    Qr) Academy of Grammar Students (1–8)

RESPONSE TO JOHN W. PADBERG

Jenny Go

We thank Fr. Padberg for sharing with us the stages of the development of the *Ratio Studiorum*. The *Ratio* as we know it has served its purpose as foundation to the first organized system of education in the western world, that of Jesuit education. But why celebrate a document that has long ago faded from major attention? I think the *Ratio* is like a diamond ring that has been kept in the safe deposit box because it does not fit our fingers anymore. But that does not change the fact that it is a precious stone. Once in a while we should take it out of the safe deposit box, admire the genius that chiseled the facets, scrutinize these facets that make it brilliant and beautiful, and analyze it for the "inclusions" that make up its flaws. In a world like ours, it is helpful to survey the past, identify and reflect on the challenges that make up our contemporary world of education, and take a proactive stance for our future course. It is good to find out what is timeless and what is time-bound in the *Ratio*.

This conference is trying to re-examine all of the *Ratio*'s facets to see the lessons or insights we can draw from the details of *how* it was put together, *why* it was commissioned, *what* it consisted of, *where* its inspiration came from, *how* it has influenced the whole Jesuit educational system, and *whether* its elements are viable for the kaleidoscopic present and future. The lessons we can draw from the details of the stages of development of the *Ratio* are very interesting to say the least. More importantly, the spirit that permeated the document is what we the followers and companions of Ignatius Loyola hope to realize through the norms and standards of Jesuit education today.

Allow me to comment on Fr. Padberg's paper by focusing on a

few questions. What does this exposition of the *Ratio*'s stages of development say about the "Jesuit way of proceeding"? What does it say about the intentionality of our schools, the aim of Jesuit education? How does it speak to us about the role of formation of teachers and students, about the curriculum, about pedagogy and the place of the humanities in Jesuit education of times gone by and today? What does it show us regarding consistency and freedom of opinion on what we teach? What message does it convey to us in terms of the value and importance of the educational apostolate in the work of the Jesuits? Finally, can the educational foundation and system, this heritage and tradition built by the *Ratio*, help the smooth incorporation of committed lay people's collaborative efforts in the present-day Jesuit educational apostolate? Can the elements continue to be the blueprint for the present context and the future?

What Does the Development of the *Ratio* Say about the "Jesuit Way of Proceeding"?

It is obvious that the "Jesuit way of proceeding" is a cornerstone, a heritage, a tradition, a charism that has been handed down as part of Jesuit institutions and education throughout the world. In fact, when one analyzes the "Jesuit way of proceeding," one finds that when thoroughly and well exercised, it is what excellent leadership and good management is all about. A more appropriate term might be the "spirituality of Ignatian leadership." As examples, let us go through a number of points and analyze the *Ratio* from the "Jesuit way of proceeding," from the organizational dimension.

1. The *Ratio* underwent a number of trial editions before the definitive edition was published and promulgated. It was the product of fifty years of corporate international experience. It resulted from a process of gathering the teaching experiences of the early Fathers and reflecting on those experiences before the codification of the *Ratio* was accomplished. This process is very Jesuit. It is always trial runs before a decision is made; it is reflection on experience, articulating, interpreting experience, a discernment before action is taken. There is always a "reality check," a process of consultation, as Fr. Padberg says.

2. Very early on, even at the time of Ignatius Loyola and the early

Superiors General of the Society, the *Ratio* prepared what we today would call "job descriptions" (the functions and responsibilities) for all, from the Jesuit Provincials, Rectors, prefects of discipline, teachers, professors, to scholastics. Up to this day, most Jesuit institutions are similarly very well organized.

3. There was an effort to make the *Ratio* reflect the whole educational spectrum and to make it as *universally acceptable and applicable* as possible by integrating the comments, suggestions, and desires from most provinces into the document.

4. "Flexibility" and "adaptation" are key concepts in Jesuit documents. Provision was made for more individualized implementation of the *Ratio*, much according to the demands and needs of each province, which we today would call "adaptation to context and cultures," "inculturation," "adaptation to the needs of times, places, and persons." Take the example of Fr. Mateo Ricci, who understood inculturation very well. We can feel an overarching respect for the specific context of a school and a respect for the person, which can be expressed in lay persons' terminology: "The person on the spot sees an angle that perhaps the superior or leader does not." Again, this is meeting the people where they are, not where we think they are.

What about the Curriculum and Freedom of Opinion?

In spite of a fixed curriculum, questions of theology and philosophy could be debated; but, on the other hand, there was always accountability to norms. In the contemporary educational scene of many countries, especially in Asia, the curriculum is fixed by the government, not the religious congregations. But there is flexibility concerning how we teach the curriculum content.

What Does the *Ratio* Say to Us about the Formation of Teachers and Professors?

The detail with which the *Ratio* spelled out how professors and teachers ought to teach and how students ought to behave shows us the importance, the priority, placed on the *formation of teachers and students.* Teachers' work must reflect their best efforts toward doing the *magis*, that is, choosing the better, more effective means to help students grow. In this, however, *cura-personalis*, the personal care of students, will guide and modify generic norms. Now that more committed lay people are being incorporated into Jesuit educational apostolate, formation of lay partners must be looked upon as an all-important organizational strategy to keep our schools and universities on course in the mission of "caring for souls." Another present-day challenge is to search for ways to form our more diverse, pluralistic faculty of Muslim, Buddhist, and Taoist teachers within the broadly humanistic worldview of Ignatius.

What Does the *Ratio* Say about the Aim of Jesuit Education?

1. "The care of souls," which is the institutional vision and intentionality of Jesuit education, remains intact. Therefore, the ideal and ultimate purpose of Jesuit education remains spiritual, to develop in the individual a deep sense of love of God and service of others, which incorporates the personal and social dimensions of Jesuit education.

2. The fact that the *Ratio* spelled out that education was free for all underscores the justice component of Jesuit education—to make our schools affordable to the poor and to have our universities speak out and work for justice.

3. As I visit the different high schools in East Asia and Oceania, I see this goal expressed in different languages of the mission statements of Taiwan, Philippines, Hong Kong, Australia, Macao, Japan, Micronesia, Indonesia. How this mission statement is translated into action in schools and universities that are populated almost ninety percent with students who are not Catholics or Christians or are without any faith tradition is a huge challenge. Can we inculcate Gospel Ignatian values without naming or labeling these values as Ignatian but as universal moral values? Even in the United States scene, we can no longer nestle in an enclave where everyone is Catholic. In our schools, colleges, and universities we welcome difference in ethnicity, belief, and culture. This challenge which we face everywhere is the result of a world so compressed by the mass migration of people. People of all cultures are now our next-door neighbors.

4. Economic globalization has made the poor even poorer. Studies report that only twenty percent of the world's population will reap the benefits of economic globalization. Therefore, the big challenge is how we can make our schools affordable to the eighty percent of the world's population who are the poor. Are we pricing ourselves out of the market for the poor and lower-middle class? The all important and timeless goal to "care for souls," "to serve a faith that does justice" must continue to be emphasized to keep us true to our roots.

How Is the Apostolate of Education Viewed in the *Ratio*?

The mere fact that Superiors General of the Society of Jesus commissioned and were personally involved in the stages of the *Ratio*'s preparation demonstrates the importance of the educational apostolate amongst the works of the Jesuits. Should we not continue to emphasize, support, re-enforce this work through more, deeper, and better formation of Jesuits and committed lay people, especially in terms of understanding different cultures, our own context, and intercultural communication within the framework of the Ignatian ethos?

While the original *Ratio* of 1599, in all of its details, reflects a society and education that is significantly different from today's realities, the elements that made up the framework of the *Ratio*—its values, priorities, guiding principles—are timeless elements we can recast, revive, or sustain and continue to use according to the needs of our different assistancies and provinces. They are the facets that still make the *Ratio* an important document.

Today and Tomorrow

Over the last quarter of a century, a number of processes, projects, and documents have been developed to help guide Jesuit education. Among them we might mention *The Preamble to the JSEA Constitution, The Profile of the Teacher in a Jesuit School, The Profile of the Graduate at Graduation*, "The Colloquium on the Ministry of Teaching," *The Profile of a Member of the Board of Trustees of a Jesuit School, The Curriculum Improvement Process*, "The 19th Annotation

Retreat for Lay Teachers," "The International Jesuit Education Leadership Project," "Ignatian Leadership Seminar," "Secondary School Administration Workshop," and especially *The Characteristics of Jesuit Education* and *Ignatian Pedagogy: A Practical Approach.* All of these are helpful *guidelines* for contemporary Jesuit educational landscape. Today, too, the Jesuit educational system must be open-ended, as were Jesuit schools of a past era, to the stages of development of educational planning. This means that all these processes, these powerful approaches, must meet the people where they are. They must meet the needs and aspirations of significant but different portions of the world's population. Can we, Jesuits and lay people alike, bring to fruition the stages of development of a modern version of the *Ratio?* Can we make a smooth shift to a merger of resources of religious and lay, men and women in the Jesuit educational milieu? How can we maintain unity of goal but appropriate diversity of means in implementation of our educational mission? The *Ratio* has clearly shown us to think globally but act locally. This ability to change, for the greater good, for the "care of souls," for the good of others, for better service is needed to keep our educational apostolate relevant.

When we look at all the energy that went into the stages of development of the *Ratio*, the Jesuits must admit quite frankly that it was well worth the efforts. Just look at the products, the people, who were formed in an educational system whose roots go back to the *Ratio*, people like you—scholars and religious, committed lay people—as well as a number of Popes, prelates, presidents, and justices in many nations. We might also mention historic figures like Paul Rubens, the painter, Gianlorenzo Bernini, the sculptor, Clavius, the mathematician, Voltaire, Alexander Volta. This legacy has been kept alive because the Jesuits are ever inventive, ever creative, practical and accommodating, never losing sight of the core as well as the wider horizon. This is part of the genius of the apostolic planning we are engaged in even today, in continuity with a history of four hundred years.

Let me conclude by saying, *Seng Re Quay Lo,* "Happy Birthday, *Ratio*", and *Kong Si Jesuits, Mabuhay Jesuits,* "Congratulations, my dear Jesuit partners"!

5

Women's Ways of Knowing and Learning: The Response of Mary Ward and Madeleine Sophie Barat to the *Ratio Studiorum*

Rosemary A. DeJulio

I WISH TO BEGIN with a very wise observation made by Joan Thirsk: "A writer's hopes of documenting women's lives will always outrun the possibilities of achievement. Generally, records are sparse. . . . Therefore, every kind of ingenuity is needed to reconstruct even a fragment of their lives."[1] In spite of the difficulties one encounters when attempting to document the lives of women who played roles in early Jesuit history, hope is sustained by the possibilities of discovering and rediscovering how these women were influenced by the spirituality and pedagogy of Ignatius Loyola. There is evidence, although not abundant, to support the fact that women in history were inspired to become the *patrons, pupils, and partners* of Ignatius and his followers. But where do we find the scholarship that advances our knowledge of why these women became so attracted to the Ignatian mission of educating others and saving souls, and of the roles they actually played in cultivating that mission?

It has been nearly forty years since Hugo Rahner compiled and edited the 139 extant letters that were exchanged between Ignatius

---

[1] Joan Thirsk, "Foreword," in *Women in English Society, 1500–1800*, ed. Mary Prior (London: Methuen, 1985), 2.

and various women contemporaries.[2] Sadly, there has not been much more written since then on this provocative and timely topic. More than a quarter century ago, John Padberg wrote an informative and engaging article about women such as Isabel Roser and Princess Juana, Regent of Spain, who tried to become Jesuits.[3] In his article, we learn how Roser went so far as to initiate a lawsuit against Ignatius for dispensing her from the vows she previously gave to him in 1545; whereas Juana, perhaps because of her pedigree and influence, actually succeeded in entering the society as a "permanent scholastic" with whom Ignatius corresponded under her pseudonym Mateo Sanchez. Such revelations and many others that can be discovered in Rahner's compilation of letters offer much insight into Ignatius's relationship with the women patrons of his time, and his links to the wealthy ladies of Spanish nobility.

Indeed, the churches, houses, and colleges in Spain and Italy that were established by the early Jesuits owed much to the patronage of wealthy benefactresses. Too often the lives and contributions of such patrons as Donna Maria Frassoni del Gesso are overlooked and overshadowed by the ridicule and the cartoons that accused Ignatius and his followers of emptying the pockets of widows.[4] Fortunately, women historians are emerging to draw from Rahner's compilation of letters and from any newly discovered primary sources to add their own historical perspectives and to fashion a greater understanding of women's roles.

Rahner provided us with an explanation of how Ignatius grappled with this "contradiction" of reconciling the vital role women played in his founding mission with the patriarchal norms of his times. We know from his own writings that Ignatius clearly understood the precarious situation he created for his companions who were subject to ridicule for accepting the monetary support of women; yet, he refused to reject their worldly patronage. Those specific acts of patronage may have been only minimally documented and largely forgotten, but Ignatius saw patronage by women as serving his objective of seeking *the greater glory of God*.[5]

[2] See Hugo Rahner, S.J., *Saint Ignatius Loyola: Letters to Women* (New York: Herder and Herder, 1960).

[3] See John W. Padberg, S.J., "Juana: Princess and Jesuit Scholastic," *National Jesuit News* 4 (October 1974).

[4] See Rahner, *Saint Ignatius Loyola*.

[5] Ibid., 202.

For the purpose of today's presentation, however, I focus on two women whose lives postdate Ignatius by a century or more: Mary Ward and Madeleine Sophie Barat. Although these "pupils" of Ignatius (as I like to call them) were separated by time and gender and full inclusion in the Society of Jesus, they adopted and assimilated Ignatian spirituality and pedagogy. They became Ignatian by following his charism and developing teaching methods that have remarkable similarities to those instituted by the Society of Jesus.

Mary Ward of Seventeenth-Century England

Mary Ward was one of the most well-known pioneers who formed an autonomous company of women with an apostolic mission. Influenced by the life of Ignatius, she had the vision of a company that would not require enclosure, strict religious garb, or obedience to local clergy. Such a radical departure from the expected religious and juridical norms for women religious brought Mary much suffering. She was imprisoned, exiled, and persecuted for her pioneering spirit, and her founding status was suppressed into silence until the twentieth century.

Miraculously, she survived to the age of sixty, and until her death in 1645, she persevered in her desire to teach academic subjects to companies of young women who, like Jesuits, shared the desire to serve their communities with a profoundly different apostolic mission. According to John Padberg: "If Ignatius had had the immense good fortune to have . . . a Mary Ward . . . to work in collaboration with him, and if they had the opportunity to put together a distinct set of insights, enthusiasms, energies, and talents, along with a common devotion to the service of the church, the history of religious life from the sixteenth century on may have been far different."[6] In keeping with what Joan Thirsk stated, the hope of fully documenting Mary's life in the context of Jesuit educational history may indeed outrun the possibility of achievement. Historical documents related to her mission and plan were in many instances intentionally burned. For more than a century after her death, her Institute's descendents were not told that she was their original foundress. Fortunately, it

---

[6] Padberg, "Juana," 6.

was the publication in the late nineteenth century of Mary Catherine Chambers's seminal two-volume work that generated a series of inquiries into the life of the true foundress of the Institute of the Blessed Virgin Mary.[7] Some eighty years later, after the Second Vatican Council called on all religious institutes to embrace the genius and directives of their founders, there arose a renewal of interest in the founding spirit and heritage of Mary Ward's vision and work. In 1988, Pope John Paul II included her among those many "perfect" women who, despite persecution and discrimination, shared in the Church's mission of salvation.[8]

An understanding of Mary's founding charism makes a comparison with Ignatian charism not only important for Jesuits as they chart their future, particularly in their relationships with women, but also for women who can gain a greater appreciation of their own roles in and for the service of the Church.

What remains of Mary Ward's story in letters and documents reveals a woman who aspired to live an independent and public life in the service of God and the Catholic Church. She lived in an era when women religious were subject to the rules of enclosure, and all of their work, including the education of young girls, took place behind the walls and grills of the convent.[9] Jeanne Cover, a descendent of Mary's Institute, attempts to answer why there was this prevailing understanding that made enclosure an essential aspect of religious life for women.[10] It was an understanding that associated holiness with the hatred of and separation from the world. But it also was an anthropology that reflected a particular view of the nature of women. Canon law, church practice, and the rigid societal requirements and expectations of women created a tradition for women religious that succeeding generations accepted without challenge.

This prevailing view frustrated Mary Ward's distinctive vision, but it did not deter her and her followers from persevering.[11] Indeed,

---

[7] See Mary Catherine Chambers, *The Life of Mary Ward (1585–1645)*, ed. H. Coleridge, S.J., 2 vols. (London: Burns & Oates, 1882–85).

[8] John Paul II, Encyclical, *Mulieris dignatatem*, August 15, 1988, in Mary Wright, *Mary Ward's Institute:The Struggle for Identity* (Sydney: Crossing Press, 1997), xiv.

[9] See Marie Rowlands, "Recusant Women 1560 to 1640," in *Women in English Society*, ed. Prior.

[10] See Jeanne Cover, *Love, The Driving Force: Mary Ward's Spirituality, Its Significance for Moral Theology* (Milwaukee: Marquette University Press, 1997).

[11] See Imolata Wetter, "Mary Ward's Apostolic Vocation," *The Way*, supplement, 17 (1972): 70–71.

Mary's struggle against the backdrop of the Church's lack of understanding and receptivity to her vision is disheartening, but in a
strictly spiritual sense, it is uplifting. With the advice and encouragement of a number of Jesuits, Mary's courageous persistence and her
love of her faith prevailed. The impact of Jesuits, in fact, began at a
very early age, as Mary Ward was born into a family of faithful Catholics in Yorkshire in 1585, when the situation for English Catholics
was extremely perilous. Harsh penalties were imposed on Catholics
if they did not conform to the Acts of Supremacy and Uniformity of
1559. Many were punished and thrown into jail for harboring priests,
and Mary's family had enough resources to provide a safe haven for
these priests. It is quite possible it was through such covert activities
that Mary first encountered Jesuits when they were given shelter in
her parents' home.[12]

At the age of twenty-one, Mary left Yorkshire for St. Omer, a small
city in the Spanish Netherlands. St. Omer had a reputation for being
a strong Catholic center where the English branch of the Society of
Jesus ran a well-known school for boys. She began her religious vocation in the convent of Poor Clares, where her lack of freedom was
less than satisfying. She experienced difficulty adapting to the language, and was obliged as a member who adhered to the strictest
rule of St. Clare to beg for alms in the streets of the city. Within a
year, she developed the idea of a convent of Poor Clares for English-
speaking women who would not encounter her same difficulties.[13]
With the assistance and approval of the local Franciscan bishop,
Bishop Blaes, she was able to obtain the services of English Jesuits as
confessors and spiritual directors for her new company of women.[14]

The Jesuit Roger Lee was named her confessor and remained so
until his death in 1615. It is Fr. Lee who is credited with leading
Mary and her small community in the *Spiritual Exercises*. After making the *Exercises*, Mary said:

> I never read of any I can compare in likeness to it. It is not like the
> state of saints, whose holiness chiefly appears in that union with God,
> which maketh them out of themselves; I perceived then an apparent
> difference and yet feel myself drawn to love and desire this estate

---

[12] Wright, *Mary Ward's Institute*, 3–4.
[13] Ibid., 4–5. See also Chambers, *Life of Mary Ward*, vol. 1, 107–25.
[14] Wright, *Mary Ward's Institute*, 6.

more than all those favours. The felicity of this course . . . was a *singular freedom* from all that could make one adhere to earthly things, with an entire application and apt disposition to all good works.[15]

This "singular freedom" to which Mary refers motivated her to a new vision, one that would not make the Order of Poor Clares the final stop on her personal spiritual journey. While recovering from a serious illness in 1611, in a moment strikingly similar to that of Ignatius, Mary experienced a vision and described this critical juncture in her life: "[B]eing alone, in some extraordinary repose of mind, I heard distinctly, not by voice, but intellectually understood these words, *Take the same of the Society. Father General will never permit it. Go to him.* So understood as that we were to take the same both in matter, and manner that only excepted which God by diversity of sex has prohibited."[16] The decision to remain steadfast to the adoption of the Jesuit model dominated the rest of Mary's life and the work of her Institute. In response to her spiritual enlightenment, Mary held fast to those famous fifteen words *Take the same of the Society. Father General will never permit it. Go to him.* Her Jesuit confessor, Fr. Lee, wanted her to proceed more cautiously, as he expected that the hierarchy of the Society of Jesus would render considerable opposition. He offered her other choices, but Mary was adamant that "there was no remedy, but [to] refuse them, which caused [her and her followers] infinite troubles."[17]

Although no institute of religious women at this time would dare to allow the total adoption of the Jesuit *Constitutions*, Mary was not satisfied with any "pale imitation" of the Ignatian heritage because she wanted "the same" both "in matter and manner" as far as it was possible for her women.[18]

The first iteration of Mary Ward's different vision for women is found in a document entitled *Schola Beatae Mariae*. It is believed to have been written in 1612 with the assistance of Fr. Lee, and as a reflection of his caution it was more of a "bridge" between the clois-

[15] Letter from Mary Ward to Fr. Lee, November 1, 1615, quoted in Chambers, *Life of Mary Ward*, vol. 1, 345–47 (emphasis added).

[16] Letter from Mary Ward to Nuncio Antonio Albergati, May/June 1611, quoted in Chambers, *Life of Mary Ward*, vol. 1, 283–84.

[17] Letter from Mary Ward to Nuncio Antonio Albergati, May/June 1621, quoted in Wright, *Mary Ward's Institute*, 9.

[18] Wetter, "Mary Ward's Apostolic Vocation," 80.

tered life Mary already had experienced as a Poor Clare and the active apostolate she so much desired to develop. In the *Schola*, we read:

> And since so many women . . . serve God most devoutly in monastic life, . . . so we also feel that God . . . is inspiring us with the pious desire [to] . . . embrace the religious life, and yet that we should strive . . . to render to our neighbour the services of Christian charity which cannot be discharged through the monastic life . . . so that in this way we may more easily educate maidens and girls of tender years in piety, in the Christian virtues and in the liberal arts so that they may be able to undertake more fruitfully the secular and domestic life or the religious or monastic life according to the vocation of each.[19]

This document plainly went beyond promoting one's own salvation through worldly renunciation. It sought the salvation of others primarily through education. It was also based on the Ignatian model of religious life, calling for an active apostolate with several houses under the control of one superioress.[20] What was emerging here was a radical new framework that embraced, rather than shunned, a formal structure.[21] It insisted upon having Jesuits only as confessors, but it was equally clear that it would not be under any control by a male religious order.

Late in 1615, as her Institute began to grow, Mary produced a second plan entitled *Ratio Instituti*. Although her *Ratio* began like the *Schola*, noting its principal motivation the dire conditions of the Catholic Church in England, it went on to create a "congregation," like the Society of Jesus, which had the power to dismiss both novices and the professed.[22] *It stressed accountability only to the Pope.* Moreover, the apostolate went beyond education to include "any other means that are congruous to the times . . . to promote the greater glory of God."[23]

Following the death of Fr. Lee, Mary was assigned to an even more courageous and enthusiastic spiritual director, Jesuit Fr. John Gerard.

---

[19] *Schola Beatae Mariae*, 1612, ARSJ, Fondo Jesuitico, n. 1435, facsimile 1, doc. 3, English translation AIT, para. 1–3, quoted in Wright, *Mary Ward's Institute*, 18.

[20] Wright, *Mary Ward's Institute*, 18.

[21] See Wright, *Mary Ward's Institute*, 18, for a discussion of the monastic features included in the *Schola*.

[22] Ibid., 20.

[23] *Ratio Instituti*, para. 6, in Chambers, *Life of Mary Ward*, vol. 1, 377.

It was through his encouragement that a third document, *Institutum I*, was created that ultimately was presented to Pope Gregory XV. In this third plan, Mary copied the words of the *Jesuit Formula Instituti* in her charter, and the words of Ignatius and his companions replaced the more feminine character of the two previous versions.[24] Although Mary adopted the Ignatian fight against heresy and evil, she expanded her apostolate to individuals *with and without* religious vocations, or in the words of the *Schola*: "by teaching catechism and the reverent use of sacred things and by giving [girls] the education in schools and communities which will seem most suitable for the common good of the Church and their own particular good whether they choose to spend their lives in the world or in the religious state."[25]

Mary's *Institutum I* was revolutionary in that it recognized that God did not divine women religious only to save themselves, but He also empowered them with the potential to save others. Her belief in the necessity of a sound Catholic education for women to assist in the Church's fight against heresy demonstrated a high level of understanding and an extraordinary vision as to what was possible for women religious to achieve in this time period.[26] Unlike her *Ratio*, this third plan contained no mention at all of enclosure. In fact, Mary's followers would be expected to travel to foreign lands where they would conform to the customs of where they lived. Their candidates would be educated and tested; their members would vow obedience to a Superior General and would not be subject to the local authority of the bishop.

What is astonishing, and I believe attributable in great measure to her Jesuit training, is the fact that Mary developed such a detailed, comprehensive plan for women in a time when women religious were so strictly enclosed.[27] She challenged the prevailing tradition and dared to divert women, who may otherwise have been moving toward the cloistered life, toward a company of women with an apostolate that extended even beyond her native country of England.

The reaction to this most radical of her documents was, as one

---

[24] Wetter, "Mary Ward's Apostolic Vocation," 84–85.

[25] *Institutum I* (The Third Plan of the Institute), 1621, as quoted in Wright, *Mary Ward's Institute*, 21–22.

[26] Ibid., 23.

[27] Wetter, "Mary Ward's Apostolic Vocation," 86.

might expect, extremely negative. Canonical precedent, political pressures, and societal rules and expectations regarding women prevented her petition from ever being granted. The patriarchal hierarchy, the diocesan clergy in England, and even the Jesuit hierarchy, fearing that Mary's "misdeeds" would be reported to Rome to stir the pot of their own incrimination, all responded with scurrilous attacks on her and her followers, calling them a bunch of "galloping girls," English Ladies, Jesuitesses, and "noxious weeds."[28]

Yet, in spite of these attacks from both Jesuits and non-Jesuits, Mary's devotion to Ignatian charism never faltered. Although she certainly was not the first woman religious who attempted to educate women without enclosure,[29] her educational apostolate was groundbreaking in its adoption of Ignatian spirituality and, insofar as possible, the teaching methods of the *Ratio Studiorum*—all this in a

---

[28] See Elizabeth Rapley, *The Dévotes: Women and Church in Seventeenth-Century France* (Montreal: McGill-Queen's University Press, 1990).

[29] See Marie-Amelie le Bourgeois, "Ursulines of Anne de Xainctonge (1606) Contributions to the History of Communities of Non-Cloistered Women Religious" (Ph.D. diss., Catholic Institute of Paris, 1995), 101–17, 185–207. Two other sixteenth-century women, Jeanne de Lestonnac, born in 1556, and Anne de Xainctonge, born in 1567, were anguished by the Reformation and inspired by the work of the Jesuits to form schools addressing the needs of girls and young women. Each was moved toward the selfless service of education by making the *Spiritual Exercises* and wanting to do for girls what Jesuits were doing for boys. Jeanne de Lestonnac established education-oriented monastaries that generally followed the norms for women issued by the Council of Trent and Pius V. Ibid., 103. Anne de Xainctonge began her company of women who, while in pursuit of their own perfection, would also work for the education of women in the imitation of Ignatius Loyola. Anne's Institute fell between those of Jeanne de Lestonnac and Mary Ward: Jeanne reconciled the "cloister" with "education," whereas Mary refused cloister but at the same time attempted to remain in the canonical religious state, an effort that doomed her vision in its infancy. Anne, however, refused cloister but accepted a renunciation of the canonical religious state. Unlike Mary, with her Institute, Anne did not induce patriarchal wrath by attempting to disrupt the accepted legislative tenets for women's institutes. Thus, congregations of "devout women" teachers like the Company of Marie Notre Dame and the Company of Saint Ursula founded by Anne remained in the "traditional movement" of religious women and obtained timely approbation. Ibid., 112. The *Institution* of the Company of Saint Ursula, which itself has many resemblances to the Jesuit *Constitutions*, incorporated specific roles for Jesuits, first implicitly, and then explicitly in its later chapters. Jesuit fathers residing in the same locations as the "sisters" would be utilized as "spiritual fathers," confessors, consultants, and intermediaries in non-spiritual matters. Ibid., 204–5. The historic, ongoing collaboration between Anne and her followers and the members of the Society of Jesus adds more evidence of women who borrowed much from Ignatian charism to form their own distinctive charism.

historical period of limited educational opportunities for women.[30] To whatever extent sources remain available, Mary's curriculum and methods of pedagogy deserve closer attention in the context of future studies of Jesuit education.

In Ignatian fashion, Mary wanted to exert careful supervision and training of her teachers and demanded a high standard of excellence of both pupils and instructors. She challenged them to reach their full potential in a free and loving partnership.[31] There was also a careful culturation and training of the mind and character of her pupils so that the best of God's powers bestowed on both were brought forth and perfected. Habits of self-control and self-government made the mind stronger, and the fear and love of God was made stronger and more acceptable to those who would follow the holy lives they were witnessing in their instructors.[32] Because of her attempt to replicate the Jesuits' disciplinary and pedagogical methods that won such praise for their boys' schools, English Catholic families were more inclined to entrust their daughters to the high standards of training that were now being offered by Mary Ward.[33]

Generally, there existed two types of schools wherever Mary's Institute was established. The first, a boarding school for children of the English recusant population. The other, a free day school, in itself an innovation for girls, that was designed for the local daughters of poor families. First place on the curriculum at her boarding schools was reserved for the teaching of religion, especially for the children of English refugees who ultimately would return to their homeland where a Church in turmoil needed them. Although Mary was scrupulous in selecting only the best-qualified priests to teach religion and prepare girls for the sacraments, her jealous critics seized this opportunity to accuse her and her followers of taking on the tasks reserved to clerics.[34]

The teaching of Latin and other languages became a hallmark of Mary's schools. She firmly believed Latin was needed to facilitate the teaching of catechism. But not only Latin was emphasized. Ever

---

[30] Marian Norman, "A Woman for All Seasons: Mary Ward (1585–1645), Renaissance Pioneer of Women's Education," *Paedagogica Historica* 23, no. 1 (1983): 129.

[31] Ibid., 137.

[32] Chambers, *Life of Mary Ward*, vol. 2, 531.

[33] Norman, "A Woman for All Seasons," 132.

[34] Ibid., 133.

since her own experience as a Poor Clare when she could not understand the language of the Spanish Netherlands, Mary sought to have her followers become well-versed in French and in the other languages spoken where they were residing. She insisted that it should not be a superficial knowledge, but sufficient to enable them to write, and to read the best authors.[35] Mary's curriculum contained another noteworthy similarity to what was taught at the Jesuit school at St. Omer: It provided opportunities for girls to see and to produce plays, both comedies and dramas, that would help them form their tastes in later life.

The Jesuit model also influenced the structure of Mary's schools. Girls were divided into smaller groups according to their talents and abilities, and were encouraged to compete with one another. Monitors were recruited from among the students to help and assist with lessons as well as discipline. Following an essential principle in the Jesuit *Ratio Studiorum*, it was of vital importance to Mary Ward for girls to fully understand their subject matter before advancing to the next level. The Superior or Mistress interviewed new pupils to determine their ability to benefit from the course of study. Assignments were made on the basis of good manners and tractability, rather than on class or wealth.[36]

At the boarding schools, the lessons of the school day began for the children at eight in the morning and concluded with night prayers and bedtime at eight in the evening, which was a schedule nearly identical to that followed in Jesuit boys' schools. To foster "a loving partnership," pupils and teachers were always within immediate access to one another, as they shared dormitories, refectory, and meal times, normally engaging in foreign-language conversation.[37]

Especially with regard to the free day schools, Mary encouraged her Sisters to move into the towns to acquaint themselves with the families and daily existence of the young girls. This freedom of movement was a key component of Mary's vision for the propagation of faith and saving souls. As mentioned earlier, her concept of freedom was acquired from the *Spiritual Exercises*, and it had much to do with shaping the apostolic character of her Institute. Mary pos-

---

[35] Chambers, *Life of Mary Ward*, vol. 2, 531.
[36] Norman, "A Women for All Seasons," 132.
[37] Ibid.

sessed that inner freedom that enables one's life to be directed toward helping others.[38]

And so emerged the new role of the apostolic woman in the seventeenth century. Mary and her followers sought to acquire that "singular freedom"—a freedom from evil, implying an ability to discern and perform every good thing that needed to be done for the sake of their neighbors. Just as Mary believed the *Spiritual Exercises* were not meant to be restricted to males, she likewise believed the spiritual life and education in "the Christian virtues and liberal arts," which flows naturally from the *Exercises*, were also applicable to women. She envisioned the need to educate girls to carry out their *own* Christian duties in the world. Jesuit schools not only educated boys to fight heresy and evil. Now, women, too, were being exhorted through education to "imitate God and follow Christ by loving others."[39]

Clearly, Mary Ward left her Sisters a charism that was not content with only a few principles of Jesuit spirituality. With the exception of their priestly functions, she wanted it all, in "manner and matter"; and in that desire, she created an Ignatian pattern for women's lives as relevant *and as needed* today as it was in her own time.

Madeleine Sophie Barat

The English Channel and about 200 years separated the lives of Mary Ward of Yorkshire and Madeleine Sophie Barat of Joigny. Their lives are joined, however, in a marked desire to restore religious faith in troubled times, each envisioning the education of women as a means to save a struggling Church. Each also possessed an inner zeal and optimism, a charism that gave life to their vision through others, and a certain fortitude that weathered all obstacles placed in their paths. Like Mary, Sophie had "pioneer work to do."[40]

Sophie Barat's life and work coincided with the aftermath of the French Revolution. She saw the compelling need for reform, and her idea, although deeply rooted in tradition, transmitted to future

---

[38] Wetter, "Mary Ward's Apostolic Vocation," 81.

[39] Norman, "A Woman for All Seasons," 129.

[40] Janet Stuart, *The Society of the Sacred Heart* (London: Convent of the Sacred Heart, 1914), 15.

generations an adaptable spiritual and educational plan that would be illuminated and unconfined by tradition. It appeared that she was of a mind more sympathetic to the generations that would follow her than to her own contemporaries,[41] informing her daughters, "when we have disappeared you will carry on, better than we have done, the work that we began."[42]

The changing times in France commanded adaptation and use of whatever religious base remained to build a new structure to satisfy new demands. Small groups of priests seeking to link teaching with devotion began to emerge, hoping that they would spearhead a second Counter Reformation in the manner of Ignatius.[43] In 1794, a group known as the Fathers of the Sacred Heart was formed with the motto: "One heart and one mind in the heart of Jesus." (In 1799, this group joined with the Fathers of the Faith; the name Fathers of the Sacred Heart was dropped, and the merged group retained the name Fathers of the Faith.) One of the Fathers of the Sacred Heart's founders, Fr. Leonor Francois de Tournely, demonstrated an eagerness to establish a corresponding order of women, believing "it would be no good to educate men and neglect women, when the building of a new social order would be increasingly women's work."[44]

Fr. de Tournely died before a female branch of his order could be formed, but his idea was consummated by his successor, Fr. Joseph Varin. It was Fr. Varin's good fortune to have as one of his followers, Louis Barat, a solemn priest who joined the Fathers of the Faith and who was gaining a reputation as a stern professor at the College of St. Jacques in Joigny in Northern France. Eleven years older than his sister Madeleine Sophie, Louis set his little goddaughter's mind aflame with classical literature and the love of "the heroic."[45]

This vintner's daughter, born in 1779, received from her brother the best educational tradition of the *ancien regime*, learning from primary sources and studying in her home grammar, rhetoric, math,

---

[41] M. O'Leary, *Education with a Tradition* (New York: Longmans, Green, 1936), xviii.

[42] Margaret Williams, R.S.C.J., *The Society of the Sacred Heart* (London: Dartman, Longman and Todd, 1978), 12.

[43] Margaret Williams, R.S.C.J., *Saint Madeleine Sophie: Her Life and Letters* (New York: Herder and Herder, 1965), 38.

[44] Williams, *Saint Madeleine Sophie*, 40.

[45] Williams, *Society of the Sacred Heart*, 33.

history, Latin, Greek, Spanish, Italian, astronomy, and "an appreciation of all things Catholic."[46] Her parents saw no value in teaching
such a frail girl such lofty subjects considered far above her station
in life. Fortunately, her steadfast brother resisted the criticism and
found a place for his young classical scholar. Fr. Varin immediately
agreed, and this "foundation stone," as he called her, would use her
classical education and strong Catholic values to form the basis of a
Plan of Studies for her Society of the Sacred Heart. Anchored in
prayer and devotion to the Sacred Heart, and driven by an apostolate
of education and service, Sophie's first Plan reflected her own education, which embodied "the book knowledge of a boy and the home
training of a girl."[47] This frail twenty-one-year-old woman arrived in
Amiens in 1801 to begin an apostolate with a small company of
women that was destined to create a new spirit, one that would
change how the education of young girls was perceived and con-
ducted.

Notwithstanding the suppression of the Society of Jesus in 1773,
private schools during this time period were still modeled in the
Jesuit tradition. The most notable of them belonged to the Fathers
of the Faith who modeled their lives and teaching on that of the
Society of Jesus.[48] Sophie turned to these Fathers repeatedly for guidance. They led her and her followers in the *Spiritual Exercises*, which
endowed her Society with its Jesuit characteristics in the method of
teaching and in the schools' curriculum. The earliest Plan of Studies
was drawn up with the help of Fr. Loriquet, who was headmaster of
the boys' school in Amiens. Ignatius was the patron of the professed
novices who were instructed in Jesuit methods of prayer. Jesuit feasts
were celebrated, at times secretly; but openly, Sophie would state
that her Society was glorified in drawing its origins from the Society
of Jesus, as the *Constitutions* and the rules of Ignatius informed its
aims, means, structure, and rules. Sophie described Ignatius to her
followers in these words:

> [A]ssuredly he was one of the greatest contemplatives of his century
> of error. *And so there formed in the heart of our hero the plan of the
> Institute to which it is our glory to be related, this Institute which unites*

---

[46] O'Leary, *Education with a Tradition*, xix.
[47] Williams, *Saint Madeleine Sophie*, 461.
[48] O'Leary, *Education with a Tradition*, 96.

the active and contemplative life. . . . Thus this spring of humility, of
prayer, of mortification which Saint Ignatius opened up spreads over the
earth like an immense river which refreshes it and makes it fruitful. From
this river a thousand rivuletes flow, and we have the happiness of being
a small one.[49]

It is ironic that the Order of the Fathers of the Faith was dissolved
by Emperor Napoleon in 1807, in the very same year that he signed
the petition for approbation in favor of Sophie's Society of the Sacred Heart. Nine years later, when the Jesuit suppression was lifted,
the Bishop of Grenoble approved the definitive, framed constitutions that were based on the *Constitutions* and rules of Ignatius,
including a structure of provinces and Provincials, and Sophie the
newly elected Superior General.

The Society's aim, like Mary Ward's, was the mingling of the perfection of its members and the salvation of others through education.[50] Sophie saw more clearly than had been seen before how much
the future depended on the influence of women and the urgent need
for a new kind of systematic education for young girls. It would be
an education that prepared them for their responsible charges in life,
and it was viewed as one of the most powerful means to direct the
course of the coming age.[51]

Although there is no question that Sophie's Society was in constant discourse with the learned Jesuit schoolmasters, her daughters
shared a deep and fervent preoccupation with the "peculiar mission
of womanhood,"[52] and were bound by an inner force that drove them
to do the work of Christ without necessarily being bound by any one
pedagogical theory or plan of action.

Her Plan of Studies, then, became more open-ended and flexible:
a liberal arts education with theology at its core; structured on philosophy, literature, and history, and humanistic in its content; with
an integration of sciences and practical skills.[53] Sophie's earliest curriculum included Bible and Church history, and Latin only for the
more gifted pupils. Reflecting Sophie's more feminine design, pupils

---

[49] Conferences, I, 258, in Williams, *Saint Madeleine Sophie*, 500–501 (emphases
added).
[50] Williams, *Society of the Sacred Heart*, 44.
[51] Stuart, *Society of the Sacred Heart*, 11.
[52] O'Leary, *Education with a Tradition*, 100.
[53] Williams, *Society of the Sacred Heart*, 71.

were also taught drawing, needlework, instrumental music, and singing. With the inclusion of domestic economy studies and other subjects that were more specifically feminine in nature, Sophie
demonstrated her unwillingness to replicate *in its entirety* the classical "boy's education" she received at home. Her level of education,
however, generally surpassed what was given to young women of her
day. She could have been ultramodern and developed a plan that
more completely reflected the boys' curriculum at Jesuit schools. Instead, she chose to recognize the nature of her times and sought to
place her gifts to achieve a different end.[54] As Janet Stuart explains:
"While it is no apostle of 'feminism,' the Society of the Sacred Heart
is essentially a feminine Order, a woman's Order, seeking in its whole
tone and spirit and training and manner of life a *woman's excellence*,
the *perfection of womanhood*, and, so far as can be learned, God's
ideals, and Mary's, of *what a woman can be*."[55] It is important to note
that in the more democratic, post-revolutionary times in which Sophie lived, the makeup of the pupils in the schoolroom was changing, as rich and poor, aristocrats' and farmers' daughters, were
beginning to sit side by side in the classroom. This meant girls in the
same school with different learning capacities, some who would not
be able to comprehend more advanced study. The social evolution
Sophie was witnessing would not allow her to take an "all or nothing" position on the education of Catholic girls. Sophie's curriculum
was not so rigid as to preclude the practical training that would help
prepare certain girls for what would ultimately be their mission in
life. The rigidity of the Jesuit *Ratio Studiorum* would not satisfy her
needs. The great value of her educational plan, during a time when
young women were so poorly educated, was not so much the content
of her curriculum but the *quality* of it and her insistence on a pedagogy that stressed *strong character formation*.[56]

In addition, Sophie had great confidence in the ways in which her
own Sisters would guide their charges. Her educators were to maintain attentive interest in the individual pupil and illustrate maternal
care. She believed they possessed expressly feminine gifts that would
relate to young girls in their schools, including affection, tact, in-

---

[54] O'Leary, *Education with a Tradition*, 91–92.
[55] Stuart, *Society of the Sacred Heart*, 76 (emphasis added).
[56] Williams, *Society of the Sacred Heart*, 71.

sight, intuition, humility, reserve, and sympathy. Because of these feminine gifts, Sophie insisted that her Order, although greatly influenced by the Fathers of the Faith and the Society of Jesus, could never be a total copy of a male order. She was adamant that her Sisters retain their own identity and remain true to the conviction that their relationship to the Jesuits should be *more like sister to brother*.[57]

Because of her orientation toward adaptation and change, there have been successive editions of Sophie's Plan of Studies, each the product of collaborative efforts. She never looked upon what was drawn up as a finished product, wisely insisting that "older methods should not be despised nor the newer neglected."[58] Each Plan edition, however, would contain certain identifiable hallmarks: a diversity of curriculum, exacting requirements for both teachers and pupils, and an unflagging devotion to the "spirit." The Religious of the Sacred Heart adopted a number of other characteristics of the Jesuit schools. For example, the advancement of students from one grade to another was dependent on each student's talent and how much each was capable of learning. The teaching of individual subjects had to be conceived according to the age of each student. There was also an underlying attention given to each child according to the child's capacity and a view of the child's future as a Christian, both in family life and society as a whole.[59] The teaching rules for the Sisters of the Sacred Heart placed high value on the individual child, and through their individual example they would lead each girl to develop her character, her own sense of worth, and an inner strength of principle that was deeply rooted in Christian faith.[60]

It has been said that Sophie had the head of St. Ignatius with the heart of St. Therese.[61] Her Plan evolved throughout the years to meet the needs of changing times; *its spirit never wavered*. Timelessness, especially when referring to spirit, does not depend on rigidity. It was Sophie's greatest gift to future generations to develop a Plan of Studies that was grounded on a permanent base and contained a harmonious program—one that had the ability of being revised so as to

[57] Stuart, *Society of the Sacred Heart*, 77.
[58] Ibid., 68.
[59] *Spirit and Plan of Studies*, 14.
[60] Stuart, *Society of the Sacred Heart*, 65.
[61] Williams, *Saint Madeleine Sophie*, 501.

find its own balance in any setting or any time period without losing any of its individuality and spirit.[62]

CONCLUSION

Mary Ward and Madeleine Sophie Barat followed in the path of the pilgrim. With the guidance of Jesuit mentors and confessors, both of these women made the *Spiritual Exercises* authored by Ignatius Loyola. They were deeply motivated by the Ignatian charism of finding God in all things, blending the contemplative with the active apostolate of serving God in this world, and striving always to do more.[63] Both wanted to reform society through character formation, and they adopted the style, manner, and philosophy of the Jesuit educational system that prevailed during their lifetime. Because these women discerned the value of Ignatian spirituality, pedagogy, and curriculum, young women of the seventeenth, eighteenth, and early nineteenth centuries began to receive the kind of education that had previously been reserved for young boys.

In the spirit of Ignatius, Mary and Sophie recognized the importance of the apostolate of education for women and, to varying degrees, were flexible enough to blend the Jesuit educational tradition with innovations more suitable for young women in the society in which they were situated. They each fought hard to achieve their visions. Mary caught only a fleeting glimpse of its actualization before the English Civil War swept her work asunder during her lifetime. Her followers struggled for many years to recapture her charism, and after three centuries, the Institute of the Blessed Virgin Mary recognized her as its foundress. Today, the I.B.V.M. as well as the Sisters of Loretto flourish worldwide. Sophie, the vintner's daughter, was able to see more of her labors in the vineyards of the Lord achieved during her lifetime. This afternoon a number of her daughters are seated in this audience, and they are proof that the Sisters of the Religious of the Sacred Heart continue globally to do the work that Sophie inspired.

---

[62] Stuart, *Society of the Sacred Heart*, 70.

[63] Joseph A. O'Hare, S.J., "What Are the Odds of Jesuit Higher Education Surviving in America?" (address presented to the AJCU conference on *Jesuit Education* 21, Philadelphia, Saint Joseph's College, June 1999).

Presently, I do not have the documentation to support whether Mary and Sophie had actually seen a copy of the *Ratio Studiorum*. Nevertheless, the similarities in curriculum design and pedagogy create a strong presumption that they each were, in some way, exposed to this extraordinary plan of study. The fact remains that both women were strongly influenced by their Jesuit mentors and copied much from the Jesuit schools in St. Omer and Amiens where they began their apostolates.

Fr. John O'Malley wrote that the "study of the past helps to locate us better in the present which enables us to plan more judiciously for the future."[64] In fewer than eighty days, we will enter a new century and a new millennium. Our eyes and our hearts are focused on what is in store for the future of Jesuit education. While I do not purport to have all the answers, I would like to suggest a more determined and cooperative effort to discuss and reflect on the roles women have played in the past in adopting Ignatian spirituality and pedagogy. This will serve as a means to locate us in the present and amplify women's roles in the next chapter of Jesuit history. The continuance of a Jesuit/lay partnership, the "sister to brother relationship" as it was envisioned by Madeleine Sophie, needs to be nurtured amidst the declining number of Jesuits.

It cannot be overstated that a more precise understanding of Ignatian spirituality by the laity, particularly women, is paramount if we expect the distinctive characteristics of our Jesuit educational institutions to survive. These characteristics have to be lifted off the pages of our lofty mission statements and recruiting materials, and thoroughly enlivened by a reflection on the lives of those men and women, *patrons, pupils, and partners*, who embody them, both in the past and in the present.

In order to do this, the richness of the Ignatian heritage and the lessons of the *Spiritual Exercises*, the *Constitutions*, and the *Ratio Studiorum* must be brought to a much wider audience of women in the Jesuit educational enterprise. We should discover more creative ways to show how Ignatian spirituality is relevant to the actual experience of women. By examining the lives and visions of Mary Ward

---

[64] John W. O'Malley, S.J., "The Jesuit Educational Enterprise in Historical Perspective," in *Jesuit Higher Education: Essays on an American Tradition of Excellence*, ed. Rolando E. Bonachea (Pittsburgh: Duquesne University Press, 1989), 10.

and Madeleine Sophie Barat, I have attempted to reveal how women and Jesuits have been historically connected by the spirit of the pilgrim. I am confident we can do much more in the future to enable Ignatius Loyola's tenet of apostolic discernment to take hold in each of us so that men and women together will strive to become, as Fr. Joseph O'Hare recently stated, more "great-hearted"[65] in our quest for the *magis*, to become more and do more *ad majorem dei gloriam*.

---

[65] O'Hare, "What Are the Odds of Jesuit Higher Education Surviving in America?"

6

From the 1599 *Ratio Studiorum* to the Present: A Humanistic Tradition?

John W. O'Malley, S.J.

THE TOPIC on which I was asked to write is huge and filled with perils for anybody rash enough to address it. My experience has been, however, that sometimes tackling an issue in such global terms can, though frustrating, be helpful in flushing out our assumptions and thus helping us deal with them more effectively. I warn you that we will hurl through the centuries as in a fast-moving rocket.

Before moving to the Jesuits for that panoramic rush, I want to review the history of the humanistic tradition before the Jesuits appeared on the scene and to do this review in a much fuller fashion than in my first contribution to this seminar. I realize that many of you already know the story well, but I hope a review of it can sharpen our discussion by providing a common base for it.

Our terms "humanism" and "the humanities" derive from the Italian Renaissance and its promotion of what was called the *studia humanitatis*, which I freely translate as literature dealing with what it means to be a human being. That literature consisted, as I indicated yesterday, in the Greek and especially Latin works of poetry, oratory, drama, and history that, when properly taught, were believed to develop an upright, articulate, and socially committed person. I hardly need add that this meaning of "humanist" and "humanism," which arose in a Christian context, bears little, if any, relationship to the way the terms are often used today to indicate somebody with faith in humanity but no faith in God.[1]

---

[1] See especially Paul Oskar Kristeller, *Renaissance Thought and Its Sources*, ed. Michael Mooney (New York: Columbia University Press, 1979).

Let us begin at the beginning by moving for just a moment back to the Athens of the philosophers Plato and Aristotle and of the Sophist Isocrates. We are all familiar with the battle Plato waged with the Sophists through his dialogues, in which he had Socrates attack those teachers of public speaking on two grounds: first, for their intellectual shallowness—they spoke of justice but could not define what it meant; second, for their moral deviance—they perverted their skills in the art of persuasion by being willing to teach their students how to argue either side of a moral issue; to *win* the case was what was important. Plato made the Sophists look like charlatans and peddlers of bombast.

Plato may have bested the Sophists in philosophical argument, but it was the Sophists who through their most eminent thinker Isocrates and his followers won the battle to educate fourth-century Greece and subsequently the Hellenistic and Roman worlds.[2] Isocrates was basically a teacher of oratory, that is, of rhetoric. A younger contemporary of Socrates, he was stung by the criticisms Plato leveled against his kind, and he to a considerable extent refashioned the Sophistic tradition to try to make it intellectually and morally responsible. He too wanted to be known as a philosopher, that is, a lover of wisdom.

But he clearly recognized the gap that separated his wisdom from that of Plato, to say nothing of the even wider gap that would separate it from Aristotle. For Isocrates and his disciples the education Plato envisaged was ridiculous, for it required most of the years of a man's life, and it also isolated the student from the urgent concerns of society. It produced ivory-tower intellectuals, not the men of action society required. The kind of learning that later Aristotle pursued, especially in "natural philosophy," that is, in the sciences of physics, astronomy, zoology, and so forth, was even further removed from life in the polis. It did not deal with human issues.

If Plato and Aristotle based their education on the idea of Truth

---

[2] The basic study remains H. I. Marrou, A *History of Education in Antiquity*, trans. George Lamb (New York: New American Library, 1944). See also Marrou's *Saint Augustin et la fin de la culture antique*, 4th ed. (Paris: Éditions E. de Boccard, 1958); Werner Jaeger, *Paideia: The Ideals of Greek Culture*, trans. Gilbert Highet, 2d ed., 3 vols. (New York: Oxford University Press, 1963); and Helen North, *Sophrosyne: Self-Knowledge and Self-Restraint in Greek Literature* (Ithaca: Cornell University Press, 1966), esp. 121–96.

with a capital T, Isocrates based his on the virtues of speech, which for him and his followers was what distinguishes human beings from animals. The burden of speech was to convey noble and uplifting ideals. The goal of education was to produce eloquent and morally effective speakers. The axiom beloved in the nineteenth century by British educators in this tradition captured the goal for their times by saying it was to produce "gentlemen," that is, persons who said what they meant and meant what they said. "Said what they meant"—that is, their words accurately transmitted their thoughts. "Meant what they said"'—they were men of moral integrity who stood by their words.

Such a goal required in students diligent study of "good literature," for through such study they would acquire an eloquent style of speaking and, just as important, be inspired by the examples of virtuous and even heroic behavior they would encounter in the best authors. Through such study they would especially acquire a practical prudence in human affairs, a wisdom that would enable them to influence others—for the good—in the law courts, in the senates, in the antechambers of power. They would be, as we in the education business love to say today, "leaders."

The curriculum itself, centered on the Greek and Roman literary classics, could be mastered in a relatively short time, so that the young man could be sent into society to play his part when he was in his late teens. Rhetoric, the art of speaking persuasively, the art needed by a man committed to public life, became the central discipline in the curriculum.

Thus was created within one or two generations the basic design of the humanistic tradition of education that would prove itself so resilient for the next 2500 years. Bit by bit the ideal took firm institutional forms in the ancient world and produced Cicero and Quintilian, as well as Sts. Ambrose, Augustine, Jerome, and Gregory the Great. Cicero summed up the broad moral ideal of this tradition in a line in his *De officiis* that Renaissance humanists and then the Jesuits loved to quote: *Non nobis solum nati sumus*—"We are not born for ourselves alone." The most succinct Roman articulation of the "ideal graduate" of the system was Cicero's simple description of the orator: *Vir bonus, dicendi peritus*—"a good man, skilled in speaking." This combination of probity, eloquence, and commitment to the public weal would be the unwavering ideal of rhetorical, or humanistic, education through the centuries, but it would often be compromised, diluted, mystified, and made subservient to other ideals.

As the Roman Empire declined, the educational system declined as well, surviving in barely vestigial form until it experienced a resurgence in the twelfth century. And then came the fuller and more lasting one in Italy in the fifteenth century that we indeed call the Renaissance, principally because it caused this cult of "good literature" (*bonae litterae*) and this ideal of education to be reborn in a particularly effective way.[3]

Fifteenth-century humanists, as they tried to recreate the educational program and ideals of the *studia humanitatis*, in effect created the basic design of "good" primary and secondary schools that persisted in the Western world until the middle of this century. (I use "secondary" as convenient but not perfectly accurate shorthand.) The principles upon which these schools were based were essentially the following: First, the curriculum was centered in works of Latin history, oratory, drama, and poetry, for these taught eloquent expression; second, these works also had a didactic purpose, that is, they gave guidance in morals and in practical affairs; third, the assumption behind the curriculum was classicist, that is, the best thoughts had been thought, the best style fashioned, so that what was needed in the student was to appropriate such thoughts and style; fourth, formal schooling was to end when a boy was in his late teens; fifth, the formation of an upright person was the goal of the system, which Erasmus would later specify with the word *pietas*.[4] As I said yesterday, *pietas* in this context included and was conditioned by Christian godliness, but it more directly denoted maturity of character. Although Erasmus and other Renaissance writers on the subject believed *pietas* was imbibed through the works in the curriculum, they

---

[3] The basic sources can be found in William Harrison Woodward, *Vittorino da Feltre and Other Humanist Educators* (1897; reprint, New York: Bureau of Publications, Teachers College, Columbia University, 1963) and his *Desiderius Erasmus Concerning the Aim and Method of Education* (1904; reprint, New York: Bureau of Publications, Teachers College, Columbia University, 1964). For the historical background, see Paul F. Grendler, *Schooling in Renaissance Italy: Literacy and Learning, 1300–1600* (Baltimore: Johns Hopkins University Press, 1989).

[4] On this concept in Erasmus, see John W. O'Malley, "Introduction," in *Collected Works of Erasmus*, ed. John W. O'Malley (Toronto: University of Toronto Press, 1988), 66:ix–li.

gave perhaps even more emphasis to the moral and human qualities required in the teacher in order to accomplish the goal, an emphasis the Jesuits later enthusiastically appropriated.

In a sense this model can be called a *pure* embodiment of the humanistic tradition in that, despite the centuries that had elapsed, it so faithfully recapitulated the program of ancient Greece and Rome. But the humanist movement in the Italian Renaissance had at least one important characteristic that distinguished it from its ancient counterpart.[5] The Italian humanists were Christians. This meant, for instance, that the way they developed certain aspects of the discipline of rhetoric, combined with certain traditions of Christian doctrine and theology, resulted in a new and often resounding surfacing of the theme of human dignity. Thus, this new rhetoric tended to promote a more optimistic Christian anthropology than the more pessimistic emphasis in the so-called Augustinian tradition, with its often dour fixation on human depravity and moral impotence.[6]

I need also to mention another aspect of the humanists' enterprise that qualifies some of the generalizations I have been making. They developed the basic techniques and principles of textual criticism and, while not lacking some prototypes in the ancient world like St. Jerome, constructed for the first time in history critical editions of classical and patristic texts. In other words, they created the highly technical discipline of philology, more or less as we know it today, that, because it required such long and disciplined study, was not open to the young generalists whom the humanistic schools themselves produced. As textual critics the humanists were professionals. In 1516, for instance, Erasmus, "the prince of the humanists," published the first critical edition of the Greek New Testament.[7]

---

[5] An international consensus on the nature of Renaissance Humanism has developed over the past thirty years; see, e.g., Albert Rabil Jr., ed., *Renaissance Humanism: Foundations, Forms, and Legacy*, 3 vols. (Philadelphia: University of Pennsylvania Press, 1998). See also, however, Kenneth Gouwens, "Perceiving the Past: Renaissance Humanism after the 'Cognitive Turn,'" *The American Historical Review*, 103 (1998): 55–82.

[6] The classic study remains Charles Trinkaus, *"In Our Image and Likeness": Humanity and Divinity in Italian Renaissance Thought*, 2 vols. (Chicago: University of Chicago Press, 1970). See also John W. O'Malley, *Praise and Blame in Renaissance Rome: Rhetorique, Doctrine, and Reform in the Sacred Orators of the Papal Court, c. 1450–1521* (Durham: Duke University Press, 1979).

[7] See, e.g., Jerry H. Bentley, *Humanists and Holy Writ: New Testament Scholarship in the Renaissance* (Princeton: Princeton University Press, 1983).

The mention of "professionals" allows us to backtrack to the striking innovation in education that took place in the twelfth and thirteenth centuries with the creation of the universities. It was, as mentioned yesterday, somewhat in reaction to the educational ethos of the universities that the humanists of the fifteenth century developed their schools. There are several characteristics of the university that made it almost the polar opposite of the humanist ideal.

First of all, the content that beginners principally studied when in the "undergraduate" or "Arts Faculty" of the university was not literature but Aristotelian science, with some admixture of metaphysics and ethics. Literature and history as such had no place in this system. Second, the goal of the university was not to produce an upright person ready for public life but to pursue truth through ongoing analysis and refinement of argument. The university was not about *pietas* but *veritas* (as Harvard's motto has it). It was not centered on the development of the student or the betterment of society but on the solving of intellectual problems. It gloried not in the *vita activa* of public engagement but in the *vita contemplativa* of study and research.

Third, rhetoric, the art of persuasion, played second fiddle in this system to dialectics, the art of debate. This is a shift from the art of winning consensus to the art of winning an argument, from the art of finding common ground to the art of proving your opponent wrong. Fourth, a full course of study might last fifteen or more years because the five or six years in the Arts Faculty that I have been describing were really preparation for entering one of the higher faculties of law, medicine, or theology—"graduate school."

Finally, this meant for the first time in the history of the West the systematic professionalization of learning, because this style of education could be pursued only within the highly sophisticated and elaborate institution known as the university. The gentleman scholar who ruminated over his texts of Virgil or the Bible was replaced with the professional, who brandished his degrees and licenses to prove he had mastered all the technicalities of his profession. Further proof of his mastery lay in his being able to speak a technical jargon that nobody outside academia could possibly understand—for eloquence he cared not a whit!

In the sixteenth century, Erasmus saw this system as the mortal enemy of all that the *studia humanitatis* stood for. Yet, these two modes of education, despite the great differences that separated them, had an important link in that the medieval *trivium* of grammar, rhetoric, and logic were taught in both the Arts Faculty of the university and in the humanistic schools, albeit with different purposes, methods, and emphasis; and they were taught to students of approximately the same age. As early as the fourteenth century, the poet Petrarch, rightly regarded as the Father of Humanism, taught rhetoric in the Arts Faculty of the University of Padua, and later other humanists did the same in other universities. By the middle of the sixteenth century, Peter Ramus proposed for the Arts Faculty of the University of Paris a seven-and-a-half-year program in the subjects contained in the original humanist curriculum that would lead to a Master of Arts degree; the idea was that that degree would enable the student to pursue further studies in a graduate faculty.[8]

This incorporation of the humanist curriculum into the university system is what Anthony Grafton and Lisa Jardine call the transformation of humanism into the humanities. By this they mean that education even in the *studia humanitatis* was for pursuing information and skills, not for inspiring the development of good citizens. Incorporation into the university curriculum thus meant a radical reordering of the scope of *studia* as they were transformed into skills to aid professional advancement.[9]

By the mid-sixteenth century, therefore, the humanistic tradition had found a home in two locations that would persist in the Western world down to the present century—the secondary school and the Arts College of the university, and they thereby manifested two quite distinct modalities. It is precisely at this point, mid-sixteenth century, that the Jesuits enter the scene. The original ten companions, graduates of the University of Paris, after 1540 had their headquarters in Italy, where humanistic secondary schools had already been in existence for at least a century.

In 1548, the Jesuits opened their first real school in Messina, Sicily, and others followed in rapid succession. All at once they had become a religious Order whose principal and most distinctive ministry was the managing and staffing of schools—at both the secondary and

---

[8] See Anthony Grafton and Lisa Jardine, *From Humanism to the Humanities: Education and the Liberal Arts in Fifteenth- and Sixteenth-Century Europe* (Cambridge: Harvard University Press, 1986), esp. 161–200.

[9] Grafton and Jardine, *Humanism*, esp. 58–98.

university level, though the former were almost incomparably more numerous than the latter. They could not avoid the issue of the *studia humanitatis*, nor did they want to.[10]

In this regard they took two fateful decisions in 1547–48 that manifest the two somewhat competing aspects of their relationship to those *studia*. In 1547, Juan de Polanco, Ignatius's secretary, wrote a letter justifying the study by young Jesuits themselves of the *cosas de humanidad*. The reasons he adduced favoring such study were borrowed from the humanists themselves but were not the ones that made the broadest claims. The study of *humanidad*, Polanco argued, helps in the understanding of Scripture, is a traditional propaedeutic to philosophy, and fosters the skills in verbal communication essential for the ministries in which Jesuits engaged. These are basically utilitarian arguments that see the *studia humanidad* not as goods in their own right but as fitting into a broader program of professional education. Missing in Polanco's letter is any suggestion that the *studia* have anything to do with making the Jesuits better human beings.[11]

Yet, the very next year Jerónimo Nadal, Ignatius's most trusted agent in the field, prescribed for the new school in Messina a basically humanistic curriculum for young boys from important families, most of whom would not go on for further professional training in a university. With the founding of Messina, no matter what the original plan was there, the Jesuits entered into the field of what we can call secondary education, where the training ended in a boy's late teens and was considered complete in and of itself.[12]

Why did the Jesuits enter this field? As I tried to make clear yesterday, there is no simple answer, but I am convinced that even from

---

[10] On these foundational years, see Grendler, *Schooling*, 363–81; Allan P. Farrell, *The Jesuit Code of Liberal Education: Development and Scope of the Ratio Studiorum* (Milwaukee: Bruce Publishing, 1938), 3–216; Gabriel Codina Mir, *Aux sources de la pédagogie des jésuites: Le "Modus parisiensis"* (Rome: Institutum Historicum Societatis Iesu, 1968); and John W. O'Malley, *The First Jesuits* (Cambridge: Harvard University Press, 1993), 200–42, 253–64.

[11] See O'Malley, *First Jesuits*, 210, 256.

[12] Technically speaking, the school at Messina was a university, but at the beginning the Jesuits were frustrated in their hopes of teaching subjects beyond the *studia humanitatis*; see Daniela Novarese, *Istituzioni politiche e studi di diritto fra Cinque e Seicento: Il Messanense Studium Generale tra politica gesuitica e istanze egemoniche cittadine* (Milan: Giuffrè Editore, 1994).

the beginning they saw a correlation between the *pietas* beloved of the humanists and the kind of personal conversion and transformation that were the traditional goals of Christian ministry, in which the Jesuits were so assiduously engaged. They saw a correlation between *pietas* and *Christianitas*. In 1552, Nadal explicitly asserted the primacy of *pietas* in the educational system the Jesuits were beginning to build and of which he was the first architect: "Everything is to be so arranged," he said, "so that in the pursuit of these studies *pietas* holds first place."[13]

A few years later, Polanco wrote his important letter to the members of the Society giving fifteen reasons why the Society had so resolutely undertaken formal schooling, especially on the secondary level, as its principal ministry. Although he does not explicitly mention *pietas*, he in the last of his reasons well captures the humanistic ideal of producing leaders in the polis, as you will recall: "Those who are now only students will grow up to be pastors, civic officials, administrators of justice, and will fill other important posts to everybody's profit and advantage."[14]

We often read that the Jesuits founded schools so that they would be bastions of orthodoxy to train young Christian soldiers to do battle against the Protestant threat. In Polanco's fifteen reasons, however, there is not a single one that even suggests such a preoccupation. The same can be said about the section on education in the Jesuit *Constitutions* written by Ignatius and Polanco, and for the most part about Nadal's early writings on the subject. The Jesuits had many and complex motives for undertaking the ministry of formal education, but absolutely fundamental to them was their faith in the almost limitless potential for the individual and for society of the *studia humanitatis*, as this was preached by earlier Renaissance humanists.

Nonetheless, there can be no denying that with varying degrees of emphasis, depending partly on where in Europe the schools were located, concern for orthodoxy affected what the moral and religious formation of the student entailed, and it in that regard changed it from its earlier even Christian manifestations. As Europe moved into

---

[13] O'Malley, *First Jesuits*, 212.
[14] Ibid., 212–13.

the Confessional Age, Jesuit schools to a greater or lesser degree even on the secondary level became ever more clearly confessional institutions, which added a further conservative dimension to what was already a fundamentally conservative educational ideal.

Two other factors that derived from the Jesuits' religious commitments affected, I believe, the humanistic ideals they adopted for their schools and almost seem to cancel each other out. The first was the call to interiority of the *Spiritual Exercises* that correlated well with the inner-directedness of the leader envisaged by the humanists. That leader would when necessary defy convention to follow what in these concrete circumstances was the better choice. He would be a person of discernment.

The second was an ever-increasing emphasis within the Society and within the Church on exacting obedience to rules and church discipline. This emphasis arose partly out of the Observantist Movement of the late Middle Ages whereby strict adherence to rules was almost the very essence of religious life—a belief to which many Jesuits gradually succumbed and which made a resoundingly strong comeback in religious Orders in the nineteenth and early twentieth centuries. It also arose more broadly in Catholicism from the strong social disciplining that permeated Catholicism in the wake of the Council of Trent. The social disciplining that the Jesuits to a large degree adopted for themselves and that broadly characterized both Protestant and Catholic churches in the late sixteenth century had to have an impact on the ideal Jesuits communicated to their students—or imposed upon them. Aldo Scaglione in his book on Jesuit education spoke of an "authoritarian humanism" as the Jesuit legacy in education.[15]

In any case, after a half century in the education business, the Jesuits produced in 1599 the definitive version of their *Ratio Studiorum*, a document basically structured as a collection of job descriptions of everybody directly connected with the process of education in the Jesuit system.[16] For teachers this job description includes the

---

[15] See Aldo Scaglione, *The Liberal Arts and the Jesuit College System* (Amsterdam and Philadelphia: John Benjamins Publishing, 1986), 95.

[16] On the *Ratio*, see Farrell, *Jesuit Code*, 219–362; John W. Donohue, *Jesuit Education: An Essay on the Foundations of Its Idea* (New York: Fordham University Press, 1963), 32–62; Gian-Mario Anselmi, "Per un'archeologia della *Ratio*: dalla 'pedagogia' al 'governo,'" in La "*Ratio studiorum*": *Modelli culturali e pratiche educative dei Gesuiti in Italia tra Cinque e Seicento*, ed. Gian Paolo Brizzi (Rome: Bulzoni

texts they are to teach, the order in which they are to teach them, and some pedagogical techniques and procedures, often pedantically detailed, to make their teaching more effective. The *Ratio* is concerned with doing a job in the most effective way possible without very clearly declaring the philosophy of education that might make the job worth doing in the first place. That philosophy, the authors surely but perhaps mistakenly presumed, would be known to those involved in doing the job.

The *Ratio* is an altogether top-down document in two crucial ways. It begins with the Jesuit Provincial Superior and works down eventually to the students. It also begins with the so-called "higher faculties"—Scripture, scholastic theology, cases of conscience or ethics—and works down the program through philosophy to rhetoric and grammar, the "lowest" disciplines in this system but the heart of the matter in the traditionally humanistic program.

Three observations are apposite. First, it is clear from some details in the "Rules for the Provincial" that the *Ratio* is designed first and foremost as a master plan for the training of Jesuits themselves.[17] We know from other sources that in the Jesuit system relatively few besides Jesuits ever got as far as the "higher," that is, the theological, disciplines—even diocesan seminarians were not expected to study theology beyond "cases of conscience." This fact gives the *Ratio* a rather curious twist as a blueprint for the wide range of institutions and the diverse student bodies the Jesuit network of schools embraced.

Second, the design of the *Ratio* reduces the *studia humanitatis* to a preparatory program for academic specialization, namely, for further studies in science and theology. It is true that in the "Common Rules for the Teachers of the Lower Classes" the *Ratio* takes as its focus young boys in Jesuit secondary schools and indicates ways teachers can train the boys in "Christian conduct" (*mores etiam Christianis dignos*) through certain devout practices like requiring

---

Editore, 1981), 11–42. For the text in English, see *The Jesuit Ratio Studiorum of 1599*, trans. Allan P. Farrell (Washington: Conference of Major Superiors of Jesuits, 1970). The new critical edition of the Latin text is to be found in *Monumenta Paedagogica Societatis Iesu*, ed. Ladislaus Lukács (Monumenta Historica Societatis Iesu, vol. 129) (Rome: Institutum Historicum Societatis Iesu, 1986), 5:357–454, with an excellent "Introductio Generalis" by Lukács, 1*–34*.

[17] See *Jesuit Ratio*, 3, 6–7.

daily attendance at Mass, but it falls short of suggesting the inner-directed wisdom implicit in Erasmian *pietas*.[18]

Third, the *Ratio* insists that the acquisition of the power of self-expression or eloquence is the scope of the class devoted to rhetoric and, more broadly, of the "lower" disciplines, with the acquisition of information a secondary goal. Missing in the *Ratio* are the highfalu-tin claims of the humanists, Jesuits included, that this training will produce the leaders society needs, but such claims were surely pre-sumed by the authors as not needing to be stated.[19]

I think just these few observations about the *Ratio* alert us to the danger of trying to recreate what happened in the past through the exclusive study of official and normative documents like the *Ratio*. The vast majority of Jesuit schools implemented only a truncated version of the grand design envisaged by the *Ratio*, and many, per-haps most, schools in that majority went little beyond the so-called "lower" disciplines. Rhetoric, "humanity," and grammar were what practically every Jesuit taught at sometime in his career and were much more important in the total network of Jesuit schools through the centuries than the *Ratio* suggests. We need more studies, espe-cially of the secondary schools like those by Scaglione and others, but my hunch is that in them the *studia humanitatis* retained more of the scope originally claimed for them by the humanists than the *Ratio* suggests.[20] Just how successfully that scope was actually at-tained is another question for which we have no secure answer, but Grafton and Jardine have alerted us to how plodding and lowly much teaching was in humanistic schools, and we should not automatically assume Jesuit schools were an exception.

In neither the university nor even in the humanistic secondary schools was any provision made for any appreciation of arts like painting and sculpture, and this deficiency is reflected in the *Ratio*. These were text-based systems. The humanists did make provision for dance, a "performing art," as a requisite for the gentleman, and

---

[18] Ibid., 62–63.

[19] See, e.g, Donohue, *Jesuit Education*, 159–85.

[20] See, e.g., Scaglione, *Liberal Arts*; Brizzi, ed., *"Ratio studiorum"*; Gian Paolo Brizzi, *La formazione delle classe dirigenti nel Sei-Settecentro: I seminaria nobilium nell'Italia centro-settentrionale* (Bologna: Il Mulino, 1976); François de Dainville, *L'éducation des jésuites (XVIe–XVIIIe siècles)* (Paris: Les Éditions de Minuit, 1978); and John W. Padberg, *Colleges in Controversy: The Jesuit Schools in France from Revival to Suppression, 1815–1880* (Cambridge: Harvard University Press, 1969).

therefore dance, though not mentioned in the *Ratio*, was taught in at least some Jesuit schools, with notable success in Paris in the seventeenth century at the Collège Louis-le-Grand.[21] Theater, another performing art, is mentioned, but in restrictive terms. We know from other sources, however, of the theatrical pieces that were produced in the Jesuit schools in such number and with such exuberance and excellence that they must be considered an integral part of those schools' self-definition.[22] The two new books from the University of Toronto Press provide incontrovertible evidence of how important the arts were in the corporate culture of the Society of Jesus, and they thus raise interesting questions about how the arts impacted formal schooling in the Jesuit system.[23]

We also know, especially through the studies of Marc Fumaroli, that Jesuits in the sixteenth and seventeenth centuries produced serious and important books on rhetoric and other aspects of what we might call literary studies, so that we cannot say categorically that in the Jesuit system such studies inevitably and invariably were reduced to pragmatic uses, without appreciation for their aesthetic qualities.[24]

---

[21] See Judith Rock, *Terpsichore at Louis-Le-Grand: Baroque Dance on the Jesuit Stage in Paris* (St. Louis: The Institute of Jesuit Sources, 1996).

[22] The literature on the subject is abundant. Of special importance are the works by Jean-Marie Valentin, e.g., *Le théâtre des jésuites dans les pays de langue allemande (1554–1680)*, 3 vols. (Bern: Peter Lang, 1978); *Le théâtre des jésuites dans les pays de langue allemande: Répertoir chronologique des pièces représentées et des documents conservés (1555–1773)* 2 vols. (Stuttgart: A. Hiersemann, 1983–84); "Gegenreformation und Literatur: Das Jesuitendrama im Dienste der religiösen und moralischen Erziehung," *Historisches Jahrbuch*, 100 (1980): 240–56. See also now on the broader program of "extra-curriculars," Joseph M. O'Keefe, "The Pedagogy of Persuasion: The Culture of the University of Pont-à-Mousson," *Paedagogica Historica*, 34 (1998): 421–42.

[23] John W. O'Malley et al., eds., *The Jesuits: Cultures, Sciences, and the Arts, 1540–1773* (Toronto: University of Toronto Press, 1999), and Gauvin Alexander Bailey, *Art on the Jesuit Missions in Asia and Latin images au XVIIe siècle America, 1542–1773* (Toronto: University of Toronto Press, 1999).

[24] See Marc Fumaroli, e.g., *L'âge de la éloquence: Rhétorique et "res literaria" au seuil de l'époque classique* (Geneva: Droz, 1980); "Définition et description: Scholastique et rhétorique chez les jésuites des XVIe et XVIIe siècles," *Travaux de Linguistique et de Literature*, 18 (1980): 37–48; "Baroque et classicisme: L'Imago Primi Saeculi Societatis Jesu (1640) et ses adversaires," in his *L'école du silence: Le sentiment des images au XVIIe siècle* (Paris: Flammarion, 1994), 343–65; "The Fertility and Shortcomings of Renaissance Rhetoric: The Jesuit Case," in *The Jesuits*, ed. O'Malley, 90–106. See also, e.g., Debora K. Shuger, *Sacred Rhetoric: The Christian*

Until fifty years ago, the Jesuits in theory stuck adamantly to the Greek and Latin classics as without question "the best literature," which therefore required a privileged and unassailable place in the curriculum, but we know that already in the seventeenth century vernacular literatures were to some degree and in certain places making inroads into the Jesuit schools. The Jesuits at least in France seem to have been slower to make room for such literature than were other educators, including members of other religious orders.[25]

In 1773, the Society of Jesus was by papal edict suppressed throughout the world. I think most scholars would agree that when the Society was restored in the early nineteenth century it at least on the normative level approached the *studia humanitatis*, as well as many other matters treated in the *Ratio*, with a tired and defensive formalism. In 1903, for instance, Robert Schwickerath published an important book on Jesuit education exalting the perennial value of the *Ratio* down to its last detail and attacking modern educational theorists who dared propose such heresy as elective courses. He vigorously advocated the Greek and Latin classics as the indispensable cornerstone of any genuine education. He practically ignored the traditional rationales for them by substituting the vague argument that they were "the best means for training the mind."[26] I recall from my own training as a young Jesuit that that same argument was adduced for our intensive study of the classics, but I could never quite understand just how they were making my brain so much better. In my malevolence I sometimes speculated that they had not done much for the brains of my teachers.

But, besides helping us get better brains, the classics were also supposed to help us young Jesuits achieve "perfect eloquence"— *eloquentia perfecta*. I did not find this claim absurd even for the twentieth century because I knew that Winston Churchill and Franklin Roosevelt, perhaps the last truly great political orators in the English-language world, were products of schools where the clas-

---

Grand Style in the English Renaissance (Princeton: Princeton University Press, 1988).

[25] See Scaglione, *Liberal Arts*, 131–32.

[26] Robert Schwickerath, *Jesuit Education: Its History and Principles Viewed in the Light of Modern Educational Problems* (St. Louis: B. Herder, 1904), 297–331. See also Francis P. Donnelly, *Principles of Jesuit Education in Practice* (New York: Kenedy & Sons, 1934).

sics were central to the curriculum. But I also knew all too many products of Jesuit classical education who were windbags.

In any case, sometime shortly after the middle of this century, the *Ratio* went into semi-official but definitive retirement, and the *studia humanitatis* and all they stood for were in colleges and universities left to fend for themselves.[27] This was not such a dramatic trauma as my words imply, for those *studia* had in actual fact been fending for themselves for a long time, certainly on the college and university level. On that level, classics departments were fast shrinking and being absorbed by other departments, and even English and history departments, the most obvious core of humanistic disciplines, were, though heavily enrolled, just departments among other departments. Philosophy departments, which in the course of time had come to be considered a humanities discipline, went the same way. To the ordinary observer, Jesuit colleges and universities in these regards did not look much different from other colleges and universities.

"The sixties" in the view of some people stand for nothing but drugs, sex, rock and roll, and the decline of the West. For persons involved in Jesuit educational institutions, however, they should stand for the first radical attempt to re-examine the whole system since the sixteenth century. They should stand for intelligent and less defensive attempts to discover and update the most vital and life-giving elements in the tradition, while sloughing off old pieties. The Jesuit high schools, as a result of hard work beginning in that decade, have refashioned themselves in this way so that, within the severe limitations of that very imperfect instrument known as formal schooling, they have with notable success produced informed, articulate, well-read, and socially committed young leaders—"men and women for others," to use the words of our beloved Pedro Arrupe, words which of course sound almost like a paraphrase of Cicero's "we are not born for ourselves alone."

Jesuit colleges and universities have not been so successful, due to a number of factors, not least of which is their almost infinitely greater complexity, as well as the long-standing ambivalences about

---

[27] I believe the last effort to revise and impose it was the edition published in 1941, which dealt only with the program of theological studies for Jesuits themselves: *Ratio Studiorum Superiorum Societatis Iesu, Mandato Congregationis Generalis XXVIII Exarata* (Rome: Curia Praepositi Generalis, 1941).

the humanistic tradition in the university system. However, as early as 1964, a thoughtful and, for the times, persuasive and thorough rethinking of what Jesuit colleges and universities were about appeared in the book *Christian Wisdom and Christian Formation*, edited by Jesuit educators; and many studies along the same line have appeared since then, including Martin Tripole's and Michael Buckley's new books, which take up many of the issues I have been describing.[28] Of special import in recent years has been the serial entitled *Conversations*, which this spring published its fifteenth number.

As with other colleges and universities, the sixties marked a profound shift in every aspect of Jesuit higher education, at least in the United States. The impact of the GI Bill, for instance, had by then drastically affected Jesuit schools as it had others. But there were two important forces that were, in the first instance, peculiar to Catholic schools and, in the second, peculiar to Jesuit schools. They are of great importance.

The first is the impact of the Second Vatican Council, which met between 1962 and 1965. The Council shook Catholicism and with it the Society of Jesus to its foundations. The aspect of the Council to which I want to call attention, however, is something quite specific. It is my conviction that the Council in adopting the rhetorical style of discourse of the Fathers of the Church unwittingly adopted the great themes and issues present in the humanistic tradition from its inception, themes and issues that were baptized by the humanists of the Renaissance—social commitment, human dignity, freedom of conscience, respectful dialogue. Like some other scholars, I have gone so far as to describe Vatican II "an Erasmian council," for it was Erasmus who gave particularly powerful voice to these ideals in the Renaissance.[29]

Second, what the Council helped the Jesuits to do was to discover

---

[2] J. Barry McGannon et al., eds. *Christian Wisdom and Christian Formation: Theology, Philosophy, and the Catholic College Student* (New York: Sheed and Ward, 1964); and Michael J. Buckley, *The Catholic University as Promise and Project: Reflections in a Jesuit Idiom* (Washington: Georgetown University Press, 1998). See also, e.g., Rolando E. Bonachea, *Jesuit Higher Education: Essays on an American Tradition of Excellence* (Pittsburgh: Duquesne University Press, 1989).

[29] See John W. O'Malley, "Erasmus and Vatican II: Interpreting the Council," in *Cristianesimo nella storia: Saggi in onore di Giuseppe Alberigo*, ed. A. Melloni et al. (Bologna: Il Mulino, 1998), 195–211.

and affirm in their own spiritual tradition fundamental themes along the same line that had lain dormant or that had for a long time lacked clear articulation. Fortunately, scholarship on Jesuit sources like the *Spiritual Exercises* and the *Constitutions* was already at the time of the Council producing results consonant with what the Council expounded. I refer to such things as the discovery of the centrality of discernment in the process of the *Exercises* and of spiritual freedom as the goal toward which discernment is geared; and I refer to the vision, in the final exercise in the book, of the world as suffused with grace and charged with the grandeur of God. As to the *Constitutions*, I refer to the basic harmony between nature and grace that runs as a leitmotif through them, a far cry from Augustinian or Jansenist views that the world is corrupt and human nature depraved—and all human actions little more than disguised plays for power.

In sum, what I have been trying to say is that in answering our question about how humanistic the Jesuit tradition in education is, we, while making use of normative documents like the *Ratio*, must move back from them to try to see what the actual practice was. We must move back even from that point to examine the specific context in which that tradition was located, whether in university or secondary school. We must examine as well the national context. And we must move still further back to locate the tradition in the even broader traditions of the Jesuit Order and, of course, in the mood and ethos of Catholicism at any given period of history.

You are all acutely aware of another context that is profoundly affecting our subject today. I refer to postmodernism, postcolonialism, multiculturalism, and the revolution in education being effected by the electronic media, all of which challenge premises upon which the traditional *studia humanitatis* rested. These contemporary realities are pervasively and aggressively present in higher education, affecting every aspect of our enterprise. The cultural wars are no less vicious for being fought on such small turf.[30]

---

[30] See, e.g., Thomas Bender et al., "The Transformation of Humanistic Studies in the Twenty-First Century: Opportunities and Perils," ACLS Occasional Paper, No. 40 (New York: American Council of Learned Societies, 1997); Eugene Goodheart, "Reflections on the Cultural Wars," *Daedalus*, 126 (1997): 153–75; Charles Bernstein, "A Blow Is Like an Instrument," ibid., 177–200. See, more broadly, the recent number of *Daedalus* entitled "Distinctively American: The Residential Liberal Arts College," 128 (1999).

"How humanistic is the Jesuit tradition—from 1599 to the present?" That is the question before us. I think we can answer it by saying the tradition has been deeply and consistently humanistic on two levels. First, on the level of belief in both the practical and the more broadly humanizing potential of the humanities, and second, on the level of concern for the yearnings of the human heart arising from Ignatian spirituality—the two levels that Professor Fumaroli has designated as *rhetorica humana* and *rhetorica divina* in the Jesuit tradition.[31] In an ideal world these two "rhetorics" should have impact on every aspect and every discipline of the educational enterprise.

The Jesuit humanistic tradition has been filled, I believe, with much light but also with many shadows. It has always for better or worse been much affected by larger contexts in which it has found expression, and thus it is not a uniform or easily defined tradition. It was humanistic, but it also had a deep concern for science. It believed passionately that education was about the formation of more fully human persons, but it also recognized the importance of professional training and esteemed it. Despite these problems and complications, I venture that it still provides us with a helpful legacy with which to address the new and radical issues that face the humanities today in Jesuit colleges and universities. The tradition will not make our decisions for us, but it provides, I think, a privileged vantage point from which we can do so.

---

[31] Fumaroli, "Fertility and Shortcomings." See also Mabel Lundberg, *Jesuitische Anthropologie und Erziehungslehre in der Frühzeit des Ordens (ca.1540–ca.1650)* (Uppsala: University of Uppsala, 1966).

7

A New *Ratio* for a New Millennium?

Vincent J. Duminuco, S.J.

AN ANNIVERSARY recaptures a past: Twenty-five years of married life, a university's centennial, a millennium of human experience. It is good to reflect on an anniversary in order to understand our roots and development, the joys and struggles that have brought us to a new plateau. *This* occasion also allows us both to focus on four centuries of a worldwide pedagogical tradition that has been successful in helping to form leaders in civic society, and to express thanks—to God and to the countless men and women who have contributed so many years of service in the tradition of Jesuit education.

But ours is a *living* tradition. This anniversary is not merely a retrospective celebrating past accomplishments, "Laudatur Temporis Acti." A *living tradition* spurs us to look more urgently to the *future*. And this raises the question—Do we need a new *Ratio* for a new millennium? The question of a new *Ratio* has been raised at significant points in the past. The *Ratio* of 1599 rendered immediate and valuable service for its own era by successfully guiding and governing hundreds of Jesuit schools in Europe, Latin America, and Asia for more than a century and a half. Harry Broudy observes with admiration that the history of Jesuit education illustrates "how schooling can be organized and systematized to make materials, methods of instruction, and teachers uniformly effective over broad regions of space and time."[1] Speaking of the *Ratio Studiorum* of 1599, Paul Shore observes: "Its tremendous influence on the development of education can be attributed to both the organization it provided to hundreds of schools that the Jesuits established worldwide, and to

---

[1] Harry Broudy, "Historic Exemplars of Teaching Method", in *Handbook of Research on Teaching*, ed. N. L. Gage (Chicago: Rand McNally, 1963), 22.

the vision of the teacher embedded in the Ratio."[2] Since the present Jesuit education system takes its origins from 1599, the *Ratio* cannot be dismissed as wholly unrelated to our more complex situation today.

THE *RATIO* AFTER THE SUPPRESSION

The *Ratio* of 1599 remained in effect with significant success for 174 years, until the suppression of the Society of Jesus in 1773. But the world changed rapidly in the brief forty-one years before the Jesuit Order was restored. The rise of nation states, development of vernacular languages and distinct cultural traditions, governmental control of curricula and instruction shattered the uniformity of the European educational model, which was the norm throughout the sixteenth, seventeenth, and eighteenth centuries. In the newly restored Society of Jesus, Jesuits learned to their regret that to think of a uniform plan of studies was an illusion.

Fr. Jan Roothan, first Superior General of the restored Society of Jesus, strongly supported drafting a new *Ratio*, which appeared in 1832.[3] When he sent it to the provinces, it was rejected outright. For it was simply impossible to follow an educational plan that would be universally valid in the face of rapidly changing societies and diverse cultures. And so the draft *Ratio* of 1832 was never implemented.

On January 1, 1893, Fr. Luis Martin, then Superior General of the Jesuits, while addressing the students of Exaaten in Holland, pointed out: "[I]t is true that today we are not free as regards to courses; their content is prescribed for us. But we are still free as regards to spirit and method of our teaching." His distinction between curriculum content on the one hand and methodology on the other is significant.[4]

---

[2] Paul Shore, "The Ratio Studiorum At 400," *Conversations* (Spring 1999), 37.

[3] Gabriel Codina, S.J., "Our Way of Proceeding in Education: The Ratio Studiorum", *Educatio S.J.*, Rome, no. 1 (1999), 1.

[4] Father Martin urged that his hearers not confound the Jesuit method of studies with the matter to which that method is applied. For the first he claimed stability, to the second he conceded change. Concerning this matter he employs the Scholastic terminology of "matter" and "form." Answering the objection of those who would maintain that the *Ratio Studiorum* was good in its own day but was at that time (1893) outmoded, he holds that anyone who maintains this position fails to

The 25th General Congregation in 1906 refused to adopt a common *Ratio* for all the schools for the Society, given the variety of secular legislation in effect. They left it to individual provinces to see how to apply what was still useful from the 1599 *Ratio*.[5] That same congregation at the beginning of the twentieth century made the grudging admission that the study of non-classical authors "is not contrary to our Institute."

To insure certification and approval of their education programs, Jesuit schools and universities gradually accommodated their programs to the requirements of states and ministries of education. Thus, several of the Jesuit schools, even when they retained *Ratio* terminology in curricula, like classes in grammar, poetry, rhetoric, and the like, in reality were distancing themselves from the definitive *Ratio* of 1599, while paying lip service to that norm. Perhaps that is why I have met so many Jesuits and other colleagues who refer to "the *Ratio*," but who give conclusive evidence of never having read it.

At the opening of the twentieth century, what still gave unity to Jesuit education was not a common document but a common spirit and worldview—that of Ignatius Loyola—and methodologies consistent with that spirit. It would take almost a century before this fact was fully recognized and formally acted upon.

A New Key

In the early 1960s, Fr. John Donohue observed that "it may be possible to disengage from the documentary sources of the Jesuit educational tradition certain key-categories or master themes, rudimentary

---

understand the *Ratio Studiorum*, and this "because he confines himself to a consideration of its 'matter' instead of taking into consideration the 'form' or 'method,' he claims, which is distinctive of us (*speciale aliquid quod ei maizime proprium est*)—and this 'form' or method we are for the most part still free to retain, even though the 'matter' must be changed because of pressure from the outside." Fr. Martin urged that this distinctive "form" or method should be retained in schools of the Society, and the *Ratio Studiorum* can and should be employed in so far as it presents this distinctive method of the Society. Cf. "Woodstock Letters," vol. 22 (Woodstock, Md.: 1893), 102.

[5] *Acts of the 25th General Congregation of the Society of Jesus* (Rome: The General Curia of the Society of Jesus, 1906).

perhaps or barely implicit, which constitute a portion of Christian educational theory and retain significance for places, persons and times very different from those of 1599."[6] Donohue goes further: "Certain principles of sixteenth-century Jesuit education may be applied to our contemporary school actualities but they will usually require transposition into a new key."[7] For instance, the rhetorical ideal of "Ciceronian grace" has a wider aim that "rests on the conviction that the truly human man must possess both wisdom and eloquence; must know something and be able to say what he knows; must be able to think and to communicate."[8]

Donohue offers another example describing the prelection as "the characteristic tool" for bringing students to an understanding of the materials and aims of the study. "[I]t is clear that the basic pattern and purpose of the prelection can and ought to be adapted to all teaching and to any subject. It is only too easy, unfortunately, to neglect this work of preparing students for individual study since it is always easier to tell them *what* than to teach them *how*."[9]

Donohue lists a number of pedagogical principles derived from the *Ratio*, which, with necessary adaptation, apply to Jesuit teaching everywhere, even today. "Mastery is to be sought, and this means student activity—exercise and more exercise." Sequence of studies, an orderly progression throughout studies according to the capacities of students, is essential. This is closely tied to individual care and concern for each student. Organization and supervision were essential and still are. Realistically some form of emulation was encouraged to capitalize on young people's desire for glory and fear of dishonor. Donohue wryly observes, "Of course, the *Ratio* proposed to baptize this pursuit of glory. Rule 31 for teachers of the lower classes confidently assumes the possibility of such a transformation when it speaks of *honesta aemulatio, quae magnum ad studia incitamentum est*—'honorable rivalry which is a powerful incentive to studies.'"[10]

---

[6] John W. Donohue, S.J., *Jesuit Education: An Essay on the Foundations of Its Idea* (New York: Fordham University Press, 1963), 69.

[7] Ibid., 121

[8] Ibid., 70

[9] Ibid., 150–51

[10] John W. Donohue, S.J., "A School Plan's 400th Birthday," *America*, 180 (May 22, 1999), 25.

ENDS AND MEANS

The early Jesuits were engaged in the actual labor of the classroom and so were looking for specific and useful pedagogical guidance. But they assumed a common view of the ideal human person, which set criteria for their methods. The records of the meetings of the Committee of Six that prepared the first draft of the *Ratio Studiorium* in 1586 state that "the spirit of Ignatius presided over the deliberations." They often consulted Ignatius's guidelines set forth in the book of the *Spiritual Exercises*, which was the record of Ignatius's only concrete teaching; in the *Constitutions* of the Society of Jesus; and in his letters. Throughout these writings we find a stress upon *means* as well as ends in education.

His own painful educational experience had proven to Ignatius that enthusiasm was not enough for success in study. *How* a student was directed, the method for teaching employed, was crucial. When he set out in the *Spiritual Exercises* to teach others to consider fundamental questions of the human condition, he took exquisite care to provide detailed methods that Charmot has well described as radically pedagogical.[11] Thus, a worldview *and the need for concrete means* to implement it were important legacies of Ignatius to Jesuit education.

The success of the Jesuits' efficient and carefully organized educational code, embodied eventually in the *Ratio* of 1599, can best be explained by acknowledging that they did not merely resurrect and restore the *modus Parisiensis* or principles of Quintillian, but they impregnated them with their own distinctive spirit, purpose, and worldview, subjected them to prolonged tests in many different countries, and then shared their results after practical experience. But in the formulation of the 1599 *Ratio*, the origins of that spirit were not expressed. They were assumed in the desire to respond to specific questions of schoolmasters who wanted very practical guidance in curriculum, methods, organizational structure of schools, and standards of conducts to be expected.

But today, given the impact of developments in human psychology, of mass media and their penetrating effect upon young people, of the repeated dashing of ideals seen even among the most promi-

---

[11] G. Charmot, *La Pedagogie des Jesuites*, (Paris: Editions Spes, 1943).

nent figures of the twentieth century, of a growing awareness of social justice and its demands upon us all, are the methods of
yesteryear truly the most effective to bring to reality a living example
of men and women after the mind of Ignatius? I believe that the
Ignatian pedagogical principles of order, sequence, individualization,
and personalization of instruction *(alumnorum cura personalis)*; the
necessity of clear goals and objectives; the paramount importance of
self-activity on the part of the student; concern for the affective domain in learning—all of these are essential in creating an educational
community of faith and trust in which an alternative can be lived to
the cynicism and duplicity, the materialism and fatalism of many in
the world around us.

The question remains now whether or not these principles are
effective in the attitudes and practices of our administrators and
faculty members. If they are not, our students may well perceive us
as talking a good game by enunciating Ignatian ideals but failing to
practice them. On the other hand, we have seen that much research
and writing in the field of curriculum within the last twenty-five
years has dealt exclusively with questions of method influenced
heavily by educational psychologists. And yet there is disillusionment here as well, for they seem to have generated a naïve faith on
the part of many in method and technology without substantive vision unifying and impelling the whole educational process. In brief,
vision without appropriate method may be perceived as sterile platitude. Method without unifying vision is frequently little more than
gadgetry. I believe a synthesis of both is essential if our schools are
to effectively bear the name "Jesuit" at any point in time.

A NEW *RATIO*?

It would seem that the core of the *Ratio* "in a new key," a *Ratio* for
the new millennium, has been developed over the last two decades.
This did *not* happen as a deliberate effort to revise the document of
1599. It happened rather as the product of a series of responses to
the urgent need expressed by Jesuit educators, lay and religious, from
all continents as they faced the challenges of a rapidly changing
world where values and assumptions were turned upside down in
the midst of a dramatic, worldwide paradigm shift—social, religious,

cultural, political, and economic. Jesuit educators, in daily touch with young people, experienced first hand the challenges and the opportunities of such times of change. In the turbulent context of the 1960s and 1970s, the need for an integrated worldview and mode of proceeding in Jesuit education became a central concern.

A CONTEMPORARY IDENTITY STATEMENT

It was at a meeting of Jesuit secondary school educators in Rome, called by Father General Pedro Arrupe in 1980, that a strong need was expressed for a contemporary identity document for Jesuit education. In light of significant shifts that impacted Jesuit schools, colleges, and universities, Jesuit educators felt that the *Ratio* of 1599 no longer spoke adequately to the need to clarify what Jesuit education is and aims to do in such a challenging new context. Now they were experiencing the shift from a coherent cultural and religious context to a pluralism of views and values, from a respect for rational discourse to postmodern distance from reason and the glorification of the individual and affective experience, from contentment with a social structure that acknowledged and often accepted social class and correlative privileges and deprivations to a demand for social justice for all, from a faculty and staff that was overwhelmingly Jesuit in composition to one characterized by ever-increasing percentages of lay men and women on staff.[12]

In response, Fr. Arrupe established the International Commission on the Apostolate of Jesuit Education.[13] Its first task was to produce the contemporary identity statement so strongly called for by Jesuit secondary education. That Commission, with one representative from each continent, worked for over four years through six drafts in moving toward its goal. Copies of drafts four and five were sent to educators in every province of the Society of Jesus around the world

---

[12] The concluding address of this meeting has been published in "Documentation S. J.," July 1980. See Pedro Arrupe, S.J., "Our Secondary Schools Today and Tomorrow," in *Acta Romana Societatis Iesu*, vol. 18 (Rome: Gregorian University Press, 1981); English text, 257–76.

[13] This Commission was established as advisory to the Secretary of Education of the Society of Jesus. The Commission was deliberately small (one member from each continent) so that it could be an effective working group.

for their reactions, criticisms, and suggestions. Harmonizing the responses received was at times especially challenging, for the Commission wished to respect regional differences where possible when preparing a universal document.

Upon completion of the Commission's work in 1986, our current Superior General, Fr. Peter Hans Kolvenbach, made this document his own, sending *The Characteristics of Jesuit Education* to all Jesuit Provincials.[14] He called for a wide distribution of this document (it has been translated into 13 different languages) to be made available to all teachers, administrators, and members of governing boards of Jesuit educational institutions, as well as to students, parents, and alumni/ae. Fr. Kolvenbach specified the nature of this document. He wrote in his letter accompanying the document sent to all Jesuit major superiors around the world:

> A document listing the characteristics of Jesuit education is not a new Ratio Studiorum. However, like the Ratio produced at the end of the 16th century and as a continuation of the tradition begun then, it can give us a common vision and a common sense of purpose; it can be a standard against which we measure ourselves.
>
> The *Characteristics* can be the basis for renewed reflection on the experience of the educational apostolate and, in light of that reflection, for evaluation of school policies and practices: not only negatively ("What are we doing wrong?"), but especially positively ("How can we do better?"). This must take account of "continually changing" local circumstances: Individual countries or regions should reflect on the meaning and implications of the characteristics for their own local situations, and should develop supplementary documents that apply this present universal document to their own concrete and specific needs.[15]

Fr. Kolvenbach wrote also of a more universal application of this document.

> The Commission, established in 1980 to help further renewal in Jesuit secondary education, has naturally made secondary education the direct focus of their work. But much of this document is applicable to all areas of Jesuit education, while the principles can be applied to all

---

[14] *The Characteristics of Jesuit Education* (Rome: Jesuit Curia, 1986), 64. (Appendix A of this book reproduces the entire text of *The Characteristics* document.)

[15] Peter Hans Kolvenbach, S.J., "A Letter to All Jesuit Major Superiors," Rome, December 8, 1986.

Jesuit apostolates. Those working in other Jesuit educational institutions, especially in universities and university colleges, should make the adaptations that are needed, or develop from this present document a new one, which will fit their situation more appropriately. Those in other Jesuit apostolates, whether in parishes or retreat work or the social apostolate, can use the document as a basis for their own apostolic discernment.[16]

Reactions to *The Characteristics* document were overwhelmingly positive. And in some parts of the world, where the need was felt strongly for inculturation, that is, India and Latin America, specific adaptations of *The Characteristics* were developed with good results.[17]

REQUESTS FOR PRACTICAL PEDAGOGICAL METHODS

But some three years after its publication, new requests began to be heard from many parts of the world. People reported genuine satisfaction with *The Characteristics*. They were proving to be truly helpful in clarifying the nature and mission of Jesuit schools in the final decade of the twentieth century. For this, teachers, administrators, boards were grateful. But they asked, "In order to realize the goals, to make the principles take life, how can we make the characteristics real in the daily interaction between teacher and student, so that we can move from theory into practice, from rhetoric into reality?"[18] The question showed that teachers and others were taking *The Characteristics* seriously. But the difficulty of moving to specific pedagogical methods on a universal level that would be coherent with *The Characteristics of Jesuit Education* was a daunting challenge.

Once again the International Commission on the Apostolate of Jesuit Education focused its efforts to reply to this need. And it did so not by proposing a monolithic plan of studies for all, but by expli-

---

[16] Ibid.

[17] See a number of publications issued by the Jesuit Education Association of India, 1987 to 1993, under the title *Magis*. See also *Desafios De America Latina y Proprestas Educativas* (Bogota, Columbia: Asociacion De Universidades Confiadas A La Compania De Jesus En America Latina, 1995), 55.

[18] Archivum Historicum Societatis Jesu, Rome, Italy. Unpublished correspondence with the Secretariat of Jesuit Education, 1989–91.

cating for our times the fundamental Ignatian worldview *and* a methodology that was coherent with this view. This Ignatian inspiration doubtless was latent in the *Ratio* of 1599. "But," Codina observes, "perhaps never as much as today has it become clear that the raison d'être of education in the Society is rooted in the vision of Ignatius and in the mission of the Society of Jesus, in the framework of a four-century-old spiritual and pedagogical inheritance."[19] We are reminded of John Donohue's insistence: "The real Ignatian flavor is found in that insistence on keeping simultaneously and steadily in sight the most exalted ends with the most exact and concrete means for achieving them."[20]

IGNATIAN PEDAGOGY: A PRACTICAL APPROACH

In 1993, after some four years of research, study, and consultation, the International Commission's response to those repeated requests for a practical pedagogy was the publication of *Ignatian Pedagogy: A Practical Approach*. From the outset this document insists upon the need for coherence between vision and method in any worthwhile pedagogy:

> Pedagogy is the way in which teachers accompany learners in their growth and development. Pedagogy, the art and science of teaching, cannot simply be reduced to methodology. It must include a worldview and a vision of the ideal human person to be educated. These provide the goal, the end towards which all aspects of educational tradition are directed. They also provide criteria for choices of means to be used in the process of education. The worldview and ideal of Jesuit education for our time has been expressed in *The Characteristics of Jesuit Education*. Ignatian Pedagogy assumes that worldview and moves one step beyond suggesting more explicit ways in which Ignatian values can be incarnated in the teaching-learning process.[21]

What is the goal? *The Characteristics of Jesuit Education* offers a description, which has been amplified by Father General Kolvenbach:

---

[19] Codina, "Our Way of Proceeding in Education," 16.

[20] Donohue, *Jesuit Education*, 16.

[21] *Ignatian Pedagogy: A Practical Approach* (Rome: Jesuit Curia, 1993), 6. (Appendix B reproduces the entire text of the *Ignatian Pedagogy* document.)

The pursuit of each student's intellectual development to the full measure of God-given talents rightly remains a prominent goal of Jesuit education. Its aim, however, has never been simply to amass a store of information or preparation for a profession, though these are important in themselves and useful to emerging Christian leaders. The ultimate aim of Jesuit education is, rather, that full growth of the person which leads to action—action, especially, that is suffused with the spirit and presence of Jesus Christ, the son of God, the Man-for-Others. This goal of action, based on sound understanding and enlivened by contemplation, urges students to self-discipline and initiative, to integrity and accuracy. At the same time, it judges slip-shod or superficial ways of thinking unworthy of the individual and, more important, dangerous to the world he or she is called to serve.[22]

Fr. Arrupe summarized this by pointing to our educational goal as "forming men and women for others."[23] Fr. Kolvenbach has described the graduate of a Jesuit school who is hoped for: a person "well-rounded, intellectually competent, open to growth, religious, loving, and committed to doing justice in generous service to the people of God."[24] Fr. Kolvenbach also states our goal when he says that we aim to form leaders in service, "men and women of competence, conscience and compassionate commitment."[25]

Such a goal requires a full and deeper formation of the human person, an educational process of formation that calls for excellence—a striving to excel, to achieve one's potential. This goal encompasses the intellectual, the academic, and more. It calls for a *human* excellence, an excellence that reflects the mystery and reality of the Incarnation, an excellence that reveres the dignity of all people as well as the holiness of all creation. There are sufficient examples from history of educational excellence narrowly conceived, of people extraordinarily advanced intellectually who, at the same time, remain emotionally underdeveloped and morally immature. Fortunately, in our time we are beginning to realize that education does

---

[22] Ibid., 6.

[23] Pedro Arrupe, S.J., *Men For Others* (Washington, D.C.: J.S.E.A, 1974).

[24] Address of Father General Peter Hans Kolvenbach, S.J., at St. Paul's High School, Winnepeg, Canada, May 14, 1986; published in the Newsletter of the Upper Canadian Jesuit Province, June 1986, 7-8.

[25] Address of Father General Peter Hans Kolvenbach, S.J., at the International Workshop on "Ignatian Pedagogy: A Practical Approach," Villa Cavalletti, Frascati, April 29, 1993.

not inevitably humanize people and society. We are losing faith in the naïve notion that all education, regardless of its quality or thrust or purpose, will lead to virtue. Increasingly, then, it becomes clear that we must insist that the process of education take place in a moral as well as an intellectual framework. This is not to suggest a program of indoctrination that suffocates the spirit; neither does it look for the introduction of theoretical courses that are speculative and remote from reality. *What is needed is a framework of inquiry that encourages the process of wrestling with significant issues and complex values of life, and professors capable and willing to guide that inquiry.*

Let me mention but a few Ignatian themes that enlighten and give impetus to our work in education; let us put up front some of the Jesuit values we stand for.

> The Ignatian worldview is world-affirming, comprehensive, places emphasis on freedom, faces up to sin, personal and social, but points to God's love as more powerful than human weakness and evil; it is altruistic, stresses the essential need for discernment, and gives ample scope to intellect and affectivity in forming leaders. Are not these and other Ignatian themes also essential to the values a Jesuit school, college or university endorses? In doing so Jesuit education challenges much that contemporary society presents as values.[26]

If these are prominent goals of Jesuit education, can we specify further the means, the methodologies, to attain these goals? For how a student is directed, the method of teaching employed, can be crucial. When we page through the *Ratio*, our first impression is that of a massive welter of regulations: for time schedules, for careful graduation of classes, for the selection of authors to be read, for the diverse methods to be employed at various times of the morning and afternoon, for correction of papers and the assignment of written work, for the precise degree of skill the students of each class will be expected to possess before moving upward. But all these particulars were designed to create a firm and reassuring framework of order and clarity within which both teacher and student could securely pursue their objectives.

---

[26] Address of Father General Peter Hans Kolvenbach, S.J., at the U.S. Jesuit Higher Education Assembly, Georgetown University, June 7, 1989; published in "Documentation S. J.," no. 64 (August 1989), 2.

Ignatius saw the importance of methodology in learning as well as in prayer. His notes to a person who would direct another in the *Spiritual Exercises* (the Annotations) are profoundly pedagogical. In their attempt to move from *The Characteristics* to practical Ignatian pedagogy, the International Commission highlighted the pedagogical paradigm that emerges from Ignatian spirituality. (See diagram next page.)

The central element in this paradigm focuses Jesuit education upon the human *meaning* imbedded in what one studies.

> At this level of *Reflection*, the memory, the understanding, the imagination and the feelings are used to capture the *meaning and the essential value* of what is being studied, to *discover its relationship* with other aspects of knowledge and human activity, and to *appreciate* its implications in the ongoing search for truth and freedom.
>
> *We use the term reflection to mean a thoughtful reconsideration of some subject matter, experience, idea, purpose, or spontaneous reaction, in order to grasp its significance more fully. Thus, reflection is the process by which meaning surfaces in human experience:*
>
> - by understanding the truth being studied more clearly.
> - by understanding the sources of the sensations or reactions I experience in this consideration.
> - by deepening my understanding of the implications of what I have grasped for myself and for others.
> - by achieving personal insights into events, ideas, truth, or the distortion of truth.
> - by coming to some understanding of . . . what moves me, and why . . . and who I might be in relation to others.[27]

Through reflection upon what he or she is studying, a student is challenged to discover its significance, its implications, likely effects upon his or her own life and those of others, and possible choices to be made. This moves learning beyond the realm of an objective grasp of facts, principles, and skills to the level of personal meaning. Such a focus motivates student learning and is more likely to lead to action based upon conviction.

Over the last forty years, much research has been done on innovations, changes in education. Results are clearly replicated time and

---

[27] *Ignatian Pedagogy: A Practical Approach* (Rome: Jesuit Curia, 1993), 19–20.

400 Years of Best Practice
The Jesuit Tradition of Ignatian Pedagogy

The Challenge

Ignatian education strives to go beyond academic excellence. It is a collaborative process between and among teachers and students which fosters personal and cooperative study, discovery and creativity, and reflection to promote life-long learning and action in service to others. Its ultimate goal is to develop men and women of competence, conscience and compassion.

The Process

Ignatian pedagogy is a way in which teachers accompany learners; it is a process that includes context, experience, reflection, action and evaluation. It is a continuous and repeated cycle of learning and growth.

Context—

Teachers consider the context of students' lives: family, society, politics, economics, culture, religion and other realities which affect the learning process.

Experience—

Teachers foster a broad base of experience which requires application, analysis, synthesis and evaluation so that learners are attentive to the human reality that confronts them.

Reflection—

Teachers formulate questions and guide discussion, journal-keeping, reaction/reflection papers and other activities helping students reconsider subject matter so that they discover meaning in their experiences and learning.

Action—

Through experience that has been reflected upon, students make the truth their own and serve others. They become impelled to act upon their convictions for the welfare of society.

Evaluation—

Teachers evaluate the whole person using effective methods such as assessment, peer tutoring, mentoring, journal reflections and critical skill application. Teachers congratulate and encourage students for their progress.

[from International Commission on the Apostolate of Jesuit Education, Ignatian Pedagogy: A Practical Approach, 1993.

again. Research finds that teachers will agree with something that makes sense, but they will *do* that with which they are comfortable. Because the Society of Jesus wants Ignatian pedagogy to be effective, it insists that it must involve a three- to four-year staff development program, during which teachers are given the opportunity to master a variety of methods that are appropriate for each step in the Ignatian Pedagogical Paradigm.[28] Ignatian pedagogy urges that teachers be given opportunities to practice and master these methods in a relatively non-threatening setting, for example, microteaching with immediate TV feedback.

IS THIS A NEW *RATIO?*

I believe that Father General Kolvenbach was correct in 1986 when he wrote in promulgating *The Characteristics of Jesuit Education*, the identity document, to the whole Society of Jesus that it was not a new *Ratio Studiorum*. It was not, because while clarifying the purposes and mission of Jesuit education it lacked the practical guidelines and norms that could incarnate what was intended in the teaching-learning process. But with the questions from the schools pressing for more specific guidelines in moving from theory into practice (not unlike many of the reactions of Jesuit schoolmen to the draft *Ratio* of 1586), the development of *Ignatian Pedagogy: A Practical Approach* completes the requirements in providing a worldview *and* method that now are enabling a much more effective renewal in Jesuit education worldwide.

What we have today is a contemporary identifying set of educational principles and a way of proceeding in accord with those principles—vision and methods that spring from the fundamental Ignatian worldview and the *Spiritual Exercises* of Ignatius. The enthusiasm with which these instruments are being used in many countries in Jesuit educational institutions at the level of Jesuit secondary education, and only beginning at the level of Jesuit higher education, witnesses to the fact that they strike a note of realism that is profound and that provides ways to involve students in their growth at a much fuller and deeper human level.[29]

---

[28] Ibid., 29.

[29] Some prior propaedeutic steps are probably essential to bring faculty members to a point of readiness to move ahead toward a new *Ratio* for today and tomorrow.

Is this a new *Ratio* for a new millennium? Certainly in form and much of its context it differs from that of 1599. It does not prescribe a fixed series of subjects in curriculum; rather, it urges the use of the Ignatian paradigm by way of infusion in all curricula wherever possible. It is not a set of norms and rules—the format is descriptive and discursive, not legalistic. It focuses upon the contemporary context, not a timeless panorama. It calls for staff development programs for ongoing growth of professors as well as development of the God-given talents of each of our students. Because it focuses on the universal level of principle and paradigm, yet insists upon inculturation by choice among specific means suggested, this new Jesuit approach receives an enthusiastic welcome in India and Indianapolis, in Bogota and Brussels, in Kinshasa and Katmandu. Its usefulness is attested in progress to train teachers and professors across vastly diverse cultures.

Like the *Ratio Studiorum* of 1599, *The Characteristics of Jesuit Education* and *Ignatian Pedagogy* have gone thorough numerous drafts, taking advantage of worldwide consultations. But over time only experience will reveal a possible lack of clarity, an omission, or a misplaced emphasis. Therefore, I view *The Characteristics of Jesuit Education* and *Ignatian Pedagogy*, taken together as a comprehensive document, as Father General Claudio Aquaviva presented the first draft of the Ratio: "not as definitive or final, for that would be very difficult and perhaps impossible; rather as an instrument which will help us encounter, because it gives the whole society one single perspective, a goal and a way to achieve it."[30] Is this a new *Ratio* for a new millennium? I think so.

Here the suggestion of Fr. Howard Gray at the opening of this seminar is important. He observes that faculty research scholars and staff are dedicated "to help people" in dedicated teaching, mentoring of excellence, care for their students. "It is here where I find the Ignatian strategy of attention, reverence, and devotion capable of bridging gaps and translating competing values into generous, shared concerns about creating a new kind of academic community in which we can speak to one another in order to learn from one another." See Howard Gray, S.J., "The Experience of Ignatius Loyola: Background to Jesuit Education," chapter 1 of this book.

[30] Cited in Father General Kolvenbach's letter To All Major Superiors, introducing *The Characteristics of Jesuit Education*, December 3, 1986. Also available in *Ratio atque Instituto Studiorum Societatis Iesu (1586, 1591, 1599). Monumenta Paedagogica Societatis Iesu*, V. Ed. Ladislaus Lukacs, S.J. (Rome: Institutum Historicum Societatis Iesu, 1986).

Appendix A

The Characteristics of Jesuit Education, 1986

Reproduced with permission from The General Curia of the Society of Jesus, Borgo Santo Spiritu, 5, 00193 Rome, Italy, December 3, 1986.

CONTENTS

7. Jesuit Education emphasizes activity on the part of the
   student in the learning process.   182
       personal study
       opportunities for personal discovery
       reflection

8. Jesuit Education encourages life-long openness
   to growth.   182
       joy in learning; desire to learn
       adult members open to change

9. Jesuit Education is value-oriented.   183
       knowledge joined to virtue
       school regulations; system of discipline
       self-discipline

10. Jesuit Education encourages a realistic knowledge, love,
    and acceptance of self.   184
        Christian humanism; sin and its effects
        obstacles to growth
        development of a critical faculty

11. Jesuit Education provides a realistic knowledge of the
    world in which we live.   185
        awareness of the social effects of sin
        realization that persons and structures can change

12. Jesuit Education proposes Christ as the model of
    human life.   186
        inspiration from the life and teaching of Christ
        for Christians, personal friendship with Jesus

13. Jesuit Education provides adequate pastoral care.   187
        religious faith and religious commitment
        the *Spiritual Exercises*
        response to a personal call from God

14. Jesuit Education celebrates faith in personal and
    community prayer, worship and service.   188
        progressive initiation to personal prayer
        community worship
        for Catholics, Eucharist and the Sacrament of
            Reconciliation
        faith leads to commitment to follow Christ

concrete experiences of church life
promote Christian Life Communities

21. Jesuit education pursues excellence in its work of
   formation.   198
   "human excellence"
   excellence depends on the needs of the region
   fullest possible development of individual capacities
   leaders in service
   excellence in faith commitment: to do "more"
   competition

22. Jesuit education witnesses to excellence.   200
   excellence in school climate
   adult members witness to excellence
   cooperation with other schools and educational agencies

23. Jesuit Education stresses lay-Jesuit collaboration.   201
   a common mission
   willingness to assume responsibilities
   the Jesuit attitude

24. Jesuit Education relies on a spirit of community among: 202
   teaching staff and administrators
   people chosen to join the educational community;
      common sense of purpose
   the Jesuit community life witness; life within the
      community; provide knowledge and appreciation of
      Ignatius; hospitality; priestly activities; relations with
      school director
   governing boards
   parents
   close cooperation with parents; understanding the school
      character; consistency between values promoted in the
      school and those promoted in the home
   students
   former students
   benefactors

25. Jesuit Education takes place within a structure that
   promotes community.   206
   shared responsibility
   mission of the Director

INTRODUCTION

(1)   In September of 1980 a small international group, Jesuit and lay, came together in Rome to discuss several important issues concerning Jesuit secondary education. In many parts of the world, serious questions had been raised about the present effectiveness of Jesuit schools: Could they be instrumental in accomplishing the apostolic purposes of the Society of Jesus? Were they able to respond to the needs of the men and women in today's world? The meeting was called to examine these questions and to suggest the kinds of renewal that would enable Jesuit secondary education to continue to contribute to the creative and healing mission of the church, today and in the future.

(2)   During the days of discussion, it became evident that a renewed effectiveness depended in part on a clearer and more explicit understanding of the *distinctive nature* of Jesuit education. Without intending to minimize the problems, the group asserted that Jesuit schools can face a challenging future with confidence *if they will be true to their particularly Jesuit heritage*. The vision of Ignatius of Loyola, founder of the Society of Jesus, had sustained these schools for four centuries. If this spiritual vision could be sharpened and activated, and then applied to education in ways adapted to the present day, it would provide the context within which other problems could be faced.

(3)   Father Pedro Arrupe, who was then Superior General of the Society of Jesus, reaffirmed this conclusion when he spoke at the closing session of the meeting. He said that a Jesuit school

> should be easily identifiable as such. There are many ways in which it will resemble other schools. . . . But if it is an authentic Jesuit school—that is to say if our operation of the school

flows out of the strengths drawn from our own specific charism, if we *emphasize our essential characteristics and our basic options*—then the education which our students receive should give them a certain "Ignacianidad," if I can use such a term. I am not talking about arrogance or snobbery, still less about a superiority complex. I simply refer to the logical consequence of the fact that *we live and operate out of our own charism.* Our responsibility is to provide, through our schools, what we believe God and the church ask of us.[1]

(4)   The delegates at the Rome meeting recommended the establishment of a permanent international group to consider questions related to secondary education, and urged that one of the first responsibilities of this group be to clarify the ways in which the vision of Ignatius continues to make Jesuit secondary education distinctive today.

(5)   In response to the recommendation, the International Commission on the Apostolate of Jesuit Education (ICAJE) was established; it held its first meeting in 1982. The members are Daven Day, S.J. (Australia), Vincent Duminuco, S.J. (U.S.A.), Luiz Fernando Klein, S.J. (Brazil, since 1983), Raimondo Kroth, S.J. (Brazil, until 1983), Guillermo Marshall, S.J. (Chile, until 1984), Jean-Claude Michel, S.J. (Zaïre), Gregory Naik, S.J. (India), Vicente Parra, S.J. (Spain), Pablo Sada, S.J. (Venezuela), Alberto Vasquez (Chile, since 1984), Gerard Zaat, S.J. (The Netherlands), and James Sauvé, S.J. (Rome).

(6)   This present document, composed by ICAJE, is the fruit of four years of meetings and worldwide consultations.

(7)   Any attempt to speak about Jesuit education today must take account of the profound changes which have influenced and affected this education—since the time of Ignatius, but especially during the present century. Government regulations or the influence of other outside agencies affect various

---

[1] Pedro Arrupe, S.J., "Our Secondary Schools, Today and Tomorrow" [hereinafter OSS], § 10. Given in Rome, September 13, 1980; published in *Acta Romana Societatis Iesu*, vol. 28 (Rome: Gregorian University Press, 1981). English text, 257–76 (emphasis added).

aspects of school life, including the course of study and the textbooks that are used; in some countries the policies of the government or high costs threaten the very existence of private education. Students and their parents seem, in many cases, to be concerned only with the academic success that will gain entrance to university studies, or only with those programs that will help to gain employment. Jesuit schools today are often coeducational, and women have joined lay-men and Jesuits as teachers and administrators. There has been a significant increase in the size of the student body in most Jesuit schools, and at the same time a decline in the number of Jesuits working in those schools. In addition:

a. The course of studies has been altered by modern advances in science and technology: the addition of scientific courses has resulted in less emphasis on, in some cases a certain neglect of, the humanistic studies traditionally emphasized in Jesuit education.

b. Developmental psychology and the social sciences, along with advances in pedagogical theory and education itself, have shed new light on the way young people learn and mature as individuals within a community; this has influenced course content, teaching techniques, and school policies.

c. In recent years, a developed theology has explicitly recognized and encouraged the apostolic role of lay people in the church; this was ratified by the Second Vatican Council, especially in its decree *"On the Apostolate of the Laity."*[2] Echoing this theology, recent General Congregations of the Society of Jesus have insisted on lay-Jesuit collaboration, through a shared sense of purpose and a genuine sharing of responsibility, in schools once exclusively controlled and staffed by Jesuits.

d. The Society of Jesus is committed to "the service of faith, of which the promotion of justice is an absolute require-

---

[2] The official document is in Latin: *Apostolicam Actuositatem*; an English translation can be found in *The Documents of Vatican II*, ed. Walter Abbott S.J. (New York: The America Press, 1966), 489–521.

ment"[3]; it has called for a "reassessment of our traditional apostolic methods, attitudes and institutions with a view to adapting them to the needs of the times, to a world in process of rapid change."[4] In response to this commitment, the purposes and possibilities of education are being examined, with renewed concern for the poor and disadvantaged. The goal of Jesuit education today is described in terms of the formation of "multiplying agents" and "men and women for others."[5]

e. Students and teachers in Jesuit schools today come from a variety of distinct social groups, cultures and religions; some are without religious faith. Many Jesuit schools have been deeply affected by the rich but challenging complexity of their educational communities.

(8)   These and many other developments have affected concrete details of school life and have altered fundamental school policies. But they do not alter the conviction that *a distinctive spirit still marks any school which can truly be called Jesuit. This distinctive spirit can be discovered through reflection on the lived experience of Ignatius, on the ways in which that lived experience was shared with others, on the ways in which Ignatius himself applied his vision to education in the Constitutions and in letters, and on the ways in which this vision has been developed and been applied to education in the course of history, including our present times.* A common spirit lies behind pedagogy, curriculum and school life, even though these may differ greatly from those of previous centuries, and the more concrete details of school life may differ greatly from country to country.

---

[3] The 32nd General Congregation of the Society of Jesus, Decree 4, "Our Mission Today: The Service of Faith and the Promotion of Justice," no. 2. Published in English in *Documents of the 31st and 32nd General Congregations of the Society of Jesus* (St. Louis: Institute of Jesuit Sources, 1977).

[4] Ibid., no. 9.

[5] The two phrases were repeatedly used by Fr. Pedro Arrupe in his writings and talks. The first use seems to have been in an address to the Tenth International Congress of Jesuit Alumni of Europe held in Valencia, Spain on July 31, 1973; this address has been published by several different offices under the title "Men for Others," e.g., by the International Center for Jesuit Education, Rome, Italy.

(9) "Distinctive" is not intended to suggest "unique" either in spirit or in method. The purpose is rather to describe "our way of proceeding"[6]: the inspiration, values, attitudes and style which have traditionally characterized Jesuit education, which must be characteristic of any truly Jesuit school today wherever it is to be found, and which will remain essential as we move into the future.

(10) To speak of an inspiration that has come into Jesuit schools through the Society of Jesus is in no sense an exclusion of those who are not members of this Society. Though the *school* is normally called "Jesuit," the *vision* is more properly called "Ignatian" and has never been limited to Jesuits. Ignatius was himself a layman when he experienced the call of God which he later described in the *Spiritual Exercises*, and he directed many other lay people through the same experience; throughout the last four centuries, countless lay people and members of other religious congregations have shared in and been influenced by his inspiration. Moreover, lay people have their own contribution to make, based on their experience of God in family and in society, and on their distinctive role in the church or in their religious culture. This contribution will enrich the spirit and enhance the effectiveness of the Jesuit school.

(11) The description that follows is for Jesuits, lay people and other Religious working in Jesuit schools; it is for *teachers, administrators, parents* and *governing boards* in these schools. All are invited to join together in making the Ignatian tradition, adapted to the present day, more effectively present in the policies and practices that determine the life of the school.

---

[6] The expression is found in the *Constitutions of the Society of Jesus* and in other writings of Ignatius. Fr. Pedro Arrupe used the phrase as the theme for one of his last talks: "Our Way of Proceeding," given on January 18, 1979, during the "Ignatian Course" organized by the Center for Ignatian Spirituality (CIS); published as "Documentation No. 42" by the Information Office of the Society of Jesus, Rome.

THE CHARACTERISTICS OF
JESUIT EDUCATION

(12)   Though many of the characteristics on the following pages describe all Jesuit education, the specific focus is the basic education of the Jesuit high school, or colegio or collège. (Depending on the country, this may be only secondary education, or it may include both primary and secondary levels.) Those in other Jesuit institutions, especially universities and university colleges, are urged to adapt these characteristics to their own situations.

(13)   A short historical summary of the life of Ignatius and the growth of Jesuit education appears in Appendix I. Reading this summary will give those less familiar with Ignatius and early Jesuit history a better understanding of the spiritual vision on which the characteristics of Jesuit education are based.

(14)   In order to highlight the relationship between the *characteristics of Jesuit education* and the *spiritual vision of Ignatius* the twenty-eight basic characteristics listed on the following pages are divided into nine sections. Each section begins with a statement from the Ignatian vision, and is followed by those characteristics that are applications of the statement to education; the individual characteristics are then described in more detail. A tenth section suggests, by way of example, some characteristics of Jesuit pedagogy.

(15)   *The introductory statements come directly from the world vision of Ignatius. The characteristics of Jesuit education come from reflection on that vision, applying it to education in the light of the needs of men and women today.*

(16)   Some characteristics apply to specific groups: students, former students, teachers or parents. Others apply to the educational community as a whole; still others, concerning the policies and practices of the institution as such, apply primarily to the school administrators or the governing board.

(17)   These pages do not speak about the very real difficulties in the lives of all those involved in education: the resistance of students and their discipline problems, the struggle to meet a host of conflicting demands from school officials, students, parents and others, the lack of time for reflection, the discouragement and disillusions that seem to be inherent in the work of education. Nor do they speak of the difficulties of modern life in general. This is not to ignore or minimize these problems. On the contrary, it would not be possible to speak of Jesuit education at all if it were not for the dedication of all those people, Jesuit and lay, who continue to give themselves to education in spite of frustration and failure. This document will not try to offer facile solutions to intractable problems, but it will try to provide a vision or an inspiration that can make the day-to-day struggle have greater meaning and bear greater fruit.

(18)   The description of Jesuit Education lies in *the document as a whole*. A partial reading can give a distorted image that seems to ignore essential traits. A commitment to the faith that does justice, to take one example, must permeate the whole of Jesuit education—even though it is not described in this document until section five.

(19)   Because they apply to Jesuit secondary schools throughout the world, the characteristics of Jesuit education are described in a form that is somewhat general and schematic. They need amplification and concrete application to local situations. This document, therefore, is a resource for reflection and study rather than a finished work.

(20)   Not all of the characteristics of Jesuit education will be present in the same measure in each individual school; in some situations a statement may represent an ideal rather

than a present reality. "Circumstances of times, places, persons and other such factors"[7] must be taken into account: the same basic spirit will be made concrete in different ways in different situations. To avoid making distinctions which depend on local circumstances and to avoid a constant repetition of the idealistic "wishes to be" or the judgmental "should be," the characteristics are written in the categoric indicative: "Jesuit education *is*. . . ."

CHARACTERISTICS

(21)   1. *For Ignatius, God is Creator and Lord, Supreme Goodness, the one Reality that is absolute; all other reality comes from God and has value only insofar as it leads us to God.*[8] This God is present in our lives, "laboring for us"[9] in all things; He can be discovered, through faith, in all natural and human events, in history as a whole, and most especially within the lived experience of each individual person.

(22)

> *Jesuit education*: is world-affirming.
>   assists in the total formation of each individual within the human community.
>   includes a religious dimension that permeates the entire education.
>   is an apostolic instrument.
>   promotes dialogue between faith and culture.

---

[7] *Constitutions*, [351] and passim; English edition translated, with an introduction and a commentary, by George E. Ganss, S.J. (St. Louis: Institute of Jesuit Sources, 1970). The sentence in the text is a basic principle and a favorite phrase of Ignatius.

[8] "The other things on the face of the earth are created for man to help him in attaining the end for which he is created. Hence, man is to make use of them insofar as they help him in the attainment of his end, and he must rid himself of them insofar as they prove a hindrance to them" (*Spiritual Exercises*, § 23). This is often referred to as the "tantum-quantum," from the words used in the Latin text. Various translations of the *Spiritual Exercises* are available in English; one common text is David L. Fleming, S.J., *The Spiritual Exercises of St. Ignatius: A Literal Translation and a Contemporary Reading* (St. Louis: Institute of Jesuit Sources, 1978).

[9] *Spiritual Exercises*, § 236.

1.1 *World-affirming.*

(23)   Jesuit education acknowledges God as the Author of all reality, all truth and all knowledge. God is present and working in all of creation: in nature, in history and in persons. Jesuit education, therefore, affirms the *radical goodness of the world* "charged with the grandeur of God,"[10] and it regards every element of creation as worthy of study and contemplation, capable of endless exploration.

(24)   The education in a Jesuit school tries to *create a sense of wonder and mystery* in learning about God's creation. A more complete knowledge of creation can lead to a greater knowledge of God and a greater willingness to work with God in His ongoing creation. Courses are taught in such a way that students, in humble recognition of God's presence, find joy in learning and thirst for greater and deeper knowledge.

1.2 *The total formation of each individual within community.*

(25)   God is especially revealed in the mystery of the human person, "created in the image and likeness of God"[11]; Jesuit education, therefore, *probes the meaning of human life* and is concerned with the total formation of each student as an individual personally loved by God. The objective of Jesuit education is to assist in the *fullest possible development of all of the God-given talents of each individual person as a member of the human community.*

(26)   A thorough and sound *intellectual formation* includes mastery of basic humanistic and scientific disciplines through careful and sustained study that is based on competent and well-motivated teaching. This intellectual formation includes a growing ability to reason reflectively, logically and critically.

(27)   While it continues to give emphasis to the traditional humanistic studies that are essential for an understanding of

---

[10] From "God's Grandeur," a poem by Gerard Manley Hopkins, S.J.
[11] Cf. Genesis 1:27.

the human person, Jesuit education also includes a careful and critical study of *technology* together with the *physical and social sciences.*

(28)   In Jesuit education, particular care is given to the development of the *imaginative,* the *affective,* and the *creative* dimensions of each student in all courses of study. These dimensions enrich learning and prevent it from being merely intellectual. They are essential in the formation of the whole person and are a way to discover God as He reveals Himself through beauty. For these same reasons, Jesuit education includes opportunities—through course work and through extracurricular activities—for all students to come to an appreciation of literature, aesthetics, music and the fine arts.

(29)   Jesuit schools of the 17th Century were noted for their development of communication skills or "eloquence," achieved through an emphasis on essays, drama, speeches, debates, etc. In today's world so dominated by communications media, the *development of effective communication skills* is more necessary than ever before. Jesuit education, therefore, develops traditional skills in speaking and writing and also helps students to attain facility with modern instruments of communication such as film and video.

(30)   An awareness of the pervasive *influence* of mass media on the attitudes and perceptions of peoples and cultures is also important in the world of today. Therefore Jesuit education includes programs which enable students to understand and critically *evaluate the influence of mass media.* Through proper education, these instruments of modern life can help men and women to become more, rather than less, human.

(31)   Education of the whole person implies physical development in harmony with other aspects of the educational process. Jesuit education, therefore, includes a well-developed program of *sports* and *physical education.* In addition to strengthening the body, sports programs help young men and women learn to accept both success and failure graciously; they become aware of the need to cooperate with

others, using the best qualities of each individual to contribute to the greater advantage of the whole group.

(32)   All of these distinct aspects of the educational process
have one common purpose: the formation of the *balanced
person* with a personally developed philosophy of life that
includes ongoing habits of reflection. To assist in this formation, individual courses are related to one another within a
well-planned educational program; every aspect of school life
contributes to the total development of each individual
person.[12]

(33)   Since the truly human is found only in relationships with
others that include attitudes of respect, love, and service,
Jesuit education stresses—and assists in developing—*the role
of each individual as a member of the human community*. Students, teachers, and all members of the educational community are encouraged to build a solidarity with others that
transcends race, culture or religion. In a Jesuit school, good
manners are expected; the atmosphere is one in which all
can live and work together in understanding and love, with
respect for all men and women as children of God.

1.3 *A religious dimension permeates the entire education.*

(34)   Since every program in the school can be a means to discover God, all teachers share a responsibility for the religious
dimension of the school. However, the integrating factor in
the process of discovering God and understanding the true
meaning of human life is theology as presented through *religious and spiritual education*. Religious and spiritual formation is integral to Jesuit education; it is not added to, or
separate from, the educational process.

(35)   Jesuit education tries to foster the creative Spirit at work
in each person, offering the opportunity for a *faith response*
to God while at the same time recognizing that faith cannot
be imposed.[13] In all classes, in the climate of the school, and

---

[12] "Our ideal is . . . the unsurpassed model of the Greeks, in its Christian version:
balanced, serene and constant, open to whatever is human." (OSS, § 14).
[13] The "faith response" is treated in greater detail in sections 4 and 6.

most especially in formal classes in religion, every attempt is made to present the possibility of a faith response to God as something truly human and not opposed to reason, as well as to develop those values which are able to resist the secularism of modern life. A Jesuit school does everything it can to respond to the mission given to the Society of Jesus *"to resist atheism* vigorously with united forces."[14]

(36)   Every aspect of the educational process can lead, ultimately, to *worship of God* present and at work in creation, and to *reverence for creation* as it mirrors God. Worship and reverence are parts of the life of the school community; they are expressed in personal prayer and in appropriate community forms of worship. The intellectual, the imaginative and affective, the creative, and the physical development of each student, along with the sense of wonder that is an aspect of every course and of the life of the school as a whole—all can help students to discover God active in history and in creation.

1.4 An apostolic instrument.[15]

(37)   While it respects the integrity of academic disciplines, the concern of Jesuit education is *preparation for life,* which is itself a preparation for eternal life. Formation of the individual is not an abstract end; Jesuit education is also concerned with the ways in which students will make use of their formation within the human community, in the service of others "for the praise, reverence, and service of God."[16] The success of Jesuit education is measured not in terms of academic performance of students or professional competence of teachers, but rather in terms of this quality of life.

---

[14] Pope Paul VI in a letter addressed to the Society of Jesus, *Acta Apostolicae Sedis* 57, 1965, 514; the same call was repeated by Pope John Paul II in his homily to the delegates of the 33rd General Congregation, September 2, 1983. Cf. *Documents of the 33rd General Congregation of the Society of Jesus* (St. Louis: Institute of Jesuit Sources, 1984), 81.

[15] The characteristic of being an "apostolic instrument" is treated in greater detail in section 6.1.

[16] *Spiritual Exercises,* § 23.

1.5 *The dialogue between faith and culture.*

(38)   Believing that God is active in all creation and in all human history, Jesuit education *promotes dialogue between faith and culture*—which includes dialogue between *faith and science.* This dialogue recognizes that persons as well as cultural structures are human, imperfect, and sometimes affected by sin and in need of conversion;[17] at the same time it discovers God revealing Himself in various distinct cultural ways. Jesuit education, therefore, encourages contact with and a genuine appreciation of other cultures, to be creatively critical of the contributions and deficiencies of each.

(39)   Jesuit education is adapted to meet the needs of the country and the culture in which the school is located[18]; this adaptation, while it encourages a "healthy patriotism" is not an unquestioning acceptance of national values. The concepts of "contact with," "genuine appreciation" and being "creatively critical" apply also to one's own culture and country. The goal is always to discover God, present and active in creation and in history.

(40)   2. *Each man or woman is personally known and loved by God. This love invites a response which, to be authentically human, must be an expression of a radical freedom. Therefore, in order to respond to the love of God, each person is called to be:*
         —*free to give of oneself, while accepting responsibility for and the consequences of one's actions: free to be faithful.*
         —*free to work in faith toward that true happiness which is the purpose of life: free to labor with others in the service of the Kingdom of God for the healing of creation.*

(41)
┌───┐
Jesuit education: insists on individual care and concern for
      each person.
    emphasizes activity on the part of the student.
    encourages life-long openness to growth.
└───┘

---

[17] Conversion is treated in greater detail in section 3.

[18] "Inculturation" is treated in detail in Decree 5 of the 32nd General Congregation; see note 3.

2.1 *Care and concern for each individual person.*

(42)   The young men and women who are students in a Jesuit school have not reached full maturity; the educational process recognizes the *developmental stages* of intellectual, affective and spiritual growth and assists each student to mature gradually in all these areas. Thus, the *curriculum is centered on the person* rather than on the material to be covered. Each student is allowed to develop and to accomplish objectives at a *pace suited to individual ability* and the characteristics of his or her own personality.

(43)   Growth in the responsible use of freedom is facilitated by the *personal relationship between student and teacher.* Teachers and administrators, both Jesuit and lay, are more than academic guides. They are involved in the lives of the students, taking a personal interest in the intellectual, affective, moral and spiritual development of every student, helping each one to develop a sense of self-worth and to become a responsible individual within the community. While they respect the privacy of students, they are ready to listen to their cares and concerns about the meaning of life, to share their joys and sorrows, to help them with personal growth and interpersonal relationships. In these and other ways, the adult members of the educational community guide students in their development of a set of values leading to life decisions that go beyond "self": that include a concern for the needs of others. They try to live in a way that offers an example to the students, and they are willing to share their own life experiences. "*Cura personalis*" (concern for the individual person) remains a basic characteristic of Jesuit education.[19]

---

[19] "This care for each student individually, as far as this is possible, remains and must remain the characteristic of our vocation. . . . Above all, we need to maintain, in one way or in another, this personal contact with each of the students in our schools and colleges": Father General Peter-Hans Kolvenbach, S.J., "Informal Remarks on Education," given during a meeting with the Delegates for Education of the Jesuit Provinces of Europe, November 18, 1983; *Education:SJ*, 44 (January–February, 1984): 3–6.

(44)   *Freedom includes responsibilities within the community.*
"*Cura personalis*" is not limited to the relationship between
teacher and student; it affects the curriculum and the entire
life of the institution. All members of the educational community are concerned with one another and learn from one
another. The personal relationships among students, and
also among adults—lay and Jesuit, administrators, teachers,
and auxiliary staff—evidence this same care. A personal concern extends also to former students, to parents and to the
student within his or her family.

2.2 *Activity of students in the learning process.*

(45)   Growth in the maturity and independence that are necessary for growth in freedom depends on *active participation*
rather than passive reception. Important steps toward this
active participation include *personal study, opportunities for
personal discovery and creativity,* and an attitude of *reflection.*
The task of the teacher is to help each student to become an
independent learner, to assume the responsibility for his or
her own education.

2.3 *Life-long openness to growth.*

(46)   Since education is a life-long process, Jesuit education
tries to instill a *joy in learning* and a *desire to learn* that will
remain beyond the days in school. "Perhaps even more important than the formation we give them is the capacity and
concern to continue their own formation; this is what we
must instill in them. It is important to learn; but it is much
more important to learn how to learn, to desire to go on
learning all through life."[20]

(47)   Personal relationships with students will help the adult
members of the educational community to be *open to
change,* to *continue to learn*; thus they will be more effective
in their own work. This is especially important today, given
the rapid change in culture and the difficulty that adults can

---

[20] OSS, § 13.

have in understanding and interpreting correctly the cultural pressures that affect young people.

(48)   Jesuit education recognizes that intellectual, affective, and spiritual growth continue throughout life; the adult members of the educational community are encouraged to continue to mature in all of these areas, and programs of ongoing formation are provided to assist in this growth.[21]

(49)   3. *Because of sin, and the effects of sin, the freedom to respond to God's love is not automatic. Aided and strengthened by the redeeming love of God, we are engaged in an ongoing struggle to recognize and work against the obstacles that block freedom—including the effects of sinfulness—while developing the capacities that are necessary for the exercise of true freedom.*

   a. *This freedom requires a genuine knowledge, love and acceptance of self, joined to a determination to be freed from any excessive attachment: to wealth, fame, health, power, or anything else, even life itself.*

   b. *True freedom also requires a realistic knowledge of the various forces present in the surrounding world and includes freedom from distorted perceptions of reality, warped values, rigid attitudes or surrender to narrow ideologies.*

   c. *To work toward this true freedom, one must learn to recognize and deal with the influences that can either promote or limit freedom: the movements within one's own heart; past experiences of all types; interactions with other people; the dynamics of history, social structures and culture.*

(50)
> *Jesuit education:* is value-oriented.
>   encourages a realistic knowledge, love, and acceptance of self.
>   provides a realistic knowledge of the world in which we live.

---

[21] See section 9.3 for a fuller development of ongoing formation.

3.1 *Value-oriented.*

(51)   Jesuit education includes formation in values, in attitudes, and in an ability to evaluate criteria; that is, it includes formation of the will. Since a knowledge of good and evil, and of the hierarchy of relative goods, is necessary both for the recognition of the different influences that affect freedom and for the exercise of freedom, education takes place in a moral context: *knowledge is joined to virtue.*

(52)   Personal development through the training of character and will, overcoming selfishness and lack of concern for others and the other effects of sinfulness, and developing the freedom that respects others and accepts responsibility, is all aided by the necessary and fair *regulations* of the school; these include a *fair system of discipline.* Of equal importance is the *self-discipline* expected of each student, manifested in intellectual rigor, persevering application to serious study, and conduct toward others that recognizes the human dignity of each individual.

(53)   In a Jesuit school, a framework of inquiry in which a value system is acquired through a process of wrestling with competing points of view is legitimate.

3.2 *Realistic knowledge, love and acceptance of self.*

(54)   The concern for total human development as a creature of God which is the "Christian humanism" of Jesuit education emphasizes the happiness in life that is the result of a responsible use of freedom, but it also *recognizes the reality of sin and its effects* in the life of each person. It therefore tries to encourage each student to confront this obstacle to freedom honestly, in a growing self-awareness and a growing realization that forgiveness and conversion are possible through the redemptive love and the help of God.[22]

(55)   The struggle to remove the obstacles to freedom and develop the capacity to exercise freedom is more than a recog-

---

[22] Forgiveness and conversion are religious concepts, treated in greater detail in section 6.

nition of the effects of sin; an ongoing effort to recognize *all obstacles to growth* is also essential.[23] Students are helped in their efforts to discover prejudice and limited vision on the one hand and to evaluate relative goods and competing values on the other.

(56)   Teachers and administrators assist students in this growth by being ready to challenge them, helping students to *reflect on personal experiences* so that they can understand their own experience of God; while they accept their gifts and develop them, they also accept limitations and overcome these as far as possible. The educational program, in bringing students into realistic contact with themselves, tries to help them recognize these various influences and to *develop a critical faculty* that goes beyond the simple recognition of true and false, good and evil.

3.3 A realistic knowledge of the world.

(57)   A realistic knowledge of creation sees the goodness of what God has made, but includes an *awareness of the social effects of sin*: the essential incompleteness, the injustice, and the need for redemption in all people, in all cultures, in all human structures. In trying to develop the ability to reason reflectively, Jesuit education emphasizes the need to be in contact with the world as it is—that is, in need of transformation—without being blind to the essential goodness of creation.

(58)   Jesuit education tries to develop in students an ability to know reality and to evaluate it critically. This awareness includes a *realization that persons and structures can change*, together with a *commitment to work for those changes* in a way that will help to build more just human structures, which will provide an opportunity for the exercise of freedom joined to greater human dignity for all.[24]

---

[23] Cf. the meditation on "The Two Standards in *Spiritual Exercises*, §§ 136–48.

[24] "In this sphere, as in so many others, do not be afraid of political involvement! It is, according to the Second Vatican Council, the proper role of the laity. It is inevitable, when you become involved in the struggle for structures that make the world more truly human, that bring into being the new creation that Christ prom-

(59)   4. *The worldview of Ignatius is centered on the historical person of Jesus Christ. He is the model for human life because of his total response to the Father's love in the service of others. He shares our human condition and invites us to follow him under the standard of the cross,[25] in loving response to the Father. He is alive in our midst and remains the Man for others in the service of God.*

(60)

> *Jesuit education*: proposes Christ as the model of human life.
>   provides adequate pastoral care.
>   celebrates faith in personal and community prayer, worship and service.

4.1 *Christ the model.*

(61)   Members of various faiths and cultures are a part of the educational community in Jesuit schools today; to all, whatever their beliefs, Christ is proposed as the model of human life. Everyone can draw inspiration and learn about commitment from the life and teaching of Jesus, who witnesses to the love and forgiveness of God, lives in solidarity with all who suffer, and pours out his life in the service of others. Everyone can *imitate him* in an *emptying of self*, in accepting whatever difficulties or sufferings come in the pursuit of the one goal to be achieved: responding to the Father's will in the service of others.

(62)   Christian members of the educational community strive for *personal friendship* with Jesus, who gained forgiveness and true freedom for us through his death and resurrection, is present today and active in our history. To be "Christian" is to *follow* Christ and be like him: to share and promote his values and way of life as far as possible.[26]

---

ised": Father General Peter-Hans Kolvenbach, S.J., address at the Opening Session of the World Congress of Jesuit Alumni, Versailles, France, July 20, 1986; published in ETC (Together), 40 (April–September, 1986): 7–15.

[25] Cf. *Spiritual Exercises*, §§ 143–47.

[26] "It is very important to note that the consideration of the mission of Jesus is not proposed for contemplation, or to understand Jesus better, but precisely insofar as this person is inviting us in a 'call' to which the response is a 'following'; . . . without this disposition, there can be no real understanding. In the logic of Saint

4.2 Pastoral care.[27]

(63)   Pastoral care is a dimension of *"cura personalis"* that enables the seeds of *religious faith and religious commitment* to grow in each individual by enabling each one to recognize and respond to the message of divine love: seeing God at work in his or her life, in the lives of others, and in all of creation; then responding to this discovery through a commitment to service within the community. A Jesuit school makes adequate pastoral care available to all members of the educational community in order to awaken and strengthen this personal faith commitment.

(64)   For Christians this care is centered on Christ, present in the Christian community. Students encounter the person of Christ as friend and guide; they come to know him through Scripture, sacraments, personal and communal prayer, in play and work, in other persons; they are led to the service of others in imitation of Christ the Man for others.[28]

(65)   Making the *Spiritual Exercises*[29] is encouraged as a way of knowing Christ better, loving him, and following him. The *Exercises* will also help the members of the educational community understand the vision of Ignatius, which is the spirit that lies behind Jesuit education. They can be made in various ways, adapted to the time and the abilities of each person, whether adult or student.

Ignatius (more implicitly than explicitly) it is apparent that every consideration of Jesus, including the historical Jesus, is made relevant for today's Christianity from a privileged point of view: the point of view of *following"*: Jon Sobrino, *Cristología desde America Latina*. Colección Teología Latinoamericana (México: Ediciones CRT, 1977), 329.

[27] "Pastoral care" is concerned with spiritual—that is, more than simply human—development. But it is not limited to the relationship between God and the individual; it includes also human relationships as these are an expression of, an extension of, the relationship with God. Therefore, "faith" leads to "commitment"; the *discovery* of God leads to the *service* of God in the service of others in the community.

[28] "Those who graduate from our secondary schools should have acquired, in ways proportional to their age and maturity, a way of life that is in itself a proclamation of the charity of Christ, of the faith that comes from Him and leads back to Him, and of the justice which He announced" (OSS, § 8).

[29] See Appendix I for a brief description of the *Spiritual Exercises*.

(66)   The Jesuit school encourages and assists each student to *respond to his or her own personal call from God*, a *vocation* of service in personal and professional life—whether in marriage, religious or priestly life, or a single life.

4.3 *Prayer and worship.*

(67)   Prayer is an expression of faith and an effective way toward establishing the personal relationship with God that leads to a commitment to serve others. Jesuit education offers a *progressive initiation to prayer*, following the example of Christ, who prayed regularly to his Father. All are encouraged to praise and thank God in prayer, to pray for one another within the school community, and to ask God's help in meeting the needs of the larger human community.

(68)   The faith relationship with God is communal as well as personal; the educational community in a Jesuit school is united by bonds that are more than merely human: it is a *community of faith*, and expresses this faith through appropriate religious or spiritual celebrations. For Catholics, the Eucharist is the celebration of a faith community centered on Christ. All adult members of the community are encouraged to participate in these celebrations, not only as an expression of their own faith, but also to give witness to the purposes of the school.

(69)   Catholic members of the educational community receive and celebrate the loving forgiveness of God in the Sacrament of Reconciliation. Depending on local circumstances, the Jesuit school prepares students (and also adults) for the reception of other Sacraments.

(70)   The obedience of Christ to his Father's will led him to give of himself totally in the service of others; a relationship to God necessarily involves a relationship to other persons.[30] Jesuit education promotes a *faith* that is *centered on the his-*

---

[30] This is treated in greater detail in the next section and in section 9.

torical person of Christ, which therefore *leads to a commitment* to imitate him as the "Man for others."

(71)   **5.** *A loving and free response to God's love cannot be merely speculative or theoretical. No matter what the cost, speculative principles must lead to decisive action: "love is shown in deeds."*[31] *Ignatius asks for the total and active commitment of men and women who, "to imitate and be more actually like Christ,"*[32] *will put their ideals into practice in the real world of the family, business, social movements, political and legal structures, and religious activities.*[33]

(72)
> Jesuit education: is preparation for active life commitment.
>   serves the faith that does justice.
>   seeks to form "men and women for others".
>   manifests a particular concern for the poor.

5.1 *Active life commitment.*

(73)   "Love is shown in deeds": the free human response of love to the redeeming love of God is shown in an active life of service. Jesuit education—in progressive stages that take into account the developmental stages of growth, and without any attempt at manipulation—assists in the formation of men and women who will put their beliefs and attitudes into practice throughout their lives. "We . . . challenge you and try to inspire you to put into practice—in concrete activity— the values that you cherish, the values that you have received in your formation."[34]

---

[31] *Spiritual Exercises*, § 230.

[32] Ibid., § 167.

[33] The "Formula of the Institute," which is the original description of the Society of Jesus written by Ignatius, applies this basic principle of the *Spiritual Exercises*: "Whoever desires to serve as a soldier of God beneath the banner of the cross in our Society . . . should . . . keep what follows in mind. He is a member of a Society founded chiefly for this purpose: to strive especially for the defense and propagation of the faith and for the progress of souls in Christian life and doctrine": "Formula," [3].

[34] Father General Peter-Hans Kolvenbach speaking at the World Congress of Jesuit Alumni, Versailles. See note 24.

5.2 *Education in the service of the faith that does justice.*[35]

(74)   The "decisive action" called for today is the *faith that does justice:* "The mission of the Society of Jesus today is the service of faith, of which the promotion of justice is an absolute requirement. For reconciliation with God demands the reconciliation of people with one another."[36] This service of the faith that does justice is action in imitation of Christ; it is the justice of God, which is *informed by evangelical charity:* "It is charity which gives force to faith, and to the desire for justice. Justice does not reach its interior fullness except in charity. Christian love both implies justice, and extends the requirements of justice to the utmost limits, by providing a motivation and a new interior force. Justice without charity is not evangelical."[37] The Kingdom of God is a Kingdom of justice, love and peace.[38]

(75)   The promotion of justice includes, as a necessary component, *action for peace.* More than the absence of war, the search for peace is a search for relationships of love and trust among all men and women.

(76)   The *goal* of the faith that does justice and works for peace is *a new type of person in a new kind of society,* in which each

---

[35] The "faith" is treated in sections 1 and 4; this present section concentrates on "justice." However, it is important not to separate these two concepts : "The living out of this unity of faith and justice is made possible through a close following of the historical Jesus. As essential parts of this following, we propose these points:

• In announcing the Kingdom and in his struggle against sin, Jesus ran into conflict with persons and structures which, because they were objectively sinful, were opposed to the Kingdom of God.

• The fundamental basis for the connection between justice and faith has to be seen in their inseparable connection with the new commandment of love. On the one hand, the struggle for justice is the form which love ought to take in an unjust world. On the other hand, the New Testament is quite clear in showing that it is love for men and women which is the royal road which reveals that we are loved by God and which brings us to love for God": *Reunion Latinoamericana de Educación,* Lima, Perú, July 1976 (Caracas, Venezuela: CERPE), 65.

[36] The 32nd General Congregation, Decree 4, "Our Mission Today: The Service of Faith and the Promotion of Justice," no. 4. See note 3.

[37] OSS, § 11.

[38] Cf. the "Preface" from the Roman Catholic Mass celebrating the Feast of Christ the King.

individual has the opportunity to be fully human and each one accepts the responsibility of promoting the human development of others. The active commitment asked of the students—and practiced by former students and by the adult members of the educational community—is a free commitment to the struggle for a more human world and a community of love. For Christians, this commitment is a response to the call of Christ, and is made in humble recognition that conversion is only possible with the help of God. For them, the Sacrament of Reconciliation is a necessary component of the struggle for peace and justice. But all members of the educational community, including those who do not share Christian faith, can collaborate in this work. A genuine sense of the dignity of the human person can be the starting point for working together in the promotion of justice and can become the beginning of an ecumenical dialogue which sees justice as intimately tied to faith.

(77)   In a Jesuit school, the focus is on *education* for justice. Adequate knowledge joined to rigorous and critical thinking will make the commitment to work for justice in adult life more effective. In addition to this necessary basic formation, education for justice in an educational context has three distinct aspects:

(78)   1. *Justice issues are treated in the curriculum.* This may at times call for the addition of new courses; of greater importance is the examination of the justice dimension always present in every course taught.[39] Teachers try to become more conscious of this dimension, so that they can provide students with the intellectual, moral and spiritual formation that will enable them to make a commitment to service—that will make them agents of change. The curriculum includes a *critical analysis of society,* adapted to the age level of the students; the outlines of a

---

[39] In his address to the Presidents and Rectors of Jesuit universities at their meeting in Frascati, Italy, on November 5, 1985, Father General Peter-Hans Kolvenbach gives several examples of how justice issues can be treated in various academic courses. "The Jesuit University Today," *Education:SJ,* 53 (November–December, 1985: 7–8.

solution that is in line with Christian principles is a part of this analysis. The reference points are the Word of God, church teachings, and human science.[40]

(79)   2. The *policies and programs* of a Jesuit school *give concrete witness to the faith that does justice*; they give a counter-witness to the values of the consumer society. Social analysis of the reality in which the school is located can lead to institutional self-evaluation, which may call for structural changes in school policies and practices.[41]School policy and school life encourage mutual respect; they promote the human dignity and human rights of each person, adult and young, in the educational community.

(80)   3. "There is no genuine conversion to justice unless there are *works of justice*."[42] Interpersonal relationships within the school manifest a concern for both justice and charity. In preparation for life commitment, there are opportunities in Jesuit education for actual contact with the world of injustice. The analysis of society within the curriculum thus becomes reflection based on actual contact with the structural dimensions of injustice.

(81)   Members of the educational community are *aware of* and *involved in* the *serious issues of our day*. The educational community, and each individual in it, are conscious of the influence they can have on others; school policies are made with an awareness of possible effects on the larger community and on its social structures.

5.3 Men and women for others.[43]

(82)   Jesuit education helps students to realize that *talents are gifts to be developed*, not for self-satisfaction or self-gain, but

---

[40] Cf. Gabriel Codina, S.J., "Faith and Justice within the Educational Context," *Education:SJ*, 56 (June–July, 1986): 12–13.

[41] Ibid., 11.

[42] Ibid., 14–15 (emphasis added).

[43] See note 5. The "others" in the much-repeated phrase is the "neighbor" in the Parable of the Good Samaritan (Luke 10:29–37). The quotation in the text is Fr. Arrupe's development of this idea; see note 44.

rather, with the help of God, *for the good of the human community*. Students are encouraged to use their gifts in the service of others, out of a love for God:

> Today our prime educational objective must be to form men and women for others; men and women who will live not for themselves but for God and his Christ——for the God-man who lived and died for all the world; men and women who cannot even conceive of love of God which does not include love for the least of their neighbors; men and women completely convinced that the love of God which does not issue in justice for men and women is a farce.[44]

(83) In order to promote an awareness of "others," Jesuit education *stresses community values* such as equality of opportunity for all, the principles of distributive and social justice, and the attitude of mind that sees service of others as more self-fulfilling than success or prosperity.[45]

(84) The adult members of the educational community— especially those in daily contact with students—*manifest in their lives* concern for others and esteem for human dignity.[46]

5.4 A *particular concern for the poor.*

(85) Reflecting on the actual situation of today's world and responding to the call of Christ who had a special love and concern for the poor, the Church and the Society of Jesus have made a *"preferential option"*[47] for the poor. This includes those without economic means, the handicapped, the marginalized and all those who are, in any sense, unable to

---

[44] "Men for Others," 9; see note 5.

[45] Concrete examples of a stress on community values can be found in nearly every section of this present description of the Characteristics of Jesuit Education.

[46] "Outside of the influence of the home, the example of the faculty and the climate which they create in the school will be the single most influential factor in any effort at education for faith and justice": Robert J. Starratt, S.J., "Sowing Seeds of Faith and Justice" (Washington, D.C.: Jesuit Secondary Education Association), 17.

[47] The phrase is common in recent documents of the Church and of the Society of Jesus. The exact meaning is much discussed; what it does not mean is an option for a single class of people to the exclusion of others. Its meaning within the educational context is described in this section 5.4.

live a life of full human dignity. In Jesuit education this option is reflected both in the students that are admitted and in the type of formation that is given.

(86)   Jesuit schools do not exist for any one class of students[48]; Ignatius accepted schools only when they were completely endowed so that education could be available to everyone; he insisted that special facilities for housing the poor be a part of every school foundation that he approved and that teachers give special attention to the needs of poor students. Today, although the situation differs greatly from country to country and the specific criteria for selecting students depends on "circumstances of place and persons," every Jesuit school does what it can to make Jesuit education *available to everyone*, including the poor and the disadvantaged.[49] Financial assistance to those in need and reduction of costs whenever possible are means toward making this possible. Moreover, Jesuit schools provide academic and counseling assistance to those in need of it so that all can profit from the education being offered.

(87)   In order for parents, especially the poor, to exercise freedom of choice in the education of their children, Jesuit schools join in movements that promote free educational opportunity for all. "The recovery of genuine equality of opportunity and genuine freedom in the area of education is a concern that falls within the scope of our struggle for promotion of justice."[50]

(88)   More basic than the type of student admitted is the type of formation that is given. In Jesuit education, the values

---

[48] "The Society of Jesus has one finality: we are for everyone. Rich and poor, oppressed and oppressors, everyone. No one is excluded from our apostolate. This is true also for the schools": Pedro Arrupe, S.J., "Reflections During the Meeting on Secondary Education," *Education:SJ*, 30 (October–December, 1980): 11.

[49] The question of admission of students varies greatly from country to country. Where there is no government aid, the school exists through fees and gifts. A concern for justice includes just wages and good working conditions for everyone working in the school, and this must also be taken into consideration in the option for the poor.

[50] OSS, § 8.

which the school community communicates, gives witness to, and makes operative in school policies and structures, the values which flow into the school climate, are those values that promote a special concern for those men and women who are without the means to live in human dignity. In this sense, the *poor form the context* of Jesuit education: "Our educational planning needs to be made in function of the poor, from the perspective of the poor."[51]

(89)   The Jesuit school provides students with *opportunities for contact with the poor and for service to them*, both in the school and in outside service projects, to enable these students to learn to love all as brothers and sisters in the human community, and also in order to come to a better understanding of the causes of poverty.

(90)   To be educational, this *contact is joined to reflection*. The promotion of justice in the curriculum, described above in (80), has as one concrete objective an analysis of the causes of poverty.

(91)   **6.** *For Ignatius, the response to the call of Christ is made in and through the Roman Catholic Church, the instrument through which Christ is sacramentally present in the world. Mary, the Mother of Jesus, is the model of this response. Ignatius and his first companions all were ordained as priests and they put the Society of Jesus at the service of the Vicar of Christ, "to go to any place whatsoever where he judges it expedient to send them for the greater glory of God and the good of souls."*[52]

(92)
Jesuit education: is an apostolic instrument, in service of the Church as it serves human society. prepares students for active participation in the Church and the local community, for the service of others.

---

[51] Cf. Codina, "Faith and Justice, 8. A more complete explanation of these points is given in that document.
[52] *Constitutions*, [603].

6.1 *An apostolic instrument in service of the Church.*

(93)   Jesuit schools are a part of *the apostolic mission of the Church* in building the Kingdom of God. Even though the educational process has changed radically since the time of Ignatius and the ways to express religious concepts are quite different, Jesuit education still remains an instrument to help students know God better and respond to him; the school remains available for use in response to emerging needs of the people of God. The aim of Jesuit education is the formation of principled, value-oriented persons for others after the example of Jesus Christ. Teaching in a Jesuit school, therefore, is a ministry.

(94)   Because it is characteristic of all Jesuit works, the Ignatian attitude of *loyalty to and service of the Church,* the people of God, will be communicated to the entire educational community in a Jesuit school. The purposes and ideals of members of other faiths can be in harmony with the goals of the Jesuit school and they can commit themselves to these goals for the development of the students and for the betterment of society.

(95)   Jesuit education—while respecting the conscience and the convictions of each student—is *faithful to the teachings of the Church,* especially in moral and religious formation. As far as possible, the school chooses as qualified leaders of the educational community those who can teach and give witness to the teachings of Christ presented by the Catholic Church.

(96)   The educational community, based on the example of Christ—and of Mary in her response to Christ[53]—and *reflecting on today's culture* in the light of the teachings of the Church, will promote:[54]

---

[53] Cf. Vatican Council II, "The Dogmatic Constitution on the Church," *Lumen Gentium,* nn. 66–69.

[54] The "spiritual vision" mentioned here includes the entire faith response of earlier sections. Once again, questions of justice cannot be separated from the faith and evangelical charity on which they are based.

- a spiritual vision of the world in the face of materialism;
- a concern for others in the face of egoism;
- simplicity in the face of consumerism;
- the cause of the poor in the face of social injustice.

(97)   As part of its service of the Church a Jesuit school will *serve the local civil and religious community and cooperate with the local bishop.* One example of this is that important decisions about school policy take into account the pastoral orientations of the local church; these same decisions about school policy consider their possible effects on the local church and the local community.

(98)   For greater effectiveness in its service of human needs, a Jesuit school works in *cooperation with other* Jesuit *apostolic works,* with local parishes and other Catholic and civic agencies, and with centers for the social apostolate.

(99)   All members of the educational community are active in *service as members of the local community and of their churches.* They participate in meetings and other activities, especially those related to education.

(100)   The Jesuit school community encourages *collaboration in ecumenical activities* with other churches and is active in dialogue with all men and women of good will; the community is a witness to the Gospel of Christ, in service to the human community.

6.2 *Preparation for active participation in the Church.*

(101)   Jesuit education is committed to the religious development of all students. They will *receive instruction in the basic truths of their faith.* For Christian students, this includes a knowledge of the Scriptures, especially the Gospels.

(102)   For Catholic students Jesuit education offers a *knowledge of and love for the Church and the sacraments,* as privileged opportunities to encounter Christ.

(103)   In ways proper to a school, *concrete experiences of church life are available* to all students, through participation in

church projects and activities. Lay teachers, especially those active in parish activities, can be leaders in promoting this; they can communicate to students the current emphasis on the apostolate of lay people.

(104)   Following the example of the early Jesuit schools where the Sodalities of Mary played such an important part in fostering devotion and Christian commitment, opportunities such as the *Christian Life Communities* are available for those students and adults who want to know Christ more completely and model their lives on his more closely. Similar opportunities are offered to members of other faiths who wish to deepen their faith commitment.

(105)   7. *Repeatedly, Ignatius insisted on the "magis"—the more. His constant concern was for greater service of God through a closer following of Christ and that concern flowed into all the apostolic work of the first companions. The concrete response to God must be "of greater value."*[55]

(106)

> *Jesuit education*: pursues excellence in its work of formation. witnesses to excellence.

7.1 *Excellence in formation.*

(107)   In Jesuit education, the criterion of excellence is applied to all areas of school life: the aim is the fullest possible development of every dimension of the person, linked to the development of a sense of values and a commitment to the service of others which gives priority to the needs of the poor and is willing to sacrifice self-interest for the promotion of justice.[56] The pursuit of academic excellence is appropriate in a Jesuit school, but only within the larger context of *human excellence.*[57]

---

[55] The expression is taken from the meditation on "The Kingdom of Christ" in the *Spiritual Exercises*, § 97, where the aim is to lead the person making the *Exercises* to a closer following of Christ.

[56] "The excellence which we seek consists in producing men and women of right principles, personally appropriated; men and women open to the signs of the times, in tune with their cultural milieu and its problems; men and women for others": OSS, § 9.

[57] Some criteria for excellence are given in section 9.1; they are the same as the criteria for discernment.

(108)   Excellence, like all other Ignatian criteria, is determined by "circumstances of place and persons." "The nature of the institution, its location, the number of students, the formulation of objectives for academic quality or of the publics to be served, etc., are elements which diversify the instrument in order to adapt it to the circumstances in which it is being employed."[58] To seek the *magis*, therefore, is to provide the type and level of education for the type and age-group of students that best responds to the *needs of the region in which the school is located.*

(109)   "More" does not imply comparison with others or measurement of progress against an absolute standard; rather is it the *fullest possible development of each person's individual capacities* at each stage of life, *joined to the willingness to continue this development* throughout life *and the motivation to use those developed gifts for others.*

(110)   A traditional aim of Jesuit education has been to train "leaders": men and women who assume responsible positions in society through which they have a positive influence on others. This objective has, at times, led to excesses which call for correction. Whatever the concept may have meant in the past, the goal of Jesuit education in today's understanding of the Ignatian worldview is not to prepare a socioeconomic elite, but rather to educate *leaders in service.* The Jesuit school, therefore, will help students to develop the qualities of mind and heart that will enable them—in whatever station they assume in life—to work with others for the good of all in the service of the Kingdom of God.

(111)   Service is founded on a *faith commitment* to God; for Christians this is expressed in terms of the following of Christ. The decision to follow Christ, made in love, leads to a desire to always do "more"—enabling us to become multiplying agents.[59] The desire, in turn, is converted into the nec-

---

[58] OSS, § 6.

[59] "The strange expression which Fr. Pedro Arrupe used so frequently—that we are to produce "multiplying agents"—is, in fact, in complete accord with the apostolic vision of Ignatius. His correspondence of 6,815 letters amply proves that Ignatius never ceased to seek out and encourage the widest possible collaboration, with

essary personal preparation in which a student dedicates himself or herself to study, to personal formation, and ultimately to action.

(112)   The *Ratio Studiorum* recommends *competition*—normally between groups rather than individuals—as an effective stimulus to academic growth. Jesuit education today faces a different reality: a world of excessive competitiveness reflected in individualism, consumerism, and success at all costs. Although a Jesuit school values the stimulus of competitive games, it urges students to distinguish themselves by their ability to work together, to be sensitive to one another, to be committed to the service of others shown in the way they help one another. "A desire for Christian witness . . . cannot thrive in an atmosphere of academic competition, or where one's personal qualities are judged only by comparison to those of others. These things will thrive only in an atmosphere in which we learn how to be available, how to be of service to others."[60]

7.2 *Witness to excellence.*

(113)   The *school policies* are such that they create an ambience or "climate" which will promote excellence. These policies include ongoing evaluation of goals, programs, services and teaching methods in an effort to make Jesuit education more effective in achieving its goals.

(114)   The *adult members* of the educational community *witness to excellence* by joining growth in professional competence to growth in dedication.

(115)   The teachers and directors in a Jesuit school cooperate with other schools and educational agencies to discover more effective institutional policies, educational processes, and pedagogical methods.[61]

---

all types of people": Fr. Kolvenbach, S.J., at the World Congress of Jesuit Alumni, Versailles. See note 24.

  [60] OSS, § 12.

  [61] "We need to learn, and we have an obligation to share. There are enormous advantages to be gained through collaboration of every type. It would be foolish to

(116)   8. *As Ignatius came to know the love of God revealed through Christ and began to respond by giving himself to the service of the Kingdom of God he shared his experience and attracted companions who became "friends in the Lord,"[62] for the service of others. The strength of a community working in service of the Kingdom is greater than that of any individual or group of individuals.*

(117)

> Jesuit education: stresses lay-Jesuit collaboration.
>   relies on a spirit of community among:
>   teaching staff and administrators;
>   the Jesuit community;
>   governing boards;
>   parents;
>   students;
>   former students;
>   benefactors.
>   takes place within a structure that
>   promotes community.

8.1 *Lay-Jesuit Collaboration.*

(118)   Lay-Jesuit collaboration is a positive goal that a Jesuit school tries to achieve in response to the Second Vatican Council[63] and to recent General Congregations of the Society of Jesus.[64] Because this concept of a *common mission* is still new, there is a need for growing understanding and for careful planning.

---

pretend that we have nothing to learn. It would be irresponsible to think only of ourselves in our planning, without considering the need to cooperate with other secondary schools. This . . . will make us more effective apostolically, and will at the same time increase and strengthen our sense of being a part of the church": Ibid., § 25. The question of evaluation is taken up again in greater detail in section 9.

[62] Ignatius is the author of this phrase, in a letter written to Juan de Verdolay on July 24, 1537. *Monumenta Iqnatiana* Epp. vol. 12, 321 and 323.

[63] *Apostolicam Actuositatem*—"On the Apostolate of the Laity." See note 2.

[64] The 31st General Congregation, Decree 33, "The Relationship of the Society to the Laity and Their Apostolate"; Decree 28, "The Apostolate of Education," n. 27. The 32nd General Congregation, Decree 2, "Jesuits Today," n. 29. The 33rd General Congregation, Decree 1, "Companions of Jesus Sent into Today's World," n. 47. See note 3.

(119)   In a Jesuit school, there is a willingness on the part of both lay people and Jesuits to *assume appropriate responsibilities*: to work together in leadership and in service. Efforts are made to achieve a true union of minds and hearts, and to work together as a single apostolic body[65] in the formation of students. There is, therefore, a sharing of vision, purpose and apostolic effort.

(120)   The legal structure of the school allows for the fullest possible collaboration in the direction of the schools.[66]

(121)   Jesuits are active in promoting lay-Jesuit collaboration in the school. "Let Jesuits consider the importance for the Society of such collaboration with lay people, who will always be the natural interpreters for us of the modern world and so will always give us effective help in this apostolate."[67] "We must be willing to work with others . . . willing to play a subordinate, supporting, anonymous role; and willing to learn how to serve from those we seek to serve."[68] One of the responsibilities of the Religious superior is to foster this openness in the apostolic work.

8.2 *Teaching staff and administrators.*

(122)   As far as possible, people chosen to join the educational community in a Jesuit school will be men and women *capable of understanding its distinctive nature and of contributing to the implementation of characteristics that result from the Ignatian vision.*

(123)   In order to promote a *common sense of purpose applied to the concrete circumstances of school-life,* teachers, adminis-

---

[65] "We used to think of the institution as 'ours,' with some lay people helping us, even if their number was much greater than the number of Jesuits. Today, some Jesuits seem to think that the number of lay people has so increased and the control has been so radically transferred, that the institution is no longer really Jesuit. . . . I would insist that the [school itself] remains an apostolic instrument: *not of the Jesuits alone, but of Jesuits and lay people working together*": Fr. Kolvenbach, "The Jesuit University Today." See note 39.

[66] See below, sections 8.7 and 9.3.

[67] The 31st General Congregation, Decree 28, "On the Apostolate of Education," n. 27.

[68] The 32nd General Congregation, Decree 1, "Jesuits Today," n. 29.

trators and auxiliary staff, Jesuit and lay, communicate with one another regularly on personal, professional and religious levels. They are willing to discuss vision and hopes, aspirations and experiences, successes and failures.

8.3 *The Jesuit community.*

(124)   The Jesuits working in the school "should be a group of men with a clear identity, who live the true Ignatian charism, closely bound together by union of minds and hearts *ad intra*, and similarly bound, *ad extra*, by their generous participation in a common mission. . . . It should be the source of inspiration and stimulation for the other components of the educational community. . . . *The witness of our lives is essential.*"[69]

(125)   The Jesuits will be more effective in their service and inspiration of the total educational community if they live in *service and inspiration to one another*, forming a true community in prayer and in life. This lived witness is one means of making their work in the school a "corporate" apostolate, and will help the larger school community be more effectively and affectively united.

(126)   At least on special occasions, other members of the educational community are invited to meals and to liturgical and social functions in the Jesuit community. Spending time together informally is a help toward building community and lay people will come to a better understanding of Jesuit life when they have opportunities to be a part of it.

(127)   In addition to their professional responsibilities in the school as teachers, administrators, or pastors, Jesuits are available to *provide* opportunities such as *discussions, workshops*, and *retreats* which can enable others in the school community to come to a better knowledge and appreciation of the worldview of Ignatius.

(128)   Education—the work of a teacher or administrator or member of the auxiliary staff—is itself apostolic. In keeping

---

[69] OSS, §§ 16, 18.

with the nature of the school as an apostolic instrument of the church, however, those Jesuits who are priests are also active in more directly sacerdotal work, including celebration of the Eucharist, being available for the Sacrament of Reconciliation, etc.

(129)   The statutes of the school define the responsibilities of the school director and the authority of the Society of Jesus (see 8.9 below). Depending on local circumstances, neither the individual Jesuit nor the group of Jesuits as a community has, as such, any power of decision-making in a Jesuit school not described in these statutes.

8.4 *Governing boards.*

(130)   General Congregation XXXI of the Society of Jesus recommended that governing boards be established in Jesuit schools, with membership that includes both lay people and Jesuits.[70] These are a further means of sharing responsibility among both lay people and Jesuits and thus promoting lay-Jesuit collaboration. They take advantage of the professional competencies of a variety of different people. The members of these boards, both Jesuits and lay, are familiar with the purposes of a Jesuit school and with the vision of Ignatius on which these purposes are based.

8.5 *Parents.*

(131)   Teachers and directors in a Jesuit school *cooperate closely with parents*, who are also members of the educational community. There is frequent communication and ongoing dialogue between the home and the school. Parents are kept informed about school activities; they are encouraged to meet with the teachers to discuss the progress of their children. Parents are offered support and opportunities for growth in exercising their role as parents, and they are also

---

[70] "It will also be advantageous to consider whether it would not be helpful to establish in some of our institutions of higher education a board of trustees which is composed partly of Jesuits and partly of lay people": The 31st General Congregation, Decree 28, "On the Apostolate of Education," n. 27.

offered opportunities to participate in advisory councils. In these and other ways, parents are helped to fulfill their right and responsibility as educators in the home and family and they in turn contribute to the work of education going on in the school.[71]

(132)   As far as possible, parents *understand, value* and *accept the Ignatian worldview* that characterizes the Jesuit school. The school community, keeping in mind the different situations in different countries, provides opportunities by which parents can become more familiar with this worldview and its applications to education.

(133)   There is *consistency between the values promoted in the school and those promoted in the home.* At the time their children first enroll in the school, parents are informed about the commitment of Jesuit education to a faith that does justice. Programs of ongoing formation are available to parents so that they can understand this aim better and be strengthened in their own commitment to it.

8.6 *Students.*

(134)   Students form a *community of understanding and support* among themselves; this is reinforced both informally and through such structures as student government and student councils. Moreover, according to their age and capacity, *student participation in the larger school community* is encouraged through membership on advisory councils and other school committees.

8.7 *Former students.*

(135)   Former students are members of the "community working in service of the kingdom"; a Jesuit school has a special responsibility to them. As far as resources permit, the school will offer *guidance and ongoing formation* so that those who

---

[71] We should cooperate with [parents] in the work of education. . . . I want to give special praise to those organizations—associations, journals, formation courses—which promote the educational formation of the parents of our students, to prepare them for a more effective collaboration with the secondary school": OSS, § 22.

received their basic formation in the school can be more effective in putting this formation into practice in adult life
and can continue to deepen their dedication to the service
of others.[72] Close bonds of friendship and mutual support
exist between the *Jesuit school and Alumni (Former Student)
Associations.*[73]

8.8 *Benefactors.*

(136)   In a similar way, the Jesuit school has a special responsibility toward its benefactors and will offer them the support
and guidance that they may need. In particular, benefactors
have opportunities to learn more about the distinctive nature of a Jesuit school, the Ignatian vision on which it is
based, and its goals, to which they contribute.

8.9 *The school structure.*

(137)   A greater degree of *shared responsibility* has developed in
recent years. Increasingly, decisions are made only after receiving advice through informal consultations, formal committees and other means; all members of the educational
community are kept informed about decisions and about important events in the life of the school. In order to be truly

---

[72] "The ongoing formation of former students is an obligation. . . . It is a work
that only we can do, practically speaking, because it is a question of redoing the
formation that we gave twenty or thirty years ago. The person that the world needs
now is different from the persons we formed then! It is an immense task, and well
beyond our own abilities; we need to seek the help of lay people who can help to
bring it about": OSS, § 23.

[73] "What is the commitment of the Society of Jesus to its former students? It is
the commitment of Ignatius, repeated by Pedro Arrupe: to make you multiplying
agents, to make you capable of incorporating the vision of Ignatius and the . . .
mission of the Society into your own lives. . . . The formation you have received
should have given you the values and the commitment that mark your lives, along
with the ability to help one another renew this commitment and apply these values
to the changing circumstances of your lives and the changing needs of the world.
We Jesuits will not abandon you—but neither will we continue to direct you! We
will be with you to guide and inspire, to challenge and to help. But we trust you
enough to carry forward in your lives and in the world the formation you have been
given": Fr. Kolvenbach, S.J., at the World Congress of Jesuit Alumni, Versailles. This
entire address is a development of the relationship between the Society of Jesus and
its former students. See note 24.

effective, a sharing of responsibility must be based on a *common vision* or common sense of purpose, noted above.

(138)   In the past the Rector of the Jesuit community, appointed by the Superior General of the Society of Jesus, was responsible for the direction of the Jesuit school; he reported regularly to the Jesuit Provincial. Today, in many parts of the world, the Rector of the community is not the "Director of the Work"; in some cases a governing board works in collaboration with the Society in the appointment of the director; more and more frequently this director is a lay person. Whatever the particular situation and whatever the mode of appointment, the responsibility entrusted to the director of a Jesuit school always includes a *mission that comes ultimately from the Society of Jesus.* This mission, as it relates to the Jesuit character of the school, is subject to periodic evaluation by the Society (normally through the Jesuit Provincial or his delegate).

(139)   The *role of the director* is that of an *apostolic leader.* The role is vital in providing inspiration, in the development of a common vision and in preserving unity within the educational community. Since the worldview of Ignatius is the basis on which a common vision is built, the director is guided by this worldview and is the one responsible for ensuring that opportunities are provided through which the other members of the community can come to a greater understanding of this worldview and its applications to education. In addition to his role of inspiration, the director remains *ultimately responsible* for the *execution of the basic educational policy* of the school and for the *distinctively Jesuit nature* of this education. The exact nature of this responsibility is described in the statutes of each school.

(140)   In many cases, responsibility for the Jesuit school is shared among several people with distinct roles (Rector, Director, President, Principal or Headmaster); the final responsibility for policy and practice is often entrusted to governing boards. All those sharing responsibility for the Jesuit school form a *directive team.* They are aware of and are open to the

Ignatian vision as this is applied to education; they are able to work together with mutual support and respect, making use of the talents of each. This type of team structure, which is an application of the principle of subsidiarity, has the advantage of bringing the abilities of more people into the leadership of the school; in addition, it ensures greater stability in carrying forward the policies that implement the basic orientation of the school.

(141)   If the school is "Jesuit," then sufficient authority and control remains in the hands of the Society of Jesus to enable that Society to respond to a call of the church through its institutions and to ensure that the Jesuit school continues to be faithful to its traditions. Except for this limitation, effective authority in the school can be exercised by anyone, Jesuit or lay, who has a knowledge of, sympathy for, identification with and commitment to the Jesuit character of education.

(142)   The structures of the school *guarantee* the *rights* of students, directors, teachers, and auxiliary staff, and *call each to his or her individual responsibilities.* All members of the community work together to create and maintain the conditions most favorable for each one to grow in the responsible use of freedom. Every member of the community is invited to be *actively engaged* in the growth of the entire community. The school structure reflects the new society that the school, through its education, is trying to construct.

(143)   9. *For Ignatius and for his companions, decisions were made on the basis of an ongoing process of individual and communal "discernment"*[74] *done always in a context of prayer.*

---

[74] The word "discernment" is used in many different contexts. Ignatius has "Rules for the Discernment of Spirits" in the *Spiritual Exercises,* §§ 313–36; in the present context it is rather the "communal apostolic discernment" practiced by the first companions and recommended by the 33rd General Congregation: a review of every work that includes "an attentiveness to the Word of God, an examination and reflection inspired by the Ignatian tradition; a personal and communitarian conversion necessary in order to become 'contemplatives in action'; an effort to live an indifference and availability that will enable us to find God in all things; and a transformation of our habitual patterns of thought through a constant interplay of experience, reflection and action. We must also always apply those criteria for action

Through prayerful reflection on the results of their activities, the companions reviewed past decisions and made adaptations in their methods, in a constant search for greater service to God ("magis").

(144)

> *Jesuit education:* adapts means and methods in order to achieve its purposes most effectively.
>
> is a "system" of schools with a common vision and common goals.
>
> assists in providing the professional training and ongoing formation that is needed, especially for teachers.

9.1 *Adaptation to achieve the purposes of Jesuit education.*

(145)   The educational community in a Jesuit school studies the needs of present-day society and then reflects on school policies, structures, methods, current pedagogical methods and all other elements of the school environment, to find *those means that will best accomplish the purposes of the school* and implement its educational philosophy. On the basis of these reflections *changes are made* in school structure, methods, curriculum, etc., when these are seen to be necessary or helpful. An educator in the Jesuit tradition is encouraged to exercise great freedom and imagination in the choice of teaching techniques, pedagogical methods, etc. *School policies and practices encourage reflection and evaluation*; they allow for change when change is necessary.

(146)   Though general norms need to be applied to concrete circumstances, principles on which this reflection is based can be found in current documents of the Church and of the Society of Jesus.[75] In addition, the Jesuit *Constitutions* provide criteria to guide discernment in order to achieve the "magis": the more universal good, the more urgent need, the more lasting value, work not being done by others, etc.[76]

---

found in the *Constitutions*, Part VII, as well as recent and more specific instructions": Decree 1, n. 40.

[75] One of the most recent and most complete sources is the letter on "Apostolic Discernment in Common" published by Father General Peter-Hans Kolvenbach in November 1986. It is a rich source of information on this topic, giving a historical perspective and also concrete suggestions.

[76] Cf. *Constitutions*, Part VII, esp. [622]–[624].

(147)   The "circumstances of persons and places" require that
courses of studies, educational processes, styles of teaching,
and the whole life of the school be *adapted to fit the specific
needs of the place* where the school is located, and the people
it serves.

9.2 *The Jesuit "system" of schools.*

(148)   The Jesuits in the first schools of the Society shared ideas
and the fruits of their experience, searching for the principles
and methods that would be "more" effective in accomplishing the purposes of their educational work. Each institution
applied these principles and methods to its own situation;
the strength of the Jesuit "system" grew out of this interchange. Jesuit schools still form a network, joined not by
unity of administration or uniformity of programs, but by a
common vision with common goals; teachers and administrators in Jesuit schools are again *sharing ideas and experiences*
in order to discover the principles and methods that will provide the most effective implementation of this common vision.

(149)   The interchange of ideas will be more effective if each
school is *inserted into the concrete reality* of the region in
which it is located and is engaged in an *ongoing exchange of
ideas and experiences with other schools* and educational
works of the local church and of the country. The broader
the interchange on the regional level, the more fruitful the
interchange among Jesuit schools can be on an international
level.

(150)   To aid in promoting this interchange of ideas and experiences an *exchange of teachers and students* is encouraged
wherever possible.

(151)   A wide variety of experimentation to discover more effective ways to make "the faith that does justice" a dimension of
educational work is going on in all parts of the world. Because
of the importance of this challenge, and the difficulty of
achieving it, these experiments need to be evaluated and the
results shared with others, so that positive experiences can be

incorporated into local school policies, practices and community. The need for an exchange of ideas and experiences in this area is especially great—not only for the individual schools, but also for the apostolate of education as such.

9.3 *Professional training and ongoing formation.*

(152)   Rapid change is typical of the modern world. In order to remain effective as educators and in order to "discern" the more concrete response to God's call, all adult members of the educational community need to take advantage of *opportunities for continuing education* and *continued personal development*—especially in professional competence, pedagogical techniques, and spiritual formation. The Jesuit school encourages this by providing staff development programs in every school and, as far as possible, providing the necessary time and financial assistance for more extended training and formation.

(153)   In order to achieve genuine collaboration and sharing of responsibility, *lay people need to have an understanding of Ignatian spirituality*, of Jesuit educational history and traditions and Jesuit life, while *Jesuits need to have an understanding of the* lived experience, challenges, and ways in which the Spirit of God also moves lay people, together with the *contributions lay people make* to the Church and to the Jesuit school. The Jesuit school provides special orientation programs to new members of staff; in addition, it provides ongoing programs and processes which encourage a growing awareness and understanding of the aims of Jesuit education, and also give an opportunity for Jesuits to learn from the lay members of the community. Where possible, special programs of professional and spiritual training are available to help lay people prepare themselves to assume directive posts in Jesuit schools.

SOME CHARACTERISTICS OF
JESUIT PEDAGOGY

(154)   Ignatius insisted that Jesuit schools should adopt the methods of the University of Paris (*"modus Parisiensis"*) because he considered these to be the most effective in achieving the goals he had in mind for these schools. The methods were tested and adapted by Jesuit educators in accordance with their religious experience in the *Spiritual Exercises* and their growing practical experience in education. Many of these principles and methods are still typical of Jesuit education because they are still effective in implementing the characteristics described in the previous sections. Some of the more widely known are listed in this final section by way of example.

A. From the experience of the *Spiritual Exercises*.[77]

(155) 1. Though there are obvious differences between the two situations, the *quality* of the relationship between the guide of the *Spiritual Exercises* and the person making them is the model for the relationship between teacher and student. Like the guide of the *Exercises*, the teacher is at the service of the students, alert to detect special gifts or special difficulties, personally concerned, and assisting in the development of the inner potential of each individual student.

---

[77] The dependence of Jesuit education on the principles and methods of the *Spiritual Exercises* has been the subject of much study. One of the classic—somewhat outdated, but still valuable—works that treat this matter in great detail is *La Pedagogie des Jesuites*, by François Charmot, S.J. (Paris, 1941). More recent treatments of the same subject can be found in "Reflections on the Educational Principles of the *Spiritual Exercises*," by Robert R. Newton, Monograph 1 (Washington, D.C.: Jesuit Secondary Education Association, 1977); and *Le Secret des Jésuites*, no. 57 of "Collection Christus" (Paris: Desclée de Brouwer, 1984).

(156)   2. The active role of the person making the *Exercises* is the model for the active role of the student in personal study, personal discovery and creativity.

(157)   3. The progression in the *Exercises* is one source of the practical, disciplined, "means to end" approach that is characteristic of Jesuit education.[78]

(158)   4. The "Presupposition" to the *Exercises*[79] is the norm for establishing personal relations and good rapport—between teachers and students, between teachers and school directors, among teachers, among students, and everywhere in the educational community.

(159)   5. Many of the "Annotations" or "suggestions for the guide to the *Exercises*" are, with appropriate adaptations, suggestions to teachers in a Jesuit school.

(160)   6. There are analogies between methods of the *Exercises* and traditional Jesuit teaching methods, many of which were incorporated into the *Ratio Studiorum*:
    a. *The "preludes" and "points" for prayer are the prelection of the course material to be covered;*
    b. *The "repetition" of prayer becomes the mastery of course material through frequent and careful repetition of class work;*
    c. *The "application of the senses" ("sentir" for Ignatius) is found in the stress on the creative and the imaginative, in the stress on experience, motivation, appreciation and joy in learning.*

---

[78] See section 1.

[79] Ignatius wrote the "Presupposition" of the *Spiritual Exercises* to indicate the relation between the guide to the Exercises and the person making them. It can be the norm for human relations in general, and especially within the educational community. What follows is a rather literal translation from the Spanish of Ignatius: "To assure better cooperation between the one who is giving the Exercises and the exercitant, and more beneficial results for both, it is necessary to suppose that every good Christian is more ready to put a good interpretation on another's statement than to condemn it as false. If an orthodox construction cannot be put on a proposition, the one who made it should be asked how he understands it. If he is in error, he should be corrected with all kindness. If this does not suffice, all appropriate means should be used to bring him to a correct interpretation, and so defend the proposition from error": *Spiritual Exercises*, § 22.

B. A few examples of directives from the *Constitutions* and *Ratio Studiorum.*

(161) 1. The curriculum is to be structured carefully in daily order, in the way that courses build on material covered in previous courses and in the way courses are related to one another. The curriculum should be so integrated that each individual course contributes toward the overall goal of the school.

(162) 2. The pedagogy is to include analysis, repetition, active reflection, and synthesis; it should combine theoretical ideas with their applications.

(163) 3. It is not the quantity of course material covered that is important but rather a solid, profound, and basic formation. (*"Non multa, sed multum."*)

CONCLUSION

(164)   The introduction refers to a meeting held in Rome in 1980, and to the address that Father Pedro Arrupe gave at the conclusion of that meeting. The address was later published under the title "Our Secondary Schools Today and Tomorrow" and has been quoted several times, both in the Characteristics themselves and in the notes.

(165)   In that address, Father Arrupe described the purpose of a Jesuit school. It is, he said, to assist in the formation of

> *New Persons*, transformed by the message of Christ, who will be witnesses to His death and resurrection in their own lives. Those who graduate from our secondary schools should have acquired, in ways proportional to their age and maturity, a way of life that is in itself a proclamation of the *charity* of Christ, of the *faith* that comes from Him and leads back to Him, and of the *justice* which he announced.[80]

(166)   More recently the present General of the Society of Jesus, Father Peter-Hans Kolvenbach, expressed the same purpose in very similar words:

> Our ideal is the well-rounded person who is intellectually competent, open to growth, religious, loving, and committed to doing justice in generous service to the people of God.[81]

(167)   The aim of Jesuit education has never been simply the acquisition of a store of information and skills or preparation for a career, though these are important in themselves and useful to emerging Christian leaders. The ultimate aim of Jesuit secondary education is, rather, that full growth of the

---

[80] OSS, § 12.

[81] "Talk of Father General Peter-Hans Kolvenbach at St. Paul's High School, Winnipeg, Canada: May 14, 1986"; published in the Newsletter of the Upper Canadian Jesuit Province, June 1986, 7–8.

person which leads to action—action that is suffused with the spirit and presence of Jesus Christ, the Man for Others.

(168)   The International Commission on the Apostolate of Jesuit Education has attempted to describe the characteristics of Jesuit education in order to help Jesuit schools to achieve this purpose more effectively. The material is not new; the paper is not complete; the work of renewal is never ended. A description of the characteristics of Jesuit education can never be perfect, and can never be final. But a growing understanding of the heritage of these schools, the Ignatian vision applied to education, can be the impetus to renewed dedication to this work, and renewed willingness to undertake those tasks which will make it ever more effective.

APPENDIX I: IGNATIUS, THE FIRST JESUIT SCHOOLS, AND THE *RATIO STUDIORUM*

A. *The Spiritual Journey of Ignatius of Loyola: 1491–1540*

> (This narration of the life of Ignatius is based on A *Pilgrim's Testament*,[82] an autobiography dictated to a fellow Jesuit three years before he died. In speaking, Ignatius consistently referred to himself in the third person.)

LOYOLA TO MONTSERRAT

(169)   Ignatius was a minor nobleman, born in 1491 in the family castle of Loyola in Basque country and brought up as a knight in the courts of Spain. In his autobiography he sums up the first twenty-six years of his life in one sentence: "he was a man given to the follies of the world; and what he enjoyed most was warlike sport, with a great and foolish desire to win fame"[83] The desire to win fame brought Ignatius to Pamplona to aid in the defense of that frontier city against French attack. The defense was hopeless; when, on May 20, 1521, he was hit by a cannon ball which shattered one leg and badly injured the other, Ignatius and the city of Pamplona both fell to the French forces.

(170)   French doctors cared for the badly wounded Ignatius and returned him to Loyola, where he spent a long convales-

---

[82] There are various translations of the Spanish and Italian original of what is often referred to as the "autobiography" of St. Ignatius. The translation used in the text is A *Pilgrim's Testament: The Memoirs of Ignatius of Loyola* [hereinafter *Memoirs*], trans. Parmananda R. Divarker (Rome: Gregorian University Press, 1983).

[83] *Memoirs*, § 1.

cence. In this forced period of inactivity he asked for books
to read and, out of boredom, accepted the only ones available—*The Lives of the Saints* and *The Life of Christ*. When
not reading, the romantic knight dreamed—at times of imi-
tating the deeds of St. Francis and St. Dominic, at times of
knightly deeds of valor in service of "a certain lady."[84] After
a time, he came to realize that "there was this difference.
When he was thinking of those things of the world, he took
much delight in them, but afterwards, when he was tired
and put them aside, he found himself dry and dissatisfied.
But when he thought of . . . practicing all the rigors that he
saw in the saints, not only was he consoled when he had
these thoughts, but even after putting them aside he remained satisfied and joyful. . . . His eyes were opened a
little, and he began to marvel at the difference and to reflect upon it. Little by little he came to recognize the difference between the spirits that were stirring."[85] Ignatius was
discovering God at work in his life; his desire for fame was
transformed into a desire to dedicate himself completely to
God, although he was still very unsure what this meant.
"The one thing he wanted to do was to go to Jerusalem as
soon as he recovered . . . with as much of disciplines and
fasts as a generous spirit, fired with God, would want to
perform."[86]

(171)   Ignatius began the journey to Jerusalem as soon as his recovery was complete. The first stop was the famous shrine of
Montserrat. On March 24, 1522, he laid his sword and dagger
"before the altar of Our Lady of Montserrat, where he had
resolved to lay aside his garments and to don the armor of
Christ."[87] He spent the whole night in vigil, a pilgrim's staff
in his hand. From Montserrat he journeyed to a town named
Manresa, intending to remain for only a few days. He remained for nearly a year.

---

[84] Ibid., § 6
[85] Ibid., § 8.
[86] Ibid., § 9.
[87] Ibid., § 17.

MANRESA

(172)   Ignatius lived as a pilgrim, begging for his basic needs and spending nearly all of his time in prayer. At first the days were filled with great consolation and joy, but soon prayer became torment and he experienced only severe temptations, scruples, and such great desolation that he wished "with great force to throw himself through a large hole in his room."[88] Finally peace returned. Ignatius reflected in prayer on the "good and evil spirits"[89] at work in experiences such as this, and he began to recognize that his freedom to respond to God was influenced by these feelings of "consolation" and "desolation." "God treated him at this time just as a schoolmaster treats a child whom he is teaching."[90]

(173)   The pilgrim gradually became more sensitive to the interior movements of his heart and the exterior influences of the surrounding world. He recognized God revealing His love and inviting a response, but he also recognized that his freedom to respond to that love could be helped or hindered by the way he dealt with these influences. He learned to respond in freedom to God's love by struggling to remove the obstacles to freedom. But "love is expressed in deeds."[91] The fullness of freedom led inevitably to total fidelity; the free response of Ignatius to the love of God took the form of loving service: a total dedication to the service of Christ who, for Ignatius the nobleman, was his "King." Because it was a response in love to God's love, it could never be enough; the logic of love demanded a response that was ever more (*"magis"*).

(174)   The conversion to loving service of God was confirmed in an experience that took place as he stopped to rest one day at the side of the river Cardoner. "While he was seated there, the eyes of his understanding began to be opened; not that

---

[88] Ibid., § 24.

[89] Ibid., § 25.

[90] Ibid., § 27.

[91] *Spiritual Exercises*, [230]. See note 8.

he saw any vision, but he understood and learned many things, both spiritual matters and matters of faith and of scholarship, and this with so great an enlightenment that everything seemed new to him. . . . He experienced a great clarity in his understanding. This was such that in the whole course of his life, after completing sixty-two years, even if he gathered up all the various helps he may have had from God and all the various things he has known, even adding them all together, he does not think he had got as much as at that one time."[92]

(175)   Ignatius recorded his experiences in a little book, a practice begun during his convalescence at Loyola. At first these notes were only for himself, but gradually he saw the possibility of a broader purpose. "When he noticed some things in his soul and found them useful, he thought they might also be useful to others, and so he put them in writing."[93] He had discovered God, and thus discovered the meaning of life. He took advantage of every opportunity to guide others through this same experience of discovery. As time went on, the notes took on a more structured form and became the basis for a small book called *The Spiritual Exercises*,[94] published in order to help others guide men and women through the experience of an interior freedom that leads to the faithful service of others in service of God.

(176)

> *The Spiritual Exercises* is not a book simply to be read; it is the guide to an experience, an active engagement enabling growth in the freedom that leads to faithful service. The experience of Ignatius at Manresa can become a personal lived experience.
>
> In the *Exercises* each person has the possibility of discovering that, though sinful, he or she is uniquely loved by God and invited to respond to His love. This response begins with an acknowledgment of sin and its

---

[92] *Memoirs*, § 30.
[93] Ibid., § 99.
[94] See note 8.

effects, a realization that God's love overcomes sin, and a desire for this forgiving and redeeming love. The freedom to respond is then made possible through a growing ability, with God's help, to recognize and engage in the struggle to overcome the interior and exterior factors that hinder a free response. This response develops positively through a process of seeking and embracing the will of God the Father, whose love was revealed in the person and life of His Son, Jesus Christ, and of discovering and choosing the specific ways in which this loving service of God is accomplished through active service on behalf of other men and women, within the heart of reality.

Jerusalem to Paris

(177)   Leaving Manresa in 1523, Ignatius continued his journey to Jerusalem. His experiences during the months at Manresa completed the break with his past life and confirmed his desire to give himself completely to God's service, but the desire was still not clearly focused. He wanted to stay in Jerusalem, visiting the holy places and serving others, but he was not permitted to remain in that troubled city. "After the pilgrim realized that it was not God's will that he remain in Jerusalem, he continually pondered within himself what he ought to do; and eventually he was rather inclined to study for some time so that he would be able to help souls, and he decided to go to Barcelona."[95] Though he was thirty years old he went to school, sitting in class beside the young boys of the city to learn grammar; two years later, he moved on to university studies at Alcala. When he was not studying he taught others about the ways of God and shared his Spiritual Exercises with them. But the Inquisition would not permit someone without training in theology to speak about spiritual things. Rather than keep silent about the one thing that

---

[95] *Memoirs*, § 50.

really mattered to him, and convinced that God was leading him, Ignatius left Alcala and went to Salamanca. The forces of the Inquisition continued to harass him until finally, in 1528, he left Spain entirely and moved to France and the University of Paris.

(178)   Ignatius remained in Paris for seven years. Though his preaching and direction in Barcelona, Alcala, and Salamanca had attracted companions who stayed with him for a time, it was at the University of Paris that a more lasting group of "friends in the Lord"[96] was formed. Peter Favre and Francis Xavier were his roommates, "whom he later won for God's service by means of the Spiritual Exercises."[97] Attracted by the same challenge, four others soon joined them. Each of these men experienced God's love personally, and their desire to respond was so complete that their lives were totally transformed. As each one shared this experience with the others, they formed a bond of community which was to last throughout their lives.

PARIS TO ROME

(179)   In 1534, this small group of seven companions journeyed together to a small monastery chapel in Montmartre, outside of Paris, and the only priest among them—Pierre Favre—celebrated a Mass at which they consecrated their lives to God through vows of poverty and chastity. It was during these days that they "determined what they would do, namely, go to Venice and Jerusalem, and spend their lives for the good of souls."[98] At Venice the six other companions were ordained as priests, Ignatius among them. But their decision to go to Jerusalem was not to become a reality.

(180)   Recurring warfare between Christian and Islamic armies made travel to the East impossible. While they waited for the tension to ease and pilgrim journeys to be resumed, the

---

[96] See note 62.
[97] *Memoirs*, § 82.
[98] Ibid., § 85.

companions spent their days preaching, giving the Exercises, working in hospitals and among the poor. Finally, when a year had passed and Jerusalem remained inaccessible, they decided that they would "return to Rome and present themselves to the Vicar of Christ so that he could make use of them wherever he thought it would be more for the glory of God and the good of souls."[99]

(181)   Their resolve to put themselves at the service of the Holy Father meant that they might be sent to different parts of the world, wherever the Pope had need of them; the "friends in the Lord" would be dispersed. It was only then that they decided to form a more permanent bond which would keep them united even when they were physically separated. They would add the vow of obedience, thus becoming a religious order.

(182)   Toward the end of their journey to Rome, at a small wayside chapel in the village of La Storta, Ignatius "was visited very especially by God. . . . He was at prayer in a church and experienced such a change in his soul and saw so clearly that God the Father placed him with Christ his Son that he would not dare doubt it—that God the Father had placed him with his Son."[100] The companions became Companions of Jesus, to be intimately associated with the risen Christ's work of redemption, carried out in and through the Church, working in the world. Service of God in Christ Jesus became service in the Church and of the Church in its redemptive mission.

(183)   In 1539 the companions, now ten, were received favorably by Pope Paul III, and the Society of Jesus was formally approved in 1540; a few months later, Ignatius was elected its first Superior General.

B. *The Society of Jesus Enters Education: 1540–1556.*

(184)   Even though all of the first companions of Ignatius were graduates of the University of Paris, the original purposes of

---

[99] Ibid.
[100] Ibid., § 96.

the Society of Jesus did not include educational institutions. As described in the "Formula" presented to Paul III for his approval, the Society of Jesus was founded "to strive especially for the defense and propagation of the faith and for the progress of souls in Christian life and doctrine, by means of public preaching, lectures, and any other ministration whatsoever of the word of God, and further by means of the Spiritual Exercises, the education of children and unlettered persons in Christianity, and the spiritual consolation of Christ's faithful through hearing confessions and administering the other sacraments."[101] Ignatius wanted Jesuits to be free to move from place to place wherever the need was greatest; he was convinced that institutions would tie them down and prevent this mobility. But the companions had only one goal: "in all things to love and serve the Divine Majesty";[102] they would adopt whatever means could best accomplish this love and service of God through the service of others.

(185)   The positive results to be obtained from the education of young boys soon became apparent, and it was not long before Jesuits became involved in this work. Francis Xavier, writing from Goa, India, in 1542, was enthusiastic in his description of the effect Jesuits there were having when they offered instruction at St. Paul's College; Ignatius responded with encouragement. A college had been established in Gandia, Spain, for the education of those preparing to join the Society of Jesus; at the insistence of parents it began, in 1546, to admit other boys of the city. The first "Jesuit school," in the sense of an institution intended primarily for young lay students, was founded in Messina, Sicily, only two years later. And when it became apparent that education was not only an apt means for human and spiritual development but also an effective instrument for defending a faith under attack by the Reformers, the number of Jesuit schools began to increase very rapidly: before his death in 1556, Ignatius personally approved the foundation of 40 schools. For centuries, religious congregations had contributed to the growth of education in

---

[101] "Formula," [3]. See notes 3 and 7.
[102] *Spiritual Exercises*, § 233.

philosophy and theology. For the members of this new order to extend their educational work to the humanities and even to running the schools, was something new in the life of the Church; it needed formal approval by Papal decree.

(186)   Ignatius, meanwhile, remained in Rome and dedicated the last years of his life to writing the *Constitutions*[103] of this new religious order.

(187)

> Inspired by the same vision embodied in the *Spiritual Exercises*, the *Constitutions* manifest the Ignatian ability to combine exalted ends with the most exact and concrete means for achieving them. The work, divided into ten "Parts," is a formative guidebook for Jesuit life.
>
> In its first draft, Part IV consisted of directives for the education of young men being formed as Jesuits. Since he was approving the establishment of new schools at the same time as he was writing the *Constitutions*, Ignatius partly revised Part IV to include the guiding educational principles for the work that was to be undertaken in these schools. This section of the *Constitutions* is, therefore, the best source for the explicit and direct thought of Ignatius on the apostolate of education, even though it was largely completed before he realized the extensive role education was to play in the apostolic work of Jesuits.
>
> The preamble to Part IV sets the goal: "The aim which the Society of Jesus directly seeks is to aid its own members and their fellowmen to attain the ultimate end for which they were created. To achieve this purpose, in addition to the example of one's life, learning and a method of expounding it are also necessary."[104]
>
> The priorities in the formation of Jesuits became priorities of Jesuit education: a stress on the humanities, to be followed by philosophy and theology,[105] a careful

---

[103] See note 7.
[104] *Constitutions*, [307].
[105] Ibid., [351].

orderly advance to be observed in pursuing these successive branches of knowledge,[106] repetition of the material and active involvement of the students in their
own education.[107] Much time should be spent in developing good style in writing.[108] The role of the Rector, as
the center of authority, inspiration and unity, is essential.[109] These were not new pedagogical methods; Ignatius was familiar with lack of method, and with the
methods of many schools, especially the careful methods of the University of Paris. He chose and adapted
those which would be most effective in achieving the
purposes of Jesuit education.

When speaking explicitly about schools for lay students in Part IV, chapter 7, Ignatius is specific about only
a few matters. He insists, for example, that the students
(at that time nearly all Christians), be "well-instructed
in Christian doctrine."[110] Also, in accordance with the
principle that there be no temporal remuneration for any
Jesuit ministry, no fees are to be charged.[111] Except for
these and a few other details, he is content to apply a
basic principle found throughout the *Constitutions*:
"Since there must be a great variety in particular cases in
accordance with the circumstances of place and persons,
this present treatment will not descend further to what
is particular, except to say that there should be rules
which come down to everything necessary in each college."[112] In a later note, he adds a suggestion: "From the
Rules of the Roman College, the part which is suitable
to the other colleges can be adapted to them."[113]

(188)   In separate correspondence, Ignatius promised further development of the rules, or basic principles, which should gov-

---

[106] Ibid., [366].
[107] Ibid., [375] and [378].
[108] Ibid., [381].
[109] Ibid., [421]–[439].
[110] Ibid., [395].
[111] Ibid., [398].
[112] Ibid., [395].
[113] Ibid., [396]. The Roman College was established by Ignatius himself in 1551;

ern all the schools. But he insisted that he could not provide these principles until he could derive them from the concrete experiences of those actually engaged in education. Before he could fulfill his promise, Ignatius died. It was the early morning of July 31, 1556.

C. *The Ratio Studiorum and More Recent History*

(189)   In the years following the death of Ignatius, not all Jesuits agreed that involvement in schools was a proper activity for the Society of Jesus; it was a struggle that lasted well into the 17th Century. Nevertheless, Jesuit involvement in education continued to grow at a rapid rate. Of the 40 schools that Ignatius had personally approved, at least 35 were in operation when he died, even though the total membership of the Society of Jesuits had not yet reached 1,000. Within forty years, the number of Jesuit schools would reach 245. The promised development of a document describing common principles for all Jesuit schools was becoming a practical necessity.

(190)   Successive Jesuit superiors encouraged an exchange of ideas based on concrete experiences so that, without violating the Ignatian principle that "circumstances of place and persons" be taken into account, a basic curriculum and basic pedagogy could be developed which would draw on this experience and be common to all Jesuit schools. A period of intense interchange among the schools of the Society followed.

(191)   The first drafts of a common document were, as Ignatius had wished, based on the "Rules of the Roman College." An international committee of six Jesuits was appointed by the Superior General Claudio Acquaviva; they met in Rome to adapt and modify these tentative drafts on the basis of experiences in other parts of the world. In 1586 and again in 1591, this group published more comprehensive drafts which were widely distributed for comments and corrections. Further in-

---

though its beginnings were very modest, he wished it to become the model for all Jesuit schools throughout the world. It developed in time into a university, whose name was changed to Gregorian University after the unification of Italy.

terchange, commission meetings and editorial work resulted, finally, in the publication of a definitive *Ratio Studiorum*[114] on January 8, 1599.

(192)

In its final form the *Ratio Studiorum*, or "Plan of Studies" for Jesuit schools, is a handbook to assist teachers and administrators in the daily operation of the school; it is a series of "rules" or practical directives regarding such matters as the government of the school, the formation and distribution of teachers, the curriculum and methods of teaching. Like Part IV of the *Constitutions*, it is not so much an original work as a collection of the most effective educational methods of the time, tested and adapted for the purposes of the Jesuit schools.

There is little explicit reference to underlying principles flowing from the experience of Ignatius and his Companions, as these were embodied in the *Spiritual Exercises* and the *Constitutions*; such principles had been stated in earlier versions, but were presupposed in the final edition of 1599. The relationship between teacher and student, to take one example, is to be modeled on the relationship between the director of the *Exercises* and the person making them; since the authors of the *Ratio*, along with nearly all the teachers in the schools, were Jesuits, this could be assumed. Even though it is not stated explicitly, the spirit of the *Ratio*—like the inspiring spirit of the first Jesuit schools—was the vision of Ignatius.

(193)   The process leading to and resulting in the publication of the *Ratio* produced a "system" of schools whose strength

---

[114] The original Latin of the *Ratio Studiorum* of 1599, along with the previous drafts, has been newly published as vol. 5 of *Monumenta Paedagogica Societatis Iesu*, ed. Ladislaus Lukacs, S.J. (Rome: Institutum Historicum Societatis Iesu, 1986). An English translation is available, *The Jesuit Ratio Studiorum of 1599*, translated with an introduction and explanatory notes by Allan P. Farrell, S.J. (Washington, D.C.: The Jesuit Conference, 1970).

and influence lay in the common spirit that evolved into common pedagogical principles. The pedagogy was based on experience, then refined and adapted through constant interchange. It was the first such educational system that the world had ever seen.

(194)   The system of Jesuit schools developed and expanded for more than two hundred years, and then came to a sudden and tragic end. When the Society of Jesus was suppressed by Papal order in 1773 a network of 845 educational institutions, spread throughout Europe and the Americas, Asia and Africa, was largely destroyed. Only a few Jesuit schools remained in Russian territories, where the suppression never took effect.

(195)   When Pius VII was about to bring the Society of Jesus back into existence in 1814, one of the reasons he gave for his action was "so that the Catholic Church could have, once again, the benefit of their educational experience."[115] Educational work did begin again almost immediately and a short time later, in 1832, an experimental revision of the *Ratio Studiorum* was published. But it was never definitively approved. The turmoil of 19th Century Europe, marked by revolutions and frequent expulsions of Jesuits from various countries—and therefore from their schools—prevented any genuine renewal in the philosophy or pedagogy of Jesuit education; often enough the Society itself was divided, and its educational institutions were enlisted in the ideological support of one or the other side of warring nations. Nevertheless, in difficult situations, and especially in the developing nations of the Americas, India, and East Asia, the schools of the Society began once again to flourish.

(196)   The 20th Century, especially in the years after the Second World War, brought a dramatic increase in the size and number of Jesuit Schools. The seeds of a renewed spirit were planted in the decrees of various General Congregations, notably the applications of the Second Vatican Council that

---

[115] From the Papal Bull *Sollicitudo Omnium Ecclesiarum* of August 7, 1814, by which the Society of Jesus was restored throughout the world.

were incorporated into decree 28 of General Congregation XXXI. Today, the Jesuit educational apostolate extends to more than 2,000 educational institutions, of a bewildering variety of types and levels. 10,000 Jesuits work in close collaboration with nearly 100,000 lay people, providing education for more than 1,500,000 young people and adults in 56 countries around the world.

(197)   Jesuit education today does not and cannot form the unified system of the 17th Century, and though many principles of the original *Ratio* remain valid today, a uniform curriculum and a structure imposed on all schools throughout the world has been replaced by the distinct needs of different cultures and religious faiths and the refinement of pedagogical methods that vary from culture to culture.

(198)   This does not mean that a Jesuit "system" of education is no longer a possibility. It was the common spirit, the vision of Ignatius, that enabled the Jesuit schools of the 16th Century to evolve common principles and methods; it was the common spirit joined to a common goal—as much as the more specific principles and methods embodied in the *Ratio*—that created the Jesuit school system of the 17th Century. This same common spirit, along with the basic goals, purposes and policies that follow from it, can be true of "Jesuit" schools of today in all countries throughout the world, even when more concrete applications are very different, or when many of the details of school life are determined by cultural factors or outside agencies.

Appendix B

Ignatian Pedagogy: A Practical Approach, 1993

Reproduced with permission from The General Curia of the Society of Jesus, Borgo Santo Spiritu, 5, 00193 Rome, Italy, December 3, 1986.

CONTENTS

FOREWORD

The publication of *The Characteristics of Jesuit Education* in 1986 aroused a renewed interest in Jesuit education among teachers, administrators, students, parents and others around the world. It has given them a sense of identity and purpose. That document, translated into 13 languages, has been the focus for seminars, workshops, and study. Reactions have been overwhelmingly positive.

In recent years a question has been heard from diverse parts of the world. How can we make the principles and orientation of *The Characteristics* more useable for **teachers**? How can Ignatian values be incorporated in a practical pedagogy for use in the daily interaction between teachers and students in the classroom?

The International Commission on the Apostolate of Jesuit Education (ICAJE) has been working for over three years to respond to this question. With help from reactions and suggestions of lay and Jesuit educators the world over, seven drafts were written for this paper introducing the *Ignatian Pedagogical Paradigm*. From the outset, however, we were convinced that no document alone would help teachers to make the adaptations in pedagogical approach and teaching method required in Ignatian education. To be successful in bringing the *Ignatian Pedagogical Paradigm* into regular use in Jesuit schools, members of the International Commission are convinced that staff development programs in each province and school are essential. Teachers need much more than a cognitive introduction to the Paradigm. They require practical training that engages and enables them to reflect on the experience of using these new methods confidently and effectively. For this reason, ICAJE has worked, from the start, on a **project** to help teachers.

THE IGNATIAN PEDAGOGY PROJECT INCLUDES:

1) **an introductory document on the *Ignatian Pedagogical Paradigm*** as a development of Part 10 of the *Characteristics*; and

2) **a program of staff development** at regional, province and school levels. The school staff development programs should last from three to four years in order to enable teachers gradually to master and be comfortable with Ignatian pedagogical approaches.

To make this project effective and introduce practical staff development programs at school level, groups of people in provinces around the world are currently being trained in the *Ignatian Pedagogical Paradigm* and appropriate teaching methods. Indeed, this whole process was initiated at an International Training Workshop held at Villa Cavalletti, just outside Rome, April 20–30, 1993. Six people from Jesuit education from each continent (a total of approximately 40 people from 26 nations) were invited to be **trained,** i.e., to learn about, practice, and master some of the key pedagogical methods involved. They, in turn, are preparing training workshops for teams of people from provinces in their areas of the world, who in turn will be equipped to initiate school level staff development programs.

Without the assistance of the training team at Villa Cavalletti and the generous participants in the international workshop there, the process of bringing the Ignatian Pedagogy Project to our teachers simply would not be possible. I am, therefore, very grateful to all of these people who are truly at the service of Jesuit education worldwide.

I offer special thanks to the members of the International Commission on the Apostolate of Jesuit Education who have worked assiduously for over three years—in writing seven drafts of this introductory paper, as well as developing the pedagogical processes which comprise the substance of the Ignatian Pedagogy Project. Members of ICAJE represent experience and cultural points of view from the far-flung corners of the world: Fr. Agustin Alonso, S.J. (Europe), Fr. Anthony Berridge, S.J. (Africa and Madagascar), Fr. Charles Costello, S.J. (North America), Fr. Daven Day S.J. (East Asia), Fr. Gregory Naik, S.J. (South Asia) and Fr. Pablo Sada, S.J. (Latin America).

In advance, I thank Provincials, their assistants for education, teachers, administrators, members of governing boards whose encouragement and cooperation in this global effort to renew our educational apostolate is crucial.

Finally, I acknowledge the generous financial assistance we have received from three foundations which wish to remain anonymous. Their participation in our efforts is a notable example of the interest and cooperation which characterizes the worldwide community of Jesuit education.

Vincent J. Duminuco, S.J.
Secretary of Education
Society of Jesus

INTRODUCTORY NOTES

(1) This document grows out of the 10th part of *The Characteristics of Jesuit Education* in response to many requests for help in formulating a practical pedagogy which is consistent with and effective in communicating the Ignatian worldview and values presented in the *Characteristics* document. It is essential, therefore, that what is said here be understood in conjunction with the substantive Ignatian spirit and apostolic thrust presented in *The Characteristics of Jesuit Education*.

(2) The field of Jesuit pedagogy has been discussed in numerous books and scholarly articles over the centuries. In this paper we treat only some aspects of this pedagogy which serve to introduce a practical teaching strategy. The Ignatian pedagogical paradigm proposed here can help to unify and incarnate many of the principles enunciated in *The Characteristics of Jesuit Education*.

(3) It is obvious that a universal curriculum for Jesuit schools or colleges similar to that proposed in the original *Ratio Studiorum* is impossible today. However, it does seem important and consistent with the Jesuit tradition to have a systematically organized pedagogy whose substance and methods promote the explicit vision of the contemporary Jesuit educational mission. Responsibility for cultural *adaptations* is best handled at the regional or local level. What seems more appropriate at a more universal level today is an Ignatian pedagogical paradigm which can help teachers and students to focus their work in a manner that is academically sound and at the same time formative of persons for others.

(4) The pedagogical paradigm proposed here involves a particular style and process of teaching. It calls for *infusion* of approaches to value learning and growth *within existing curricula*

rather than adding courses. We believe that such an approach is preferable both because it is more realistic in light of already crowded curricula in most educational institutions, and because this approach has been found to be more effective in helping learners to interiorize and act upon the Ignatian values set out in *The Characteristics of Jesuit Education.*

(5) We call this document *Ignatian Pedagogy* since it is intended not only for formal education provided in Jesuit schools, colleges and universities, but it can be helpful in every form of educational service that in one way or other is inspired by the experience of St. Ignatius recorded in the *Spiritual Exercises*, in Part IV of the *Constitutions of the Society of Jesus*, and in the Jesuit *Ratio Studiorum.*

(6) Ignatian Pedagogy is inspired by faith. But even those who do not share this faith can gather valuable experiences from this document because the pedagogy inspired by St. Ignatius is profoundly human and consequently *universal.*

(7) Ignatian pedagogy from its beginnings has been eclectic in selection of methods for teaching and learning. Ignatius Loyola himself adapted the "modus Parisiensis," the ordered pedagogical approach employed at the University of Paris in his day. This was integrated with a number of the methodological principles he had previously developed for use in the *Spiritual Exercises.* To be sure, the sixteenth-century Jesuits lacked the formal, scientifically tested methods proposed, for example, in developmental psychology in recent times. Attention to care for the individual student made these Jesuit teachers attentive to what really helped learning and human growth. And they shared their findings across many parts of the world, verifying more universally effective pedagogical methods. These were specified in the *Ratio Studiorum*, the Jesuit code of liberal education which became normative for all Jesuit schools. (A brief description of some of these methods is presented in Appendix 2.)

(8) Over the centuries a number of other specific methods more scientifically developed by other educators have been adopted within Jesuit pedagogy *insofar as they contribute to the goals of Jesuit education.* A perennial characteristic of Ignatian ped-

agogy is the ongoing systematic incorporation of methods from a variety of sources which better contribute to the integral intellectual, social, moral and religious formation of the whole person.

(9) This document is only one part of a comprehensive, long-term renewal project which has been in progress for several years with such programs as the Colloquium on the Ministry of Teaching, the Curriculum Improvement Process, the Magis Program and the like. Renewal requires a change of heart, an openness of mind and spirit to break new ground for the good of one's students. Thus, building on previous stages of renewal this document aims to move a major step ahead by introducing Ignatian Pedagogy through understanding and *practice* of methods that are appropriate to achieve the goals of Jesuit education. This paper, therefore, must be accompanied by practical staff development programs which enable teachers to learn and to be comfortable with a structure for teaching and learning the Ignatian Pedagogical Paradigm and specific methods to facilitate its use. To assure that this can happen, educators, lay and Jesuit, from all continents are being trained to provide leadership in staff development programs at regional, province and local school levels.

(10) The *Ignatian Pedagogy Project* is addressed in the first instance to teachers. For it is especially in their daily interaction with students in the learning process that the goals and objectives of Jesuit education can be realized. How a teacher relates to students, how a teacher conceives of learning, how a teacher engages students in the quest for truth, what a teacher expects of students, a teacher's own integrity and ideals—all of these have significant formative effects upon student growth. Fr. Kolvenbach takes note of the fact that "Ignatius appears to place teachers' personal example ahead of learning as an apostolic means to help students grow in values." (See Appendix 2, ¶125.) It goes without saying that in schools, administrators, members of governing boards, staff and other members of the school community also have indispensable and key roles in promoting the environment and learning processes that can contribute to the ends of Ignatian Pedagogy. It is important, therefore, to share this project with them.

IGNATIAN PEDAGOGY

(11)   Pedagogy is the way in which teachers accompany learners in their growth and development. Pedagogy, the art and science of teaching, cannot simply be reduced to methodology. It must include a worldview and a vision of the ideal human person to be educated. These provide the goal, the end towards which all aspects of an educational tradition are directed. They also provide criteria for choices of means to be used in the process of education. The worldview and ideal of Jesuit education for our time has been expressed in *The Characteristics of Jesuit Education*. Ignatian Pedagogy assumes that worldview and moves one step beyond, suggesting more explicit ways in which Ignatian values can be incarnated in the teaching-learning process.

THE GOAL OF JESUIT EDUCATION

(12)   What is our goal? *The Characteristics of Jesuit Education* offers a description which has been amplified by Father General Kolvenbach:

> The pursuit of each student's intellectual development to the full measure of God-given talents rightly remains a prominent goal of Jesuit education. Its aim, however, has never been simply to amass a store of information or preparation for a profession, though these are important in themselves and useful to emerging Christian leaders. The ultimate aim of Jesuit education is, rather, that full growth of the person which leads to action—action, especially, that is suffused with the spirit and presence of Jesus Christ, the Son of God, the Man-for-Others. This goal of action, based on sound understanding and enlivened by contemplation, urges students to self-discipline and initiative, to integrity and accuracy. At the same time, it judges slip-shod or superficial ways of thinking unworthy of the indi-

vidual and, more important, dangerous to the world he or she is called to serve.[1]

(13) Fr. Arrupe summarized this by pointing to our educational goal as "forming men and women for others." Fr. Kolvenbach has described the hoped-for graduate of a Jesuit school as a person who is "well-rounded, intellectually competent, open to growth, religious, loving, and committed to doing justice in generous service to the people of God." Fr. Kolvenbach also states our goal when he says: "We aim to form leaders in service, in imitation of Christ Jesus, men and women of competence, conscience and compassionate commitment."

(14) Such a goal requires a full and deeper formation of the human person, an educational process of formation that calls for excellence—a striving to excel, to achieve one's potential—that encompasses the intellectual, the academic and more. It calls for a human excellence modeled on Christ of the Gospels, an excellence that reflects the mystery and reality of the Incarnation, an excellence that reveres the dignity of all people as well as the holiness of all creation. There are sufficient examples from history of educational excellence narrowly conceived, of people extraordinarily advanced intellectually who, at the same time, remain emotionally undeveloped and morally immature. We are beginning to realize that education does not inevitably humanize or Christianize people and society. We are losing faith in the naive notion that all education, regardless of its quality or thrust or purpose, will lead to virtue. Increasingly, then, it becomes clear that if we in Jesuit education are to exercise a moral force in society, we must insist that the process of education takes place in a moral as well as an intellectual framework. This is not to suggest a program of indoctrination that suffocates the spirit; neither does it look for the introduction of theoretical courses which are speculative and remote from reality. What is needed is a framework of inquiry for the process of wrestling with significant issues and complex values of life, and teachers capable and willing to guide that inquiry.

---

[1] Cf. *Characteristics*, ¶167; and Peter-Hans Kolvenbach, S.J., address, Georgetown, 1989.

Towards a Pedagogy for Faith and Justice

(15)   Young men and women should be free to walk a path whereby
        they are enabled to grow and develop as fully human persons.
        In today's world, however, there is a tendency to view the aim
        of education in excessively utilitarian terms. Exaggerated em-
        phasis of financial success can contribute to extreme competi-
        tiveness and absorption with selfish concerns. As a result, that
        which is human in a given subject or discipline may be dimin-
        ished in students' consciousness. This can easily obscure the
        true values and aims of humanistic education. To avoid such
        distortion, teachers in Jesuit schools present academic sub-
        jects out of a human centeredness, with stress on uncovering
        and exploring the patterns, relationships, facts, questions, in-
        sights, conclusions, problems, solutions, and implications
        which a particular discipline brings to light about what it
        means to be a human being. Education thus becomes a care-
        fully reasoned investigation through which the student forms
        or reforms his or her habitual attitudes towards other people
        and the world.

(16)   From a Christian standpoint, the model for human life—and
        therefore the ideal of a humanely educated individual—is the
        person of Jesus. Jesus teaches us by word and example that the
        realization of our fullest human potential is achieved ulti-
        mately in our union with God, a union that is sought and
        reached through a loving, just and compassionate relationship
        with our brothers and sisters. Love of God, then, finds true
        expression in our daily love of neighbor, in our compassionate
        care for the poor and suffering, in our deeply human concern
        for others as God's people. It is a love that gives witness to
        faith and speaks out through action on behalf of a new world
        community of justice, love and peace.

(17)   The mission of the Society of Jesus today as a religious order
        in the Catholic Church is the service of faith of which the
        promotion of justice is an essential element. It is a mission
        rooted in the belief that a new world community of justice,
        love and peace needs educated persons of competence, con-
        science and compassion, men and women who are ready to

embrace and promote all that is fully human, who are committed to working for the freedom and dignity of all peoples, and who are willing to do so in cooperation with others equally dedicated to the reform of society and its structures. Renewal of our social, economic and political systems so that they nourish and preserve our common humanity and free people to be generous in their love and care for others requires resilient and resourceful persons. It calls for persons, educated in faith and justice, who have a powerful and ever growing sense of how they can be effective advocates, agents and models of God's justice, love and peace within as well as beyond the ordinary opportunities of daily life and work.

(18) Accordingly, education in faith and for justice begins with a reverence for the freedom, right and power of individuals and communities to create a different life for themselves. It means assisting young people to enter into the sacrifice and joy of sharing their lives with others. It means helping them to discover that what they most have to offer is who they are rather than what they have. It means helping them to understand and appreciate that other people are their richest treasure. It means walking with them in their own journeys towards greater knowledge, freedom and love. This is an essential part of the new evangelization to which the Church calls us.

(19) Thus education in Jesuit schools seeks to transform how youth look at themselves and other human beings, at social systems and societal structures, at the global community of humankind and the whole of natural creation. If truly successful, Jesuit education results ultimately in a radical transformation not only of the way in which people habitually think and act, but of the very way in which they live in the world, men and women of competence, conscience and compassion, seeking the *greater good* in terms of what can be done out of a faith commitment with justice to enhance the quality of peoples' lives, particularly among God's poor, oppressed and neglected.

(20) To achieve our goal as educators in Jesuit schools, we need a pedagogy that endeavors to form men and women for others in a postmodern world where so many forces are at work which

are antithetical to that aim.[2] In addition we need an ongoing formation for ourselves as teachers to be able to provide this pedagogy effectively. There are, moreover, many places where governmental entities define the limits of educational programs and where teacher training is counterproductive to a pedagogy which encourages student activity in learning, fosters growth in human excellence, and promotes formation in faith and values along with the transmission of knowledge and skill as integral dimensions of the learning process. This describes the real situation facing many of us who are teachers and administrators in Jesuit schools. It poses a complex apostolic challenge as we embark daily on our mission to win the trust and faith of new generations of youth, to walk with them along the pathway towards truth, to help them work for a just world filled with the compassion of Christ.

(21) How do we do this? Since the publication in 1986 of *The Characteristics of Jesuit Education*, a frequent question of teachers and administrators alike in Jesuit schools has been: "How can we achieve what is proposed in this document, the educational formation of youth to be men and women for others, in the face of present-day realities?" The answer necessarily must be relevant to many cultures; it must be usable in different situations; it must be applicable to various disciplines; it must appeal to multiple styles and preferences. Most importantly, it must speak to teachers of the realities as well as the ideals of teaching. All of this must be done, moreover, with particular regard for the preferential love of the poor which characterizes the mission of the Church today. It is a hard challenge and one that we cannot disregard, because it goes to the heart of what is the apostolate of Jesuit education. The solution is not simply to exhort our teachers and administrators to greater dedication. What we need, rather, is a model of how to proceed that promotes the goal of Jesuit education, a paradigm that speaks to the teaching-learning process, that addresses the teacher-learner relationship, and that has practical meaning and application for the classroom.

---

[2] Such as secularism, materialism, pragmatism, utilitarianism, fundamentalism, racism, nationalism, sexism, consumerism—to name but a few.

(22) The first decree of the 33rd General Congregation of the Society of Jesus, "Companions of Jesus Sent into Today's World," encourages Jesuits in the regular apostolic discernment of their ministries, both traditional and new. Such a review, it recommends, should be attentive to the Word of God and should be inspired by the Ignatian tradition. In addition, it should allow for a transformation of peoples' habitual patterns of thought through a **constant interplay of experience, reflection and action.**[3] It is here that we find the outline of a model for bringing *The Characteristics of Jesuit Education* to life in our schools today, through a way of proceeding that is thoroughly consistent with the goal of Jesuit education and totally in line with the mission of the Society of Jesus. We turn our consideration, then, to an Ignatian paradigm that gives preeminence to the constant interplay of EXPERIENCE, REFLECTION and ACTION.

PEDAGOGY OF THE *Spiritual Exercises*

(23) A distinctive feature of the Ignatian pedagogical paradigm is that, understood in the light of the *Spiritual Exercises* of St. Ignatius, it becomes not only a fitting description of the continual interplay of experience, reflection and action in the teaching-learning process, but also an ideal portrayal of the dynamic interrelationship of teacher and learner in the latter's journey of growth in knowledge and freedom.

(24) Ignatius' *Spiritual Exercises* is a little book that was never meant to be read, at least as most books are. It was intended, rather, to be used as a way to proceed in guiding others through experiences of prayer wherein they might meet and converse with the living God, come honestly to grips with the truth of their values and beliefs, and make free and deliberate choices about the future course of their lives. The *Spiritual Exercises*, carefully construed and annotated in Ignatius' little manual, are not meant to be merely cognitive activities or devotional practices. They are, instead, rigorous exercises of

---

[3] Decree 1, nos. 42–43 (emphasis added).

the spirit wholly engaging the body, mind, heart and soul of the human person. Thus they offer not only matters to be pondered, but also realities to be contemplated, scenes to be imagined, feelings to be evaluated, possibilities to be explored, options to be considered, alternatives to be weighed, judgments to be reached and choices of action to be made—all with the expressed aim of helping individuals to seek and find the will of God at work in the radical ordering of their lives.

(25)   A fundamental dynamic of the *Spiritual Exercises* of Ignatius is the continual call to reflect upon the entirety of one's experience in prayer in order to discern where the Spirit of God is leading. Ignatius urges reflection on human experience as an essential means of validating its authenticity, because without prudent reflection delusion readily becomes possible and without careful reflection the significance of one's experience may be neglected or trivialized. Only after adequate reflection on experience and interior appropriation of the meaning and implications of what one studies can one proceed freely and confidently towards choosing appropriate courses of action that foster the integral growth of oneself as a human being. Hence, reflection becomes a pivotal point for Ignatius in the movement from experience to action, so much so that he consigns to the director or guide of persons engaged in the *Spiritual Exercises* primary responsibility for facilitating their progress in reflection.

(26)   For Ignatius, the vital dynamic of the *Spiritual Exercises* is the individual person's encounter with the Spirit of Truth. It is not surprising, therefore, that we find in his principles and directions for guiding others in the process of the *Spiritual Exercises* a perfect description of the pedagogical role of teacher as one whose job is not merely to inform but to help the student progress in the truth.[4] If they are to use the *Ignatian Pedagogical*

---

[4] This fundamental insight into the Ignatian Paradigm of the *Spiritual Exercises* and its implications for Jesuit education was explored by François Charmot, S.J. in *La Pédagogie des Jésuites: Ses principes—Son actualité* (Paris: Aux Editions Spes, 1943). "Further convincing information may be found in the first ten chapters of the directory of the *Spiritual Exercises*. Applied to education, they place in relief the pedagogical principle that the teacher is not merely to inform, but to help the student progress in the truth." (A note summarizing a section of the book in which

Paradigm successfully, teachers must be sensitive to their own experience, attitudes, opinions lest they impose their own agenda on their students. (Cf. paragraph ¶111.)

(27) Applying, then, the Ignatian paradigm to the teacher-learner relationship in Jesuit education, it is the teacher's primary role to facilitate the growing relationship of the learner with truth, particularly in the matter of the subject being studied under the guiding influence of the teacher. The teacher creates the conditions, lays the foundations and provides the opportunities for the continual interplay of the student's EXPERIENCE, REFLECTION and ACTION to occur.

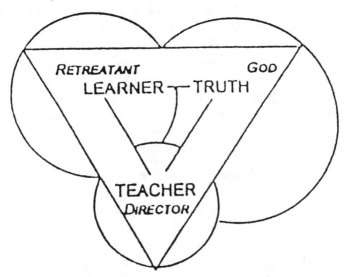

Figure 1. Ignatian Paradigm and the teacher-learner relationship.

(28) Starting with EXPERIENCE, the teacher creates the conditions whereby students gather and recollect the material of their own experience in order to distill what they understand already in terms of facts, feelings, values, insights and intuitions they bring

Charmot describes the role of the teacher according to the *Exercises*, taken from an unofficial annotation and translation of sections of Charmot's work by Michael Kurimay, S.J.).

to the subject matter at hand. Later the teacher guides the students in assimilating new information and further experience so that their knowledge will grow in completeness and truth. The teacher lays the foundations for learning how to learn by engaging students in skills and techniques of REFLECTION. Here memory, understanding, imagination and feelings are used to grasp the essential meaning and value of what is being studied, to discover its relationship to other facets of human knowledge and activity, and to appreciate its implications in the continuing search for truth. Reflection should be a formative and liberating process that so shapes the consciousness of students—their habitual attitudes, values and beliefs as well as ways of thinking— that they are impelled to move beyond knowing to ACTION. It is then the role of the teacher to see that the opportunities are provided that will challenge the imagination and exercise the will of the students to choose the best possible course of action to flow from and follow up on what they have learned. What they do as a result under the teacher's direction, while it may not immediately transform the world into a global community of justice, peace and love, should at least be an educational step in that direction and towards that goal even if it merely leads to new experiences, further reflections and consequent actions within the subject area under consideration.

(29) The continual interplay, then, of EXPERIENCE, REFLEC-TION and ACTION in the teaching-learning dynamic of the classroom lies at the heart of an Ignatian pedagogy. It is our way of proceeding in Jesuit schools as we accompany the learner on his or her journey of becoming a fully human person. It is an Ignatian pedagogical paradigm which each of us can bring to the subjects we teach and programs we run, knowing that it needs to be adapted and applied to our own specific situations.

IGNATIAN PARADIGM

(30) An Ignatian paradigm of experience, reflection and action suggests a host of ways in which teachers might accompany their

students in order to facilitate learning and growth through encounters with truth and explorations of human meaning. It is a paradigm that can provide a more than adequate response to critical educational issues facing us today. It is a paradigm with inherent potential for going beyond mere theory to become a practical tool and effective instrument for making a difference in the way we teach and in the way our students learn. The model of experience, reflection and action is not solely an interesting idea worthy of considerable discussion, nor is it simply an intriguing proposal calling for lengthy debate. It is rather a fresh yet familiar Ignatian paradigm of Jesuit education, a way of proceeding which all of us can confidently follow in our efforts to help students truly grow as persons of competence, conscience and compassion.

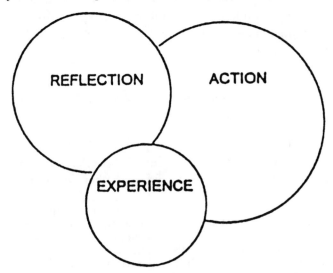

Figure 2. Ignatian Paradigm

(31) A critically important note of the Ignatian paradigm is the introduction of reflection as an essential dynamic. For centuries, education was assumed to consist primarily of accumulated knowledge gained from lectures and demonstrations.[5]

---

[5] The methodology of the lecture hall, in which the authority of the teacher (*magister*) as the dispenser of knowledge reigns supreme, became the predominant instructional model in many schools from the Middle Ages onward. The reading aloud

Teaching followed a primitive model of communications in which information is transmitted and knowledge is transferred from teacher to learner. Students experience a lesson clearly presented and thoroughly explained and the teacher calls for subsequent action on the part of students whereby they demonstrate, frequently reciting from memory, that what was communicated has, indeed, been successfully absorbed. While research over the past two decades has proven time and again, study after study, that effective learning occurs through the interaction of the learner with experience, still much of teaching continues to be limited to a two-step instructional model of EXPERIENCE → ACTION, in which the teacher plays a far more active role than the student.[6] It is a model often followed where development of memorization skills on the part of students is a primary pedagogical aim. As a teaching model of Jesuit education, however, it is seriously deficient for two reasons:

1) In Jesuit schools the learning *experience* is expected to move beyond rote knowledge to the development of the more complex learning skills of understanding, application, analysis, synthesis and evaluation.

2) If learning were to stop there, it would not be Ignatian. For it would lack the component of REFLECTION wherein students are impelled to consider the human meaning and sig-

---

of the lecture marked the "lectio" or lesson of the class the student was subsequently expected to recall and defend. Advancements in the technology of printing eventually led to the greater availability of books for private reading and independent study. In more recent times, textbooks and materials written by professionals in the field and commercially published for the mass market of education have had a significant impact on classroom teaching. In many cases, the textbook has replaced the teacher as the primary authority on curriculum and teaching, so much so that textbook selection may be the most important pedagogical decision some teachers make. Coverage of the matter in terms of chapters and pages of text that students need to know to pass a test continues to be the norm in many instances. Often little thought is given to how knowledge and ideas reflected upon within the framework of a discipline might dramatically increase not only students' comprehension of the subject but also their understanding of and appreciation for the world in which they live.

[6] One only needs to think of discipleship and apprenticeship to appreciate the fact that not all pedagogies have been so passive when it comes to the role of the learner.

nificance of what they study and to integrate that meaning as responsible learners who grow as persons of competence, conscience and compassion.

DYNAMICS OF THE PARADIGM

(32)   A comprehensive **Ignatian Pedagogical Paradigm** must consider the context of learning as well as the more explicitly pedagogical process. In addition, it should point to ways to encourage openness to growth even after the student has completed any individual learning cycle. Thus five steps are involved: **CONTEXT; EXPERIENCE; REFLECTION; ACTION; EVALUATION**.

(33)   1. *CONTEXT OF LEARNING:* Before Ignatius would begin to direct a person in the *Spiritual Exercises*, he always wanted to know about their predispositions to prayer, to God. He realized how important it was for a person to be open to the movements of the Spirit, if he or she was to draw any fruit from the journey of the soul to be begun. And based upon this pre-retreat knowledge, Ignatius made judgments about readiness to begin, whether a person would profit from the complete *Exercises* or an abbreviated experience.

(34)   In the *Spiritual Exercises* Ignatius makes the point that the experiences of the retreatant should always give shape and context to the exercises that are being used. It is the responsibility of the director, therefore, not only to select those exercises that seem most worthwhile and suitable but to modify and adjust them in order to make them directly applicable to the retreatant. Ignatius encourages the director of the *Spiritual Exercises* to become as familiar as possible beforehand with the life experience of the retreatant so that, during the retreat itself, the director will be better equipped to assist the retreatant in discerning movements of the Spirit.

(35)   Similarly, personal care and concern for the individual, which is a hallmark of Jesuit education, requires that the teacher become as conversant as possible with the life experience of the learner. Since human experience, always the starting point

in an Ignatian pedagogy, never occurs in a vacuum, we must know as much as we can about the actual context within which teaching and learning take place. As teachers, therefore, we need to understand the world of the student, including the ways in which family, friends, peers, youth culture and mores as well as social pressures, school life, politics, economics, religion, media, art, music and other realities impact that world and affect the student for better or worse. Indeed, from time to time we should work seriously with students to reflect on the contextual realities of both our worlds. What are forces at work in them? How do they experience those forces influencing their attitudes, values and beliefs, and shaping our perceptions, judgments and choices? How do world experiences affect the very way in which students learn, helping to mold their habitual patterns of thinking and acting? What practical steps can they and are they willing to take to gain greater freedom and control over their destinies?

(36) For such a relationship of authenticity and truth to flourish between teacher and student, mutual trust and respect that grows out of a continuing experience of the other as a genuine companion in learning is required. It means, too, being keenly conscious of and sensitive to the institutional environment of the school or learning center; being alert as teachers and administrators to the complex and often subtle network of norms, expectations, behaviors and relationships that create an atmosphere for learning.

(37) Praise, reverence and service should mark the relationship that exists not only between teachers and students but among all members of the school community. Ideally Jesuit schools should be places where people are believed in, honored and cared for; where the natural talents and creative abilities of persons are recognized and celebrated; where individual contributions and accomplishments are appreciated; where everyone is treated fairly and justly; where sacrifice on behalf of the economically poor, the socially deprived, and the educationally disadvantaged is commonplace; where each of us finds the challenge, encouragement and support we need to reach our fullest individual potential for excellence; where we help one

another and work together with enthusiasm and generosity, attempting to model concretely in word and action the ideals we uphold for our students and ourselves.

(38) **Teachers, as well as other members of the school community, therefore, should take account of:**

a) **the real context of a student's life** which includes family, peers, social situations, the educational institution itself, politics, economics, cultural climate, the ecclesial situation, media, music and other realities. All of these have an impact on the student for better or worse. From time to time it will be useful and important to encourage students to reflect on the contextual factors that they experience, and how they affect their attitudes, perceptions, judgments, choices. This will be especially important when students are dealing with issues that are likely to evoke strong feelings.

(39) b) **the socioeconomic, political and cultural context** within which a student grows can seriously affect his or her growth as a person for others. For example, a culture of endemic poverty usually negatively affects students' expectations about success in studies; oppressive political regimes discourage open inquiry in favor of their dominating ideologies. These and a host of other factors can restrict the freedom which Ignatian pedagogy encourages.

(40) c) **the institutional environment of the school or learning center,** i.e. the complex and often subtle network of norms, expectations and especially relationships that create the atmosphere of school life. Recent study of Catholic schools highlights the importance of a positive school environment. In the past, improvements in religious and value education in our schools have usually been sought in the development of new curricula, visual aids and suitable textbook materials. All of these developments achieve some results. Most, however, achieve far less than they promised. The results of recent research suggest that the climate of the school may well be the pre-condition necessary before value education can even begin, and that much more at-

tention needs to be given to the school environment in which the moral development and religious formation of adolescents takes place. Concretely, concern for quality learning, trust, respect for others despite differences of opinion, caring, forgiveness and some clear manifestation of the school's belief in the Transcendent distinguish a school environment that assists integral human growth. A Jesuit school is to be a face-to-face faith community of learners in which an authentic personal relationship between teachers and students may flourish. Without such a relation much of the unique force of our education would be lost. For an authentic relationship of trust and friendship between teacher and student is an indispensable dispositive condition for any growth in commitment to values. Thus *alumnorum cura personalis*, i.e., a genuine love and personal care for each of our students, is essential for an environment that fosters the Ignatian pedagogical paradigm proposed.

(41)   d) **what previously acquired concepts students bring with them to the start of the learning process**. Their points of view and the insights that they may have acquired from earlier study or picked up spontaneously from their cultural environment, as well as their feelings, attitudes and values regarding the subject matter to be studied form part of the real context for learning.

(42)   2. *EXPERIENCE* for Ignatius meant "to taste something internally." In the first place this calls for knowing facts, concepts, principles. This requires one to probe the connotation and overtones of words and events, to analyze and evaluate ideas, to reason. Only with accurate comprehension of what is being considered can one proceed to valid appreciation of its meaning. But Ignatian experience goes beyond a purely intellectual grasp. Ignatius urges that the whole person—mind, heart and will—should enter the learning experience. He encourages use of the imagination and the feelings as well as the mind in experience. Thus affective as well as cognitive dimensions of the human person are involved, because without internal feeling joined to intellectual grasp, learning will

not move a person to action. For example, it is one thing to assent to the truth that God is Father or Parent. But for this truth to live and become effective, Ignatius would have us feel the tenderness with which the Father of Jesus loves us and cares for us, forgives us. And this fuller experience can move us to realize that God shares this love with all of our brothers and sisters in the human family. In the depths of our being we may be impelled to care for others in their joys and sorrows, their hopes, trials, poverty, unjust situations—and to want to do something for them. For here the heart as well as the head, the human person, is involved.

(43) **Thus we use the term EXPERIENCE to describe any activity in which in addition to a cognitive grasp of the matter being considered, some sensation of an affective nature** is registered by the student. In any experience, data is perceived by the student cognitively. Through questioning, imagining, investigating its elements and relationships, the student organizes this data into a whole or a hypothesis. "What is this?" "Is it like anything I already know?" "How does it work?" And even without deliberate choice there is a concomitant affective reaction, e.g., "I like this." . . . "I'm threatened by this." . . . "I never do well in this sort of thing." . . . "It's interesting." . . . "Ho hum, I'm bored."

(44) At the beginning of new lessons, teachers often perceive how students' feelings can move them to grow. For it is rare that a student experiences something new in studies without referring it to what he or she already knows. New facts, ideas, viewpoints, theories often present a challenge to what the student understands at that point. This calls for growth—a fuller understanding that may modify or change what had been perceived as adequate knowledge. Confrontation of new knowledge with what one has already learned cannot be limited simply to memorization or passive absorption of additional data, especially if it does not exactly fit what one knows. It disturbs a learner to know that he does not fully comprehend. It impels a student to further probing for understanding—analysis, comparison, contrast, synthesis, evaluation—all

sorts of mental and/or psychomotor activities wherein students are alert to grasp reality more fully.

(45) **Human experience** may be either **direct or vicarious:**

• **Direct**

It is one thing to read a newspaper account of a hurricane striking the coastal towns of Puerto Rico. You can know all the facts: wind speed, direction, numbers of persons dead and injured, extent and location of physical damage caused. This cognitive knowing, however, can leave the reader distant and aloof to the human dimensions of the storm. It is quite different to be out where the wind is blowing, where one feels the force of the storm, senses the immediate danger to life, home, and all one's possessions, and feels the fear in the pit of one's stomach for one's life and that of one's neighbors as the shrill wind becomes deafening. It is clear in this example that direct experience usually is fuller, more engaging of the person. **Direct experience** in an academic setting usually occurs in interpersonal experiences such as conversations or discussions, laboratory investigations, field trips, service projects, participation in sports, and the like.

• **Vicarious**

But in studies, direct experience is not always possible. Learning is often achieved through **vicarious experience** in reading, or listening to a lecture. In order to involve students in the learning experience more fully at a human level, teachers are challenged to stimulate students' imagination and use of the senses precisely so that students can enter the reality studied more fully. Historical settings, assumptions of the times, cultural, social, political and economic factors affecting the lives of people at the time of what is being studied need to be filled out. Simulations, role playing, use of audio visual materials and the like may be helpful.

(46) In the initial phases of experience, whether direct or vicarious, learners perceive data as well as their affective responses to it. But only by organizing this data can the experience be grasped as a whole, responding to the question: **"What is this?"** and

"How do I react to it"? Thus learners need to be attentive and active in achieving comprehension and understanding of the human reality that confronts them.

(47) **3. *REFLECTION*:** Throughout his life Ignatius knew himself to be constantly subjected to different stirrings, invitations, alternatives which were often contradictory. His greatest effort was to try to discover what moved him in each situation: the impulse that leads him to good or the one that inclines him to evil; the desire to serve others or the solicitude for his own egotistical affirmation. He became the master of discernment that he continues to be today because he succeeded in distinguishing this difference. For Ignatius to "discern" was to clarify his internal motivation, the reasons behind his judgments, to probe the causes and implications of what he experienced, to weigh possible options and evaluate them in the light of their likely consequences, to discover what best leads to the desired goal: to be a free person who seeks, finds and carries out the will of God in each situation.

(48) At this level of **REFLECTION**, the memory, the understanding, the imagination and the feelings are used to capture the **meaning and the essential value** of what is being studied, to **discover its relationship** with other aspects of knowledge and human activity, and to **appreciate** its implications in the ongoing search for truth and freedom. This **REFLECTION** is a formative and liberating process. It forms the conscience of learners (their beliefs, values, attitudes and their entire way of thinking) in such a manner that they are led to move beyond knowing, to undertake **action**.

(49) **We use the term reflection to mean a thoughtful reconsideration of some subject matter, experience, idea, purpose or spontaneous reaction, in order to grasp its significance more fully. Thus, reflection is the process by which meaning surfaces in human experience:**

(50) **—by understanding the truth being studied more clearly.** For example, "What are the assumptions in this theory of the atom, in this presentation of the history of native peoples, in this statistical analysis? Are they valid; are they fair? Are other

assumptions possible? How would the presentation be different if other assumptions were made?"

(51)   —by understanding the sources of the sensations or reactions I experience in this consideration. For example, "In studying this short story, what particularly interests me? Why?." "What do I find troubling in this translation? Why?"

(52)   —by deepening my understanding of the implications of what I have grasped for myself and for others. For example, "What likely effects might environmental efforts to check the greenhouse effect have on my life, on that of my family, and friends . . . on the lives of people in poorer countries?"

(53)   —by achieving personal insights into events, ideas, truth or the distortion of truth and the like. For example, "Most people feel that a more equitable sharing of the world's resources is at least desirable, if not a moral imperative. My own life style, the things I take for granted, may contribute to the current imbalance. Am I willing to reconsider what I really need to be happy?"

(54)   —by coming to some understanding of who I am ("What moves me, and why?") . . . and who I might be in relation to others. For example, "How does what I have reflected upon make me feel? Why? Am I at peace with that reaction in myself? Why? If not, why not?"

(55)   A major challenge to a teacher at this stage of the learning paradigm is to formulate questions that will broaden students' awareness and impel them to consider viewpoints of others, especially of the poor. The temptation here for a teacher may be to impose such viewpoints. If that occurs, the risk of manipulation or indoctrination (thoroughly non-Ignatian) is high, and a teacher should avoid anything that will lead to this kind of risk. But the challenge remains to open students' sensitivity to human implications of what they learn in a way that transcends their prior experiences and thus causes them to grow in human excellence.

(56)   As educators we insist that all of this be done with total respect for the student's freedom. It is possible that, even after

the reflective process, a student may decide to act selfishly. We recognize that it is possible that due to developmental factors, insecurity or other events currently impacting a student's life, he or she may not be able to grow in directions of greater altruism, justice, etc. at this time. Even Jesus faced such reactions in dealing with the rich young man. We must be respectful of the individual's freedom to reject growth. We are sowers of seeds; in God's Providence the seeds may germinate in time.

(57) The reflection envisioned can and should be broadened wherever appropriate to enable students and teachers to share their reflections and thereby have the opportunity to grow together. Shared reflection can reinforce, challenge, encourage reconsideration, and ultimately give greater assurance that the action to be taken (individual or corporate) is more comprehensive and consistent with what it means to be a person for others.

(58) (The terms **EXPERIENCE** and **REFLECTION** may be defined variously according to different schools of pedagogy, and we agree with the tendency to use these and similar terms to express or to promote teaching that is personalized and learner-active and whose aim is not merely the assimilation of subject matter but the development of the person. In the Ignatian tradition of education, however, these terms are particularly significant as they express a "way of proceeding" that is more effective in achieving "integral formation" of the student, that is, a way of experiencing and reflecting that leads the student not only to delve deeply into the subject itself but to look for meaning in life, and to make personal options (**ACTION**) according to a comprehensive world vision. On the other hand, we know that experience and reflection are not separable phenomena. It is not possible to have an experience without some amount of reflection, and all reflection carries with it some intellectual or affective experiences, insights and enlightenment, a vision of the world, of self and of others.)

(59) **4. *ACTION:*** For Ignatius the acid test of love is what one does, not what one says. **"Love is shown in deeds, not words."**

The thrust of the *Spiritual Exercises* was precisely to enable the retreatant to know the will of God and to do it freely. So too, Ignatius and the first Jesuits were most concerned with the formation of students' attitudes, values, ideals according to which they would make decisions in a wide variety of situations about what actions were to be done. Ignatius wanted Jesuit schools to form young people who could and would contribute intelligently and effectively to the welfare of society.

(60)   —Reflection in Ignatian Pedagogy would be a truncated process if it ended with understanding and affective reactions. Ignatian reflection, just as it begins with the reality of experience, necessarily ends with that same reality in order to effect it. Reflection only develops and matures when it fosters decision and commitment.

(61)   —In his pedagogy, Ignatius highlights the affective/evaluative stage of the learning process because he is conscious that in addition to letting one "sense and taste," i.e., deepen one's experience, affective feelings are motivational forces that move one's understanding to action and commitment. And it must be clear that Ignatius does not seek just any action or commitment. Rather, while respecting human freedom, he strives to encourage decision and commitment for the *magis*, the better service of God and our sisters and brothers.

(62)   —The term "Action" here refers to internal human growth based upon experience that has been reflected upon as well as to its manifestation externally. **It involves two steps:**

   1) Interiorized Choices.
   After reflection, the learner considers the experience from a personal, human point of view. Here in light of cognitive understanding of the experience and the affections involved (positive or negative), the will is moved. Meanings perceived and judged present choices to be made. Such choices may occur when a person decides that a truth is to be his or her personal point of reference, attitude or predisposition which will affect any number of decisions. It may take the form of gradual clarification of one's priorities. It is at this point that the student chooses to make the truth

his or her own while remaining open to where the truth might lead.

2) Choices Externally Manifested

In time, these meanings, attitudes, values which have been interiorized, made part of the person, impel the student to act, **to do something consistent with this new conviction.** If the meaning was positive, then the student will likely seek to enhance those conditions or circumstances in which the original experience took place. For example, if the goal of physical education has been achieved, the student will be inclined to undertake some regular sport during his free time. If she has acquired a taste for history of literature, she may resolve to make time for reading. If he finds it worthwhile to help his companions in their studies, he may volunteer to collaborate in some remedial program for weaker students. If he or she appreciates better the needs of the poor after service experiences in the ghetto and reflection on those experiences, this might influence his or her career choice or move the student to volunteer to work for the poor. If the meaning was negative, then the student will likely seek to adjust, change, diminish or avoid the conditions and circumstances in which the original experience took place. For example, if the student now appreciates the reasons for his or her lack of success in school work, the student may decide to improve study habits in order to avoid repeated failure.

(63)   **5. *EVALUATION:*** All teachers know that from time to time it is important to evaluate a student's progress in academic achievement. Daily quizzes, weekly or monthly tests and semester examinations are familiar evaluation instruments to assess the degree of mastery of knowledge and skills achieved. Periodic testing alerts the teacher and the student both to intellectual growth and to lacunae where further work is necessary for mastery. This type of feedback can alert the teacher to possible needs for use of alternate methods of teaching; it also offers special opportunities to individualize encouragement and advice for academic improvement (e.g., review of study habits) for each student.

(64) Ignatian pedagogy, however, aims at formation which includes but goes beyond academic mastery. Here we are concerned about students' well-rounded growth as persons for others. Thus periodic evaluation of the student's growth in attitudes, priorities and actions consistent with being a person for others is essential. Comprehensive assessment probably will not occur as frequently as academic testing, but it needs to be planned at intervals, at least once a term. A teacher who is observant will perceive indications of growth or lack of growth in class discussions, students' generosity in response to common needs, etc. much more frequently.

(65) There are a variety of ways in which this fuller human growth can be assessed. All must take into account the age, talents and developmental levels of each student. Here the relationship of mutual trust and respect which should exist between students and teachers sets a climate for discussion of growth. Useful pedagogical approaches include mentoring, review of student journals, student self-evaluation in light of personal growth profiles, as well as review of leisure time activities and voluntary service to others.

(66) This can be a privileged moment for a teacher both to congratulate and encourage the student for progress made, as well as an opportunity to stimulate further reflection in light of blind spots or lacunae in the student's point of view. The teacher can stimulate needed reconsideration by judicious questioning, proposing additional perspectives, supplying needed information and suggesting ways to view matters from other points of view.

(67) In time, the student's attitudes, priorities, decisions may be reinvestigated in light of further experience, changes in his or her context, challenges from social and cultural developments and the like. The teacher's gentle questioning may point to the need for more adequate decisions or commitments, what Ignatius Loyola called the *magis*. This newly realized need to grow may serve to launch the learner once again into the cycle of the Ignatian learning paradigm.

An Ongoing Process

(68)   This mode of proceeding can thus become an effective ongoing pattern for learning as well as a stimulus to remain
open to growth throughout a lifetime.

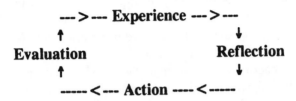

(69)   A repetition of the Ignatian paradigm can help the growth
of a student:
* who will gradually learn to discriminate and be selective
in choosing experiences;
* who is able to draw fullness and richness from the reflection on those experiences; and
* who becomes self-motivated by his or her own integrity
and humanity to make conscious, responsible choices.

(70)   In addition, perhaps most important, consistent use of the
Ignatian paradigm can result in the acquisition of life-long
habits of learning which foster attention to experience, reflective understanding beyond self-interest, and criteria for
responsible action. Such formative effects were characteristic of Jesuit alumni in the early Society of Jesus. They are
perhaps even more necessary for responsible citizens of the
third millennium.

Noteworthy Features of the Ignatian Pedagogical Paradigm

(71)   We naturally welcome an Ignatian pedagogy that speaks to
the characteristics of Jesuit education and to our own goals
as teachers. The continual interplay of CONTEXT, EXPE-
RIENCE, REFLECTION, ACTION and EVALUATION
provides us with a pedagogical model that is relevant to our

cultures and times. It is a substantial and appealing model that speaks directly to the teaching-learning process. It is a carefully reasoned way of proceeding, cogently and logically argued from principles of Ignatian spirituality and Jesuit education. It consistently maintains the importance and integrity of the interrelationship of teacher, learner and subject matter within the real context in which they live. It is comprehensive and complete in its approach. Most importantly, it addresses the realities as well as ideals of teaching in practical and systematic ways while, at the same time, offering the radical means we need to meet our educational mission of forming young men- and women-for-others. As we continue to work to make Ignatian pedagogy an essential characteristic of Jesuit education in our schools and classrooms, it may help us to remember the following about the Paradigm itself:

(72)   *—The Ignatian Pedagogical Paradigm applies to all Curricula.* As an attitude, a mentality and a consistent approach which imbues all our teaching, the *Ignatian Pedagogical Paradigm* applies to all curricula. It is easily applicable even to curricula prescribed by governments or local educational authorities. It does not demand the addition of a single course, but it does require the infusion of new approaches in the way we teach existing courses.

(73)   *—The Ignatian Pedagogical Paradigm is fundamental to the teaching-learning process.* It applies not only to the academic disciplines but also to the non-academic areas of schooling, such as extra-curricular activities, sports, community service programs, retreat experiences, and the like. Within a specific subject (history, mathematics, language, literature, physics, art, etc.), the paradigm can serve as a helpful guide for preparing lessons, planning assignments, and designing instructional activities. The paradigm has considerable potential for helping students to make connections across as well as within disciplines and to integrate their learning with what has gone before. Used consistently throughout a school's program, the paradigm brings coher-

ence to the total educational experience of the student. Regular application of the model in teaching situations contributes to the formation for students of a natural habit of reflecting on experience before acting.

(74) *—The Ignatian Pedagogical Paradigm promises to help teachers be better teachers.* It enables teachers to enrich the content and structure of what they are teaching. It gives teachers additional means of encouraging student initiative. It allows teachers to expect more of students, to call upon them to take greater responsibility for and be more active in their own learning. It helps teachers to motivate students by providing the occasion and rationale for inviting students to relate what is being studied to their own world experiences.

(75) *—The Ignatian Pedagogical Paradigm personalizes learning.* It asks students to reflect upon the meaning and significance of what they are studying. It attempts to motivate students by involving them as critical active participants in the teaching-learning process. It aims for more personal learning by bringing student and teacher experiences closer together. It invites integration of learning experiences in the classroom with those of home, work, peer culture, etc.

(76) *—The Ignatian Pedagogical Paradigm stresses the social dimension of both learning and teaching.* It encourages close cooperation and mutual sharing of experiences and reflective dialogue among students. It relates student learning and growth to personal interaction and human relationships. It proposes steady movement and progress towards action that will affect the lives of others for good. Students will gradually learn that their deepest experiences come from their relationship with what is human, relationships with and experiences of persons. Reflection should always move towards greater appreciation of the lives of others, and of the actions, policies or structures that help or hinder mutual growth and development as members of the human family. This assumes, of course, that teachers are aware of and committed to such values.

CHALLENGES TO IMPLEMENTING AN IGNATIAN PEDAGOGY

(77)   Achievement of value-oriented goals like those presented in *The Characteristics of Jesuit Education* is not easy. There are formidable challenges working at cross-purposes to our aims. Here are but a few:

1. Limited View of Education

(78)   The purpose of education is often presented as cultural transmission, i.e., passing on to new generations the accumulated wisdom of the ages. This is certainly an important function to assure coherence in human endeavors within any society and in the human family at large. Failure to inform and train youth in what we have learned would result in the need for each new generation to reinvent the wheel. In fact, in many places cultural transmission is the dominant, if not the sole purpose, of public education.

(79)   But the purpose of education in today's world, marked by rapid changes at every level of human endeavor and competing value systems and ideologies, cannot remain so limited if it is effectively to prepare men and women of competence and conscience capable of making significant contributions to the future of the human family. From a sheerly pragmatic point of view, education which is limited to cultural transmission results in training for obsolescence. This is clear when we consider programs training for technology. Less apparent, however, may be the results of failure to probe human implications of developments that inevitably affect human life such as genetic engineering, the image culture, new forms of energy, the role of emerging economic blocks of nations, and a host of other innovations that promise progress. Many of these offer hope for improved human living, but at what cost? Such matters cannot simply be left to political leaders or the captains of industry; it is the right and responsibility of every citizen to judge and act in appropriate ways for the emerging human community. People need to be educated for responsible citizenship.

(80)   In addition, therefore, to cultural transmission, preparation for significant participation in cultural growth is essential. Men and women of the third millennium will require new technological skills, no doubt; but more important, they will require skills to lovingly understand and critique all aspects of life in order to make decisions (personal, social, moral, professional, religious) that will impact all of our lives for the better. Criteria for such growth (through study, reflection, analysis, critique and development of effective alternatives) are inevitably founded on values. This is true whether or not such values are averted to explicitly. All teaching imparts values, and these values can be such as to promote justice, or work partially or entirely at cross-purposes to the mission of the Society of Jesus.

(81)   Thus, we need a pedagogy that alerts young people to the intricate networks of values that are often subtly disguised in modern life—in advertising, music, political propaganda, etc.—precisely so that students can examine them and make judgments and commitments freely, with real understanding.

2. Prevalence of Pragmatism

(82)   In a desire to meet goals of economic advancement, which may be quite legitimate, many governments are stressing the pragmatic elements of education exclusively. The result is that education is reduced to job training. This thrust is often encouraged by business interests, although they pay lip service to broader cultural goals of education. In recent years, in many parts of the world, many academic institutions have acceded to this narrow perspective of what constitutes education. And it is startling to see the enormous shift in student selection of majors in universities away from the humanities, the social and psychological sciences, philosophy and theology, towards an exclusive focus on business, economics, engineering, or the physical and biological sciences.

(83)   In Jesuit education we do not simply bemoan these facts of life today. They must be considered and dealt with. We

believe that almost every academic discipline, when honest with itself, is well aware that the values it transmits depend upon assumptions about the ideal human person and human society which are used as a starting point. Thus educational programs, teaching and research, and the methodologies they employ in Jesuit schools, colleges and universities are of the highest importance, for we reject any partial or deformed version of the human person, the image of God. This is in sharp contrast to educational institutions which often unwittingly sidestep the central concern for the human person because of fragmented approaches to specializations.

(84)   This means that Jesuit education must insist upon integral formation of its students through such means as required core curricula that include humanities, philosophy, theological perspectives, social questions and the like, as part of all specialized educational programs. In addition, infusion methods might well be employed within specializations to highlight the deeper human, ethical and social implications of what is being studied.

3. Desire for Simple Solutions

(85)   The tendency to seek simple solutions to complex human questions and problems marks many societies today. The widespread use of slogans as answers does not really help to solve problems. Nor does the tendency we see in many countries around the world towards fundamentalism on one extreme of the spectrum and secularism on the other. For these tend to be reductionist; they do not realistically satisfy the thirst for integral human growth that so many of our brothers and sisters cry out for.

(86)   Clearly Jesuit education which aims to form the whole person is challenged to chart a path, to employ a pedagogy, that avoids these extremes by helping our students to grasp more comprehensive truth, the human implications of their learning, precisely so that they can more effectively contribute to healing the human family and building a world that is more human and more divine.

4. Feelings of Insecurity

(87) One of the major reasons contributing to a widespread quest for easy answers is the insecurity many people experience due to the breakdown of essential human institutions that normally provide the context for human growth. Tragically, the family, the most fundamental human society, is disintegrating in countries around the world. In many first world countries, one out of two marriages ends in divorce with devastating effects for the spouses, and especially for the children. Another source of insecurity and confusion is due to the fact that we are experiencing a historic mass migration of peoples across the face of the earth. Millions of men, women and children are being uprooted from their cultures due to oppression, civil conflicts, or lack of food or means to support themselves. The older émigrés may cling to elements of their cultural and religious heritage, but the young are often subject to culture conflict, and feel compelled to adopt the dominant cultural values of their new homelands in order to be accepted. Yet, at heart, they are uncertain about these new values. Insecurity often expresses itself in defensiveness, selfishness, a "me-first" attitude, which block consideration of the needs of others. The emphasis that the Ignatian paradigm places upon reflection to achieve meaning can assist students to understand the reasons underlying the insecurities they experience, and to seek more constructive ways to deal with them.

5. Government-Prescribed Curricula

(88) Cutting across all of these factors is the reality of pluralism in the world today. Unlike Jesuit schools of the sixteenth century, there exists no single universally recognized curriculum like the Trivium or Quadrivium that can be employed as a vehicle for formation in our times. Curricula today justifiably reflect local cultures and local needs that vary considerably. But in a number of countries, governments strictly prescribe the courses that form curricula at the level of elementary and secondary education. This can impede

curriculum development according to formational priorities of schools.

(89)   Because the Ignatian learning program requires a certain style of teaching, it approaches existing curricular subjects through infusion rather than by changes or additions to course offerings. In this way it avoids further crowding of overburdened school curricula, while at the same time not being seen as a frill tacked on to the "important" subjects. (This does not rule out the possibility that a specific unit concerning ethics or the like may on occasion be advisable in a particular context.)

THEORY INTO PRACTICE: STAFF DEVELOPMENT PROGRAMS

(90)   Reflecting on what has been proposed here, some may wonder how it can be implemented. After all, very few teachers really practice such a methodology consistently. And lack of know-how is probably the major obstacle to any effective change in teacher behavior. The members of the International Commission on the Apostolate of Jesuit Education can understand such reservations. Research has shown that many educational innovations have foundered precisely because of such problems.

(91)   We are convinced, therefore, that **staff development programs** involving in-service training are essential in each school, province or region where this **Ignatian Pedagogical Paradigm** will be used. Since teaching skills are mastered only through practice, teachers need not only an explanation of methods, but also opportunities to practice them. Over time staff development programs can equip teachers with an array of pedagogical methods appropriate for Ignatian pedagogy from which they can use those more appropriate for the needs of students whom they serve. Staff development *programs* at the province or local school level, therefore, are an essential, integral part of the Ignatian Pedagogy Project.

(92)   Accordingly, we are convinced of the need to identify and train teams of educators who will be prepared to offer staff development programs for province and local groups of teachers in the use of the **Ignatian Pedagogical Paradigm**. Therefore, training workshops are now being planned. These will, of course, encourage local adaptations of specific methods which are consistent with the Ignatian pedagogy proposed.

Some Concrete Helps to Understand the Paradigm

(93)   The appendices to this document provide a further understanding of the roots of Ignatian Pedagogy in Ignatius' own notes (Appendix 1) and in Fr. Kolvenbach's address (Appendix 2). A brief list of the variety of concrete processes and methods which can be used by teachers in each step of the paradigm is provided (Appendix 3). Fuller training protocols, utilizing these pedagogical methods, will form the substance of local or regional staff development programs to assist teachers to understand and use this pedagogy effectively.

An Invitation to Cooperate

(94)   Greater understanding of how to adapt and apply the Ignatian Pedagogical Paradigm to the wide variety of educational settings and circumstances which characterize Jesuit schools around the world will come about as we work with the Paradigm in our relationships with students both in and outside the classroom and discover through those efforts concrete, practical ways of using the Paradigm that enhance the teaching-learning process. It can be expected, moreover, that many detailed and helpful treatments of the Ignatian Pedagogical Paradigm will be forthcoming that will be further enriched by the experience of teachers trained and practiced in applying the Paradigm within specific academic fields and disciplines. All of us in the work

of Jesuit education look forward to benefiting from the insights and suggestions that other teachers have to offer.

(95) In the Ignatian spirit of cooperation, we hope that teachers who develop their own lessons or brief units in specific subjects of their curriculum utilizing the **Ignatian Paradigm** will share them with others. Accordingly, from time to time we hope to make brief illustrative materials available. For this reason teachers are invited to send concise presentations of their use of the **Ignatian Paradigm** in specific subjects to:

> The International Center for Jesuit Education
> Borgo S. Spirito, 4
> C.P. 6139
> 00195 Rome, Italy

Appendices: Table of Contents

N.B.: Staff development programs will explain and enable teachers to practice and master these methods.

APPENDIX 1: SOME OVERRIDING PEDAGOGICAL PRINCIPLES (IGNATIAN "ANNOTATIONS")

An adaptation of the introductory notes of St. Ignatius to one who directs another in the *Spiritual Exercises*.

(99)   There follows a translation of the "Annotations" or guiding notes to the Director of the *Spiritual Exercises* into Introductory Ignatian Pedagogical statements:

(100) 1. By "learning" is meant every method of experiencing, reflecting and acting upon the truth; every way of preparing and disposing oneself to be rid of all obstacles to freedom and growth (Annotation 1).

(101) 2. The teacher explains to the student the method and order of the subject and accurately narrates the facts. He/she stays to the point and adds only a short explanation. The reason for this is that when students take the foundation presented, go over it and reflect on it, they discover what makes the matter clearer and better understood. This comes from their own reasoning, and produces a greater sense of accomplishment and satisfaction than if the teacher explained and developed the meaning at great length. It is not much knowledge that fills and satisfies students, but the intimate understanding and relish of the truth (Annotation 2).

(102) 3. In all learning we make use of the acts of intellect in reasoning and acts of the will in demonstrating our love (Annotation 3).

(103) 4. Specific time periods are assigned to learning and generally correspond to the natural divisions of the subject. However, this does not mean that every division must necessarily consist of a set time. For it may happen at times that some are slower in attaining what is sought while some may be more diligent, some more troubled and tired. So it may be necessary at times to shorten the time, at others to lengthen it (Annotation 4).

(104) 5. The student who enters upon learning should do so with a great-heartedness and generosity, freely offering all his or her attention and will to the enterprise (Annotation 5).

(105) 6. When the teacher sees the student is not affected by any experiences, he or she should ply the student with questions, inquire about when and how study takes place, question the understanding of directions, ask what the student's reflection yielded, and ask for an accounting (Annotation 6).

(106) 7. If the teacher observes that the student is having troubles, he or she should deal with the student gently and kindly. The teacher should encourage and strengthen the student for the future by reviewing mistakes kindly and suggesting ways for improvement (Annotation 7).

(107) 8. If during reflection a student experiences joy or discouragement, he or she should reflect further on the causes of such feelings. Sharing such reflection with a teacher can help the student to perceive areas of consolation or challenge that can lead to further growth or that might subtly block growth (Annotations 8, 9, 10).

(108) 9. The student should set about learning the matter of the present as if he or she were to learn nothing more. The student should not be in haste to cover everything. "*Non multa, sed multum*" ("Treat matter selected in depth; don't try to cover every topic in a given field of inquiry.") (Annotation 11).

(109) 10. The student should give to learning the full time that is expected. It is better to go overtime than to cut the time short, especially when the temptation to "cut corners" is strong, and it is difficult to study. Thus the student will get

accustomed to resist giving in and strengthen study in the future (Annotations 12 and 13).

(110) 11. If the student in learning is going along with great success, the teacher will advise more care, less haste (Annotation 14).

(111) 12. While the student learns, it is more suitable that the truth itself is what motivates and disposes the student. The teacher, like a balance of equilibrium, leans to neither side of the matter, but lets the student deal directly with the truth and be influenced by the truth (Annotation 15).

(112) 13. In order that the Creator and Lord may work more surely in the creature, it will be most useful for the student to work against any obstacles which prevent an openness to the full truth (Annotation 16).

(113) 14. The student should faithfully inform the teacher of any troubles or difficulties he or she is having, so that a learning process might be suited and adapted to personal needs (Annotation 17).

(114) 15. Learning should always be adapted to the condition of the student engaged in it (Annotation 18).

(115) 16. (The last two annotations allow for creative adaptations to suit persons and circumstances. Such readiness to adapt in the teaching-learning experience is greatly effective.) (Annotations 19 and 20).

APPENDIX 2: IGNATIAN PEDAGOGY TODAY

Context: Christian Humanism Today

(116) I begin by setting our efforts today within the context of the tradition of Jesuit Education. From its origins in the sixteenth century, Jesuit education has been dedicated to the development and transmission of a genuine Christian humanism. This humanism had two roots: the distinctive spiritual experiences of Ignatius Loyola, and the cultural, social and religious challenges of Renaissance and Reformation Europe.

(117) The spiritual root of this humanism is indicated in the final contemplation of the *Spiritual Exercises*. Here Ignatius has the retreatant ask for an intimate knowledge of how God dwells in persons, giving them understanding and making them in God's own image and likeness, and to consider how God works and labors in all created things on behalf of each person. This understanding of God's relation to the world implies that faith in God and affirmation of all that is truly human are inseparable from each other. This spirituality enabled the first Jesuits to appropriate the humanism of the Renaissance and to found a network of educational institutions that were innovative and responsive to the urgent needs of their time. Faith and the enhancement of *humanitas* went hand in hand.

(118) Since the Second Vatican Council we have been recognizing a profound new challenge that calls for a new form of Christian humanism with a distinctively societal emphasis. The Council stated that the "split between the faith that many profess and their daily lives deserves to be counted among the more serious errors of our age" (GS 43). The world appears to us in pieces, chopped up, broken.

(119) The root issue is this: what does faith in God mean in the face of Bosnia and Sudan, Guatemala and Haiti, Auschwitz and Hiroshima, the teeming streets of Calcutta and the broken bodies in Tiananmen Square? What is Christian humanism in the face of starving millions of men, women and children in Africa? What is Christian humanism as we view millions of people uprooted from their own countries by persecution and terror, and forced to seek a new life in foreign lands? What is Christian humanism when we see the homeless that roam our cities and the growing underclass who are reduced to permanent hopelessness. What is humanistic education in this context? A disciplined sensitivity to human misery and exploitation is not a single political doctrine or a system of economics. It is a humanism, a humane sensibility to be achieved anew within the demands of our own times and as a product of an education whose ideal continues to be motivated by the great commandments—love of God and love of neighbor.

(120) In other words, late twentieth-century Christian humanism necessarily includes social humanism. As such it shares much with the ideals of other faiths in bringing God's love to effective expression in building a just and peaceful kingdom of God on earth. Just as the early Jesuits made distinctive contributions to the humanism of the sixteenth century through their educational innovations, we are called to a similar endeavor today. This calls for creativity in every area of thought, education and spirituality. It will also be the product of an Ignatian pedagogy that serves faith through reflective inquiry into the full meaning of the Christian message and its exigencies for our time. Such a service of faith, and the promotion of justice which it entails, is the fundament of contemporary Christian humanism. It is at the heart of the enterprise of Catholic and Jesuit education today. This is what *The Characteristics of Jesuit Education* refers to as "human excellence." This is what we mean when we say that the goal of Jesuit education is the formation of men and women for others, people of competence, conscience and compassionate commitment.

The Society's Reply to This Context

(121) Just a decade ago a request came from many parts of the world for a more contemporary statement of the essential principles of Jesuit pedagogy. The need was felt in light of notable changes and emerging new governmental regulations concerning curriculum, student body composition and the like; in light of the felt need to share our pedagogy with increasing numbers of lay teachers who were unfamiliar with Jesuit education, in light of the Society's mission in the Church today, and especially in light of the changing, ever more bewildering context in which young people are growing up today. Our response was the document describing the characteristics of Jesuit education today. But that document, which was very well received throughout the world of Jesuit education, provoked a more urgent question. How? How do we move from an understanding of the principles guiding Jesuit education today to the practical level of making these principles real in the daily interaction between teachers and students? For it is here in the challenge and the excitement of the teaching-learning process that these principles can have effect. This workshop in which you are participating seeks to provide the practical pedagogical methods that can answer the crucial question: how do we make *The Characteristics of Jesuit Education* real in the classroom? The *Ignatian Pedagogical Paradigm* presents a framework to incorporate the crucial element of reflection into learning. Reflection can provide the opportunity for students themselves to consider the human meaning and the implications of what they study.

(122) Amid all the conflicting demands on their time and energies, your students are searching for meaning for their lives. They know that nuclear holocaust is more than a madman's dream. Unconsciously at least, they suffer from fear of life in a world held together by a balance of terror more than by bonds of love. Already many young people have been exposed to very cynical interpretations of man: he is a sack of egoistic drives, each demanding instant gratification; he is the innocent victim of inhuman systems over which he has no control. Due to

mounting economic pressures in many countries around the world, many students in developed countries seem excessively preoccupied with career training and self-fulfillment to the exclusion of broader human growth. Does this not point to their excessive insecurity? But beneath their fears, often covered over with an air of bravado, and beneath their bewilderment at the differing interpretations of man, is their desire for a unifying vision of the meaning of life and of their own selves. In many developing countries, the young people with whom you work experience the threat of famine and the terrors of war. They struggle to hope that human life has value and a future in the ashes of devastation, which is the only world they have ever experienced. In other countries where poverty grinds the human spirit, modern media cynically project the good life in terms of opulence and consumerism. Is it any wonder that our students in all parts of the world are confused, uncertain about life's meaning?

(123) During their years in a secondary school, young men and women are still relatively free to listen and to explore. The world has not yet closed in on them. They are concerned about the deeper questions of the "why" and "wherefore" of life. They can dream impossible dreams and be stirred by the vision of what might be. The Society has committed so much of its personnel and resources to the education of young people precisely because they are questing for the sources of life "beyond academic excellence." Surely, every teacher worthy of the name must believe in young people and want to encourage their reaching for the stars. This means that your own unifying vision of life must be tantalizingly attractive to your students, inviting them to dialogue on the things that count. It must encourage them to internalize attitudes of deep and universal compassion for their suffering fellow men and women and to transform themselves into men and women of peace and justice, committed to be agents of change in a world which recognizes how widespread is injustice, how pervasive the forces of oppression, selfishness and consumerism.

(124) Admittedly, this is not an easy task. Like all of us in our pre-reflective years, your students have unconsciously accepted

values which are incompatible with what truly leads to human happiness. More than young people of a previous generation, your students have more "reasons" for walking away in sadness when they see the implications of a Christian vision of life and basic change of worldview which leads to rejection of softness and the distortedly glamorous image of life purveyed in slick magazines and cheap films. They are exposed, as perhaps no generation in history, to the lure of drugs and the flight from painful reality which they promise.

(125) These young men and women need confidence as they look to their future; they need strength as they face their own weakness; they need mature understanding and love in the teachers of all areas of the curriculum with whom they explore the awesome mystery of life. Do they not remind us of that young student of the University of Paris of four and one-half centuries ago whom Inigo befriended and transformed into the Apostle of the Indies?

(126) These are the young men and women whom you are called to lead to be open to the Spirit, willing to accept the seeming defeat of redemptive love; in short, eventually to become principled leaders ready to shoulder society's heavier burdens and to witness to the faith that does justice.

(127) I urge you to have great confidence that your students are called to be leaders in their world; help them to know that they are respected and loveable. Freed from the fetters of ideology and insecurity, they can be introduced to a more complete vision of the meaning of man and woman, and be equipped for service to their brothers and sisters, sensitive to and deeply concerned about using their influence to right social wrongs and to bring wholesome values into each of their professional, social and private lines. The example of your own social sensitivity and concern will be a major source of inspiration for them.

(128) This apostolic aim needs, however, to be translated into practical programs and appropriate methods in the real world of the school. One of the characteristic Ignatian qualities, revealed in the *Spiritual Exercises*, in the 4th part of the *Consti-*

tutions, and in many of his letters is Ignatius' insistence simultaneously upon the highest ideals and the most concrete means to achieve them. Vision without appropriate method may be perceived as sterile platitude, while method without unifying vision is frequently passing fashion or gadgetry.

(129) An example of this Ignatian integration in teaching is found in the *Protrepticon* or *Exhortation to the Teachers in the Secondary Schools of the Society of Jesus* written by Fr. Francesco Sacchini, the second official historian of the Society a few years after the publication of the *Ratio* of 1599. In the Preface he remarks: "Among us the education of youth is not limited to imparting the rudiments of grammar, but extends simultaneously to Christian formation." The Epitome, adopting the distinction between "instruction" and "education" understood as character formation, lays it down that schoolmasters are to be properly prepared in methods of instruction **and** in the art of **educating**. The Jesuit educational tradition has always insisted that the adequate criterion for success in Jesuit schools is not simply mastery of propositions, formulae, philosophies and the like. The test is in deeds, not words: What will our students **do** with the empowerment which is their education? Ignatius was interested in getting educated men and women to work for the betterment of others, and erudition is not enough for this purpose. If the effectiveness of one's education is to be employed generously, a person has to be both good and learned. If she is not educated, she cannot help her neighbors as effectively she might; if not good, she will not help them, or at least she cannot be relied upon to do so consistently. This implies clearly that Jesuit education must go beyond cognitive growth to human growth, which involves understanding, motivation and conviction.

Pedagogical Guidelines

(130) In accord with this goal to **educate** effectively, St. Ignatius and his successors formulated overriding pedagogical guidelines. Here I mention a few of them:

(131) a) Ignatius conceived of man's stance as being one of awe and wonder in appreciation for God's gifts of creation, the universe and human existence itself. In his key meditation on God's Presence in creation, Ignatius would have us move beyond logical analysis to affective response to God who is active for us in all of reality. By finding God in all things we discover God's loving plan for us. The role of imagination, affection and will, as well as intellect, are central to an Ignatian approach. Thus Jesuit education involves **formation of the whole person**. In our schools we are asked to integrate this fuller dimension precisely to enable students to discover the realm of meaning in life, which can in turn give direction to our understanding of who we are and why we are here. It can provide criteria for our priorities and crucial choices at turning points in our lives. Specific methods in teaching thus are chosen which foster rigorous investigation, understanding and reflection.

(132) b) In this adventure of finding God, Ignatius respects human **freedom**. This rules out any semblance of indoctrination or manipulation in Jesuit education. Jesuit pedagogy should enable students to explore reality with open hearts and minds. And in an effort to be honest, it should alert the learner to possible entrapment by one's assumptions and prejudices, as well as by the intricate networks of popular values that can blind one to the truth. Thus Jesuit education urges students to know and to love the truth. It aims to enable people to be critical of their societies in a positive as well as negative sense, embracing wholesome values proposed, while rejecting specious values and practices.

(133) Our institutions make their essential contribution to society by embodying in our educational process a rigorous, probing study of crucial human problems and concerns. It is for this reason that Jesuit schools must strive for high academic quality. So we are speaking of something far removed from the facile and superficial world of slogans or ideology, of purely emotional and self-centered responses; and of instant, simplistic solutions. Teaching and research and all that goes into the educational process are of the highest importance in our insti-

tutions because they reject and refute any partial or deformed vision of the human person. This is in sharp contrast to educational institutions which often unwittingly sidestep the central concern for the human person because of fragmented approaches to specializations.

(134) c) And Ignatius holds out the ideal of the fullest development of the human person. Typically he insists on the *"magis,"* the more, the greater glory of God. Thus in education Loyola demands that our expectations go beyond mastery of the skills and understandings normally found in the well-informed and competent students. *Magis* refers not only to academics, but also to action. In their training Jesuits are traditionally encouraged by various experiences to explore the dimensions and expressions of Christian service as a means of developing a spirit of generosity. Our schools should develop this thrust of the Ignatian vision into programs of service, which would encourage the student to actively experience and test his or her acceptance of the *magis*. By this service the student can be led to discover the dialectic of action and contemplation.

(135) d) But not every action is truly for God's greater glory. Consequently, Ignatius offers a way to discover and choose God's will. "Discernment" is pivotal. And so in our schools, colleges and universities **reflection and discernment** must be taught and practiced. With all the competing values that bombard us today, making free human choice is never easy. We very rarely find that all of the reasons for a decision are on one side. There is always a pull and tug. This is where **discernment** becomes crucial. Discernment requires getting the facts and then reflecting, sorting out the motives that impel us, weighing values and priorities, considering how significant decisions will impact on the poor, deciding, and living with our decisions.

(136) e) Furthermore, response to the call of Jesus may not be self-centered; it demands that we be and teach our students to be **for others**. The worldview of Ignatius is centered on the person of Christ. The reality of the Incarnation affects Je-

suit education at its core. For the ultimate purpose, the very reason for the existence of schools is to form men and women for others in imitation of Christ Jesus—the Son of God, the Man for Others par excellence. Thus Jesuit education, faithful to the Incarnational principle, is humanistic. Fr. Arrupe wrote:

(137)   "What is it to humanize the world if not to put it at the service of mankind?" But the egoist not only does not humanize the material creation, he dehumanizes people themselves. He changes people into things by dominating them, exploiting them, and taking to himself the fruit of their labor. The tragedy of it all is that by doing this the egoist dehumanizes himself: He surrenders himself to the possessions he covets; he becomes their slave—no longer a person self-possessed but an un-person, a thing driven by his blind desires and their objects.

(138) In our own day, we are beginning to understand that education does not inevitably humanize or Christianize. We are losing faith in the notion that all education, regardless of its quality or thrust or purpose, will lead to virtue. Increasingly, it becomes clear that if we are to exercise a moral force in society, we must insist that the process of education takes place in a moral context. This is not to suggest a program of indoctrination that suffocates the spirit, nor does it mean theory courses that become only speculative and remote. What is called for is a framework of inquiry in which the process of wrestling with big issues and complex values is made fully legitimate.

(139) f) In this whole effort to form men and women of competence, conscience and compassion, Ignatius never lost sight of the individual human person. He knew that God gives different gifts to each of us. One of the overriding principles of Jesuit pedagogy derives directly from this, namely, *alumnorum cura personalis*, a genuine love and personal care for each of our students.

THE ROLE OF THE TEACHER IS CRITICAL

(140) In a Jesuit school, the chief responsibility for moral as well as for intellectual formation rests finally not upon any procedure

or curricular or extra-curricular activity, but upon the teacher, under God. A Jesuit school is to be a face-to-face community in which an authentic personal relationship between teachers and students may flourish. Without such a relation of friendship, in fact, much of the unique force of our education would be lost. For an authentic relationship of trust and friendship between the teacher and pupil is an invaluable dispositive condition for any genuine growth in commitment to values.

(141) And so the *Ratio* of 1591 insists that teachers first need to know their students. It recommends that the masters study their pupils at length and reflect upon their aptitudes, their defects and the implications of their classroom behavior. And at least some of the teachers, it remarks, ought to be well acquainted with the student's home background. Teachers are always to respect the dignity and personality of the pupils. In the classroom, the *Ratio* advises that teachers should be patient with students and know how to overlook certain mistakes or put off their correction until the apt psychological moment. They should be much readier with praise than blame, and if correction is required it should be made without bitterness. The friendly spirit which is nourished by frequent, casual counseling of the students, perhaps outside class hours, will greatly help this aim along. Even these bits of advice serve only to apply that underlying concept of the very nature of the school as a community and of the teacher's role as crucial within it.

(142) In the Preamble to the 4th Part of the *Constitutions*, Ignatius appears to place **teachers' personal example** ahead of learning or rhetoric as an apostolic means to help students grow in values. Within this school community, the teacher will persuasively influence character, for better or for worse, by the example of what he himself is. In our own day Pope Paul VI observed incisively in *Evangelii Nuntiandi*: "Today students do not listen seriously to teachers but to witnesses; and if they do listen to teachers, it is because they are witnesses."

(143) As teachers, in a Jesuit school then, beyond being qualified professionals in education, you are called to be men and

women of the Spirit. Whether you like it or not, you are a city resting on a hill. What you are speaks louder than what you do or say. In today's image-culture, young people learn to respond to the **living** image of those ideals which they dimly sense in their heart. Words about total dedication, service of the poor, a just social order, a non-racist society, openness to the Spirit and the like may lead them to reflection. A living example will lead them beyond reflection to aspire to live what the words mean. Hence, our continuing growth in the realm of the Spirit of Truth must lead us to a **life** of such compelling wholeness and goodness that the example we set will challenge our students to grow as men and women of competence, conscience and compassion.

METHODS

(144) His own painful educational experience had proven to Ignatius that enthusiasm was not enough for success in study. How a student was directed, the method of teaching employed were crucial. When we page through the *Ratio*, our first impression is that of a welter of regulations for time schedules, for careful gradation of classes, for the selection of authors to be read, for the diversified methods to be employed at various times of the morning and afternoon, for correction of papers and the assignment of written work, for the precise degree of skill which the students of each class will be expected to possess before moving upward. But all these particulars were designed to create a firm and reassuring framework of order and clarity within which both teacher and student could securely pursue their objectives. Here I mention just a few of the typical methods employed in Jesuit education.

(145) a) Given this sort of environment of order and care for method, it would be relatively easy to determine **precise** and limited academic **objectives** for the individual classes. It was felt that this was the first requirement of any good learning situation—to know just what one sought and how to seek it. The characteristic tool employed here was the

prelection in which the teacher carefully prepared students for their own subsequent immanent activity which alone could generate true learning and firm habits.

(146) b) But learning objectives needed to be selected and adapted to the students. The first Jesuit teachers believed that even little boys could learn a good deal if they were not overwhelmed with too much at one time. Thus concern for **scope and sequence** became prominent **according to the abilities of each learner**. A century after the *Ratio* was published, Jouvancy remarked that youthful talents are like narrow-necked vessels. You cannot fill them by splashing everything in at once. You can, if you pour it in carefully drop-by-drop.

(147) c) Because he knew human nature well, Ignatius realized that even well-ordered experience in prayer or in academic study could not really help a person to grow unless the individual actively participated. In the *Spiritual Exercises* Ignatius proposes the importance of **self-activity** on the part of the exercitant. The second Annotation enjoins the director to be brief in his proposal of matter for each meditation so that by his own activity in prayer the exercitant may discover the truths and practices to which God calls him. This discovery tends to produce delight for the exercitant and greater "understanding and relish of the truth than if one in giving the *Exercises* had explained and developed the meaning at great length." In Annotation 15, he writes, "Allow the Creator to deal directly with the creature, and the creature directly with His Creator and Lord." Ignatius knew the tendency of all teachers, whether in teaching prayer, history or science, to discourse at great length about their views of the matter at hand. Ignatius realized that no learning occurs without the learner's own intelligent activity. Thus in numerous exercises and study, **student activities** were seen as important.

(148) d) The principle of self-activity on the part of the learner reinforced the *Ratio's* detailed instructions for repetitions— daily, weekly, monthly, annually. For these were further

devices for stimulating, guiding and sustaining that student exercise which is aimed at mastery. But repetitions were not meant to be boring re-presentation of memorized material. Rather they were to be occasions when personal reflection and appropriation could occur by reflecting on what troubled or excited the student in the lesson.

(149) e) If, as we have seen, there is no mastery without action, so too there is no successful action without **motivation**. Ignatius noted that those who studied should never go beyond two hours without taking a break. He prescribed variety in classroom activities, "for nothing does more to make the energy of youth flag than too much of the same thing." As far as possible, learning should be pleasant both intrinsically and extrinsically. By making an initial effort to orient students to the matter at hand, the teachers hoped to engage their students' interests in that subject. In this spirit, plays and pageants were produced by the students, aimed at stimulating the study of literature, since "*Friget enim Poesis sine theatro.*" Then too, contests, games, etc. were suggested so that the adolescent's desire to excel might help him to progress in learning. These practices demonstrate a prime concern to make learning interesting, and thereby to engage youthful attention and application to study.

(150) **All these pedagogical principles are, then, closely linked together.** The learning outcome sought is genuine growth, which is conceived in terms of abiding habits or skills. Habits are generated not simply by understanding facts or procedures, but by mastery and personal appropriation, which makes them one's own. Mastery is the product of continual intellectual effort and exercise; but fruitful effort of this sort is impossible without adequate motivation and a reflective humane milieu. No part of this chain is particularly original, although the strict concatenation had novelty in its day.

(151) Accordingly, to help students develop a commitment to apostolic action, Jesuit schools should offer them opportunities to explore human values critically and to test their own values experientially. Personal integration of ethical and religious val-

ues that leads to action is far more important than the ability to memorize facts and opinions of others. It is becoming clear that men and women of the third millennium will require new technological skills, no doubt; but more important, they will require skills to lovingly understand and critique all aspects of life in order to make decisions (personal, social, moral, professional, religious) that will impact all of our lives for the better. Criteria for such growth (through study, reflection, analysis, judgment and development of effective alternatives) are inevitably founded on values. This is true whether or not such values are made explicit in the learning process. In Jesuit education Gospel values as focused in the *Spiritual Exercises* are the guiding norms for integral human development.

(152) The importance of method as well as substance to achieve this purpose is evident. For a value-oriented educational goal like ours—forming men and women for others—will not be realized unless, infused within our educational programs at every level, we challenge our students to reflect upon the value implication of what they study. We have learned to our regret that mere appropriation of knowledge does not inevitably humanize. One would hope that we have also learned that there is no value-free education. But the values imbedded in many areas in life today are presented subtly. So there is need to discover ways that will enable students to form habits of reflection, to assess values and their consequences for human beings in the positive and human sciences they study, the technology being developed, and the whole spectrum of social and political programs suggested by both prophets and politicians. Habits are not formed only by chance occasional happenings. Habits develop only by consistent, planned practice. And so the goal of forming habits of reflection needs to be worked on by all teachers in Jesuit schools, colleges and universities in all subjects, in ways appropriate to the maturity of students at different levels.

CONCLUSION

(153) In our contemporary mission the basic pedagogy of Ignatius can be an immense help in winning the minds and hearts of

new generations. For Ignatian pedagogy focuses upon formation of the whole person, heart, mind and will, not just the
intellect; it challenges students to discernment of meaning in
what they study, through reflection rather than rote memory;
it encourages adaptation which demands openness to growth
in all of us. It demands that we respect the capacities of students at varied levels of their growth; and the entire process is
nurtured in a school environment of care, respect and trust
wherein the person can honestly face the often painful challenges to being human with and for **others**.

(154) To be sure, our success will always fall short of the ideal. But
it is the striving for that ideal, the greater glory of God, that
has always been the hallmark of the Jesuit enterprise.

(155) If you feel a bit uneasy today—about how you can ever measure up to the challenges of your responsibilities as you begin
this process of sharing Ignatian Pedagogy with teachers on
your continents—know that you do not stand alone! Know,
also, that for every doubt there is an affirmation that can be
made. For the ironies of Charles Dickens' time are with us
even now. "It was the best of times, it was the worst of times,
. . . it was the spring of hope, it was the winter of despair."
And I am personally greatly encouraged by what I sense as a
growing desire on the part of many in countries around the
globe to pursue more vigorously the ends of Jesuit education
which, if properly understood, will lead our students to unity,
not fragmentation; to faith, not cynicism; to respect for life,
not the raping of our planet; to responsible action based on
moral judgment, not to timorous retreat or reckless attack.

(156) I'm sure you know that the best things about any school are
not what is said about it, but what is lived out by its students.
The ideal of Jesuit education calls for a life of intellect, a life
of integrity, and a life of justice and loving service to our fellow men and women and to our God. This is the call of Christ
to us today—a call to growth, a call to life. Who will answer?
Who if not you? When if not now?

(157) In concluding I recall that when Christ left his disciples, He
said: "Go and teach!" He gave them a mission. But He also

realized that they and we are human beings; and God knows we often lose confidence in our ourselves. So He continued: "Remember you are not alone! You are never going to be alone because **I shall be with you**. In your ministry, in difficult times as well as in the times of joy and elation, I shall be with you all days, even to the end of time." Let us not fall into the trap of Pelagianism, putting all the weight on ourselves and not realizing that we are in the hands of God and working hand in hand with God in this, God's Ministry of the Word.

(158) God bless you in this cooperative effort. I look forward to receiving reports on the progress of the Ignatian Pedagogy Project throughout the world. Thank you for all you will do!

APPENDIX 3: EXAMPLES OF METHODS TO ASSIST TEACHERS IN USING THE IGNATIAN PEDAGOGICAL PARADIGM

(159) **CONTEXT OF LEARNING**
1. *The Student: Readiness for Growth*
   a) The Student's Situation: Diagnosis of Factors Affecting the Student's Readiness for Learning and Growth: physical, academic, psychological, socio-political, economic, spiritual.
   b) Student Learning Styles: How to plan for effective teaching.
   c) Student Growth Profile: A strategy for growth.
2. *Society*
   a) Reading the Signs of the Times: some tools for socio-cultural analysis.
3. *The School*
   a) School Climate: Assessment Instruments
   b) Curriculum
      —Formal/Informal.
      —Scope and Sequence; interdisciplinary possibilities.
      —Assessing values in the curriculum.
   c) Personalized Education
   d) Collegial Relationships among Administrators, Teachers, and Support Staff.
4. *The Teacher:* Expectations and Realities

(160) **EXPERIENCE**
1. *The Prelection*
   a) Continuity

      b) Advance Organizers
      c) Clear Objectives
      d) Human Interest Factors
      e) Historical Context of the matter being studied
      f) Point of View/Assumptions of Textbook Authors
      g) A Study Pattern
2. *Questioning Skills*
3. *Student Self-Activity: Notes*
4. *Problem Solving/Discovery Learning*
5. *Cooperative Learning*
6. *Small Group Processes*
7. *Emulation*
8. *Ending the Class*

(161) REFLECTION
1. *Mentoring*
9. *Peer Tutoring*
2. *Student Journals*
3. *Ignatian Style "Repetition"*
4. *Case Studies*
5. *Dilemmas/Debates/Role Playing*
6. *Integrating Seminars*

(162) ACTION
1. *Projects/Assignments: Quality Concerns*
2. *Service Experiences*
3. *Essays and Essay Type Questions*
4. *Planning and Application*
5. *Career Choices*

(163) EVALUATION
1. *Testing: Alternatives Available*
2. *Student Self-Evaluation*
3. *Assessing a Spectrum of Student Behaviors: The Student Portfolio*
4. *Teachers' Consultative Conferences*
5. *Questions for Teachers*
6. *Student Profile Survey*

CONTRIBUTORS

George A. Aschenbrenner, S.J. has devoted all of his priestly life to spiritual direction in the Ignatian tradition. He served for ten years as Master of Novices in the Jesuit Maryland Province, as Spiritual Director for lay faculty at Scranton University and at St. Joseph's University in Philadelphia. From 1985 to 1991, he served as Director of the Spiritual Formation Program, training over 100 U.S. seminarians each year at the North American College in Rome. He also taught at the Institute of Spirituality at the Gregorian University in Rome. Currently, he serves as Director of the Jesuit Center for Spiritual Growth at Wernersville, Pennsylvania. Over the past thirty years he has published numerous articles in journals such as *Review for Religious, Human Development, The Way,* and *Pastoral Life.* His book, *A God For A Dark Journey,* and his pioneering work on the centrality of the Ignatian "Consciousness Examen" are much appreciated by lay and religious persons.

Gabriel Codina, S.J., a native of Barcelona, Spain, completed his Ph.D. at the Sorbonne in Paris, and subsequently dedicated all of his efforts to Jesuit education in Bolivia. There he served as Principal of a colegio, Province Delegate for Education, Vice-President of the National Association of Private Schools, National Director of *Fe y Alegria* of Bolivia and Acting President of the International Federation of *Fe y Alegria,* the network of schools for children from poor families that now stretches across thirteen countries in Latin America. His best known work, *Aux Sources de la Pedagogie des Jesuites. Le "Modus Parisiensis,"* is recognized as the definitive work on this topic. He is currently the Secretary for Education of the Society of Jesus.

Rosemary A. De Julio is the Assistant Academic Dean of Fordham College at Lincoln Center. She has served as Director of "The College at 60 Program" and as Administrative Assistant of the Fordham

University Center for Medieval Studies. She received her Ph.D. from Fordham University in the Spring of 2000; her dissertation is entitled "Patrons, Pupils, and Partners: The Participation of Women in Ignatian Spirituality and Pedagogy." She has also delivered papers at national conferences of the National Association for Women in Catholic Higher Education.

Vincent J. Duminuco, S.J. is Director of the International Jesuit Education Leadership Project training lay persons for leadership positions in Jesuit schools, colleges, and universities in Africa, Asia, and Eastern Europe. He also serves as the delegate of the Superior General of the Society of Jesus to the World Union of Jesuit Alumni/ae. Currently, he is visiting Professor at the Graduate School of Education at Fordham University. After earning his Ph.D. at Stanford University, his whole professional career has been dedicated to renewal of the apostolate of Jesuit education. He has served as headmaster and teacher at Jesuit high schools and as professor at two Jesuit universities, Director of the Commission on Research and Development, and then President for nine years of the Jesuit Secondary Education Association. During these years, he helped to develop "The Colloquium on the Ministry of Teaching," which has been used on six continents. He was Secretary of Education of the Society of Jesus with responsibilities for Jesuit education worldwide for ten years. Fr. Duminuco served as one of the founding members of the International Commission on the Apostolate of Jesuit Education, which produced both *The Characteristics of Jesuit Education* and *Ignatian Pedagogy: A Practical Approach*.

John L. Elias is Professor of Religion and Education at Fordham University where he is on the faculty of both the School of Education and the School of Religion and Religious Education. He is presently the director of the program in Church and Society/Peace and Justice.

John Elias received his doctorate in history and philosophy of education at Temple University. He has published copiously, and has recently completed a manuscript on the history of Christian education. Elias has worked extensively with community and church groups in developing programs in adult education, notably, a leadership-training program for the South Bronx churches to prepare church, synagogue, and mosque members to work for social and political change. He has assisted many local churches in developing comprehensive programs in adult religious education. While on sabbatical in England, he founded the Centre for Adult Religious Education at St. Mary's College, Strawberry Hill, and was instrumental in establishing at the University of Sussex the first postgraduate degree in adult religious education in the United Kingdom.

Jenny H. Go has been associated with Jesuit education for all of her professional life, beginning with her studies for a Master's degree at the Fordham University School of Education. For over twenty years she served as Principal of Xavier High School, Manila, Philippines, which serves the Chinese Philippino community. She is the first lay person to serve as Executive Secretary of the East Asia and Oceania Jesuit Education Conference, advising Jesuit Provincials of that region and presenting workshops training teachers and administrators of Jesuit and many other Catholic school systems. She is one of six members of the International Commission on the Apostolate of Jesuit Education. She is co-founder of "Inigo Friends," a group of lay persons who strive to live according to the principles of Ignatian spirituality.

Howard Gray, S.J. has graduate degrees in theology and English literature, completing Ph.D. work at the University of Wisconsin, Madison. Within the Society of Jesus he has held a number of positions ranging from Director of Formation for the Detroit Province of the Society to Rector of the Jesuit community at the Weston Jesuit School of Theology to Provincial Superior of the Detroit Province. In 1989–90, Fr. Gray served as a special consultant to the Jesuits of the East Asia Assistancy. Before assuming his present position, Fr. Gray was the Director of Tertians for the U.S.A. Presently, he is Director of the Boston College Center for Ignatian Spirituality. Fr. Gray has written and lectured on Ignatian spirituality, priesthood, lay leadership, and ministry throughout the United States, Asia, India, the United Kingdom, Ireland, and Africa. He was a delegate to the Jesuits' General Congregation 33 (1983), and he was Vice President of the Conference of the Major Superiors of Men. Finally, Fr. Gray was on the papal-mandated teams that studied religious life in the U.S.A. and assessed seminary life and training in the U.S.A.

John W. O'Malley, S.J. is Distinguished Professor of Church History at Weston Jesuit School of Theology in Cambridge, Massachusetts. Author of thirteen books on the Renaissance and Reformation periods, he has received acclaim with best-book awards: "The Jacques Barzun Prize for Cultural History" for *The First Jesuits*, American Philosophical Society, 1995; "The Philip Schaff Prize for Religious History" for *The First Jesuits*, American Society of Church History, 1996; and "The Howard R. Massaro Prize for Italian History and Culture" for *Praise and Blame in Renaissance Rome*, American Historical Association, 1979. He has served as President of the Renaissance Society of America, as a fellow of the American Academy of Arts and Sciences, and as a member of the American Philosophical Society. He has served as President of the American Catholic Historical Society, Research Fellow at the National Endowment for the Humanities, Scholar in Residence at the American Academy in Rome, John Simon Guggenheim Fellow, and John Harvard Fellow: Harvard University. He has held visiting professorships and lectureships at Harvard University, the University of Michigan, Boston College, and Oxford University.

John W. Padberg, S.J. is Director of the Institute of Jesuit Sources. The Institute publishes books on the history and current status of the life, activities, and spirituality of the Society of Jesus. He has been Chairman of the National Seminar on Jesuit Higher Education and is presently Chairman of the Seminar on the Spirituality of Jesuits. Born in 1926, Fr. Padberg received his Ph.D. in the history of ideas from Harvard University in 1965. After serving as Professor of History and Academic Vice President at Saint Louis University, he was President (1975–85) of Weston Jesuit School of Theology, a national theological center in Cambridge, Massachusetts. His major interest in recent years has been the history of the Society of Jesus, and his publications include articles and monographs on that subject, such as *Colleges in Conflict: The Jesuit Schools in France from Revival to Suppression, 1815-1880* (Harvard University Press), *For Matters of Greater Moment: The First Thirty Jesuit General Congregations* (Institute of Jesuit Sources), "Ignatius, the Popes and Realistic Reverence," and "The Three Forgotten Founders of the Society of Jesus" in *Studies in the Spirituality of Jesuits*.

Louis Pascoe, S.J. is Professor of Medieval History at Fordham University. He has served on the Executive Council of the American Catholic Historical Association and has been honored by the American Council of Learned Societies, the Centro Italiano di Studi, Spoleto, and Georgetown University. His impressive list of publications includes *Jean Gerson: Principles of Church Reform* and *Church and Reform: Bishops, Theologians and Canon Lawyers in the Thought of Pierre L'Ailly*. His articles appear in scholarly historical journals in France, Germany, Italy, the Netherlands, and the United Kingdom, as well as in the United States.

Seated, from left: Jenny H. Go, Rosemary A. DeJulio, Joseph A. O'Hare, S.J., George A. Aschenbrenner, S.J., Vincent O'Keefe, S.J. Standing, from left: Regis Bernhardt, John W. Padberg, S.J., Gabriel Codina, S.J., John W. O'Malley, S.J., Louis Pascoe, S.J., Howard Gray, S.J., Vincent J. Duminuco, S.J.

INDEX